FOOD AND LOVE

FOOD AND LOVE

A Cultural History
of East and West

JACK GOODY

VERSO

London • New York

First published by Verso 1998
© Jack Goody 1998
All rights reserved

The moral rights of this author have been asserted

Verso
UK: 6 Meard Street, London W1V 3HR
US: 180 Varick Street, New York, NY 10014–4606

Verso is the imprint of New Left Books

ISBN 1–85984–829–X

British Library Cataloguing in Publication Data
A catalogue record for this book is available from the British Library

Library of Congress Cataloging-in-Publication Data
A catalog record for this book is available from the Library of Congress

Typeset by The Running Head Limited, London and Cambridge
Printed by Biddles Ltd, Guildford and King's Lynn

To Ernest Gellner, a worker in the field as well as with ideas

CONTENTS

ACKNOWLEDGEMENTS

I am grateful to those places that have given me support, especially St John's College, Cambridge, but also the European University Institute at Florence; to institutions and people that have invited me to talk, especially the Royal Anthropological Institute, the University of Liverpool, the University of Illinois, Institut français de Londres, Entretiens Franklin and the Foundation for Chinese Dietary Culture; to those bodies who have published earlier versions; to Ruth Daniel for reading the proofs and to Wendy Redgewood and Susan Mansfield of St John's College for typing and help more generally. Juliet Mitchell has read and commented upon many of the chapters; Jean-Louis Flandrin has helped with chapter 6; others have contributed at seminars.

Jack Goody
St John's College, Cambridge, August 1998

INTRODUCTION

The chapters of this book are based on revisions of contributions I have written over the last two or three years. They bear mainly upon two topics. Firstly, I look at the exaggerated claims made by Europeans for their uniqueness, in an attempt to explain the background of the developments that led to 'capitalism, industrialisation and modernisation', processes that are inter-related but have frequently been confused. In particular these claims have neglected those similarities that exist within Eurasia, between East and West, that are based, in the last analysis, upon a common heritage in the Urban Revolution of the Bronze Age, which initiated intensive agriculture, extensive craft specialisation and the wide-ranging change in the mode of communication involved in the invention of writing. The attempts of European scholars like Marx and Weber to explain the temporary advantage that Europe had after the fifteenth century, and more specifically after the later eighteenth, led them to look for the reasons in particular sequences of social development in the West and deep-seated or wide-ranging differences in the East which contemporary events make seem increasingly out of place.

Secondly, in seeing continuities between the socio-cultural systems of the major Eurasian states, I also observe some major discontinuities with societies practising extensive hoe agriculture which – as in Africa, where farming does not make use of non-human energy – does not permit levels of primary production that would support a body of full-time specialists, including scribes. Neolithic farming, let alone hunting and gathering, simply was not efficient enough except in a few unusual circumstances. The specialisation of scribes was of great cultural significance. But while writing allowed a quantum jump in human consciousness, in cognitive awareness, what emerged – forms of rationality as well as commerce and social stratification – was based upon the embryonic achievements of oral cultures. That was the case with logic (chapter 1), as it is with love (chapter 5) and scepticism (chapter 11), where I look for quite specific reasons, rather than to mentalities in general, for any perceived differences.

Some of these chapters have to do with more specific issues than the so-called European miracle and the East–West problem, and may at first appear irrelevant. Yet there are direct relationships between the themes. My earlier interest in the culture of flowers lay in the observation that in sub-Saharan Africa they were neither cultivated nor in general use. That situation contrasted dramatically with the attention given to aesthetic horticulture in Asia and Europe, where stratified luxury cultures, based on intensive and more experimental cultivation, employed them for decoration, celebration, gift-giving and worship. The same was the case with food; only in Europe and Asia did we find the development of an *haute cuisine* that was clearly class-based and marked off those continents from Africa south of the Sahara. In both these cases, flowers and food, the development of luxury behaviour encourages doubts, characteristic of these regimes, about the uneven distribution of man's worldly goods, not only among the deprived themselves but also among some members of upper groups, especially intellectuals, philosophers and preachers, who think about and doubt the existing order.

These general differences in regimes were related not only to the means of production but to the means of communication. *Haute cuisine* was both recorded and developed in writing; so too with aspects of botany and the culture of flowers. The appreciation of food and nature certainly existed in oral cultures but these features expanded and changed direction under the impact of writing. So too with love. I argue once again that those who see this notion as purely European, whether dating from the twelfth or eighteenth centuries, are quite mistaken; it exists even in oral cultures, but the idea and the practice greatly expanded under the influence of literacy.

In this introduction I want to put my perspective in very broad terms, which has to do with the importance not only of modes and the means of production (as well as the means of destruction (Goody 1971)) but also of the means and modes of communication, in particular the advent of writing, which had a profound effect on the way that society operated, including the cognitive levels. By concentrating on these, especially the means, in a rather different way from Marx and Weber, we reduce the supposed disparity between Europe and Asia, and at the same time provide a way of understanding Africa's differences. In doing this, I want to consider my work, perhaps incongruously, not only in relation to the notions of the nineteenth-century writers, especially Karl Marx, and to two most interesting recent interpreters, Perry Anderson and Robert Brenner, but also to a contemporary one, Jared Diamond, who looks at long-term developments from a very different angle. But all have dared to tackle some of the wider questions of cultural history from a comparative perspective.[1] I take these different approaches as paradigmatic. Marx followed the post-Enlightenment view in Europe, starting from that continent's undoubted contemporary success; he saw it as being especially privileged in the progressive historical sequence leading to 'modernisation', in contrast to the stagnant, despotic East characterised by Asiatic exceptionalism. That view I challenge on empirical grounds, more particularly in the first chapter. In the main, Anderson and Brenner follow this line of thinking, as do most Western historians. Diamond recognises the Eurasian continent as one, deriving its temporal advantages from the development of food production as the result of the availability of domesticable crops and animals, combined with the easy possibility of their actual East–West transmission within the same climatic zones. In other words he appeals to a neolithic commonality, based largely on geographic factors, which continues to structure the world situation down to the present day. His approach recognises that until 1500 the cultural flow from East to West was more significant than that in the other direction; until 1450 China was the more innovative society in many substantive respects (Diamond 1997: 253). The subsequent reversal he also sees as ultimately controlled by geographic factors.

Let me turn first to Marx's general scheme of development. It is well known. 'In broad outlines Asiatic, ancient, feudal, and modern bourgeois modes of production can be designated as progressive epochs in the economic formation of society' (Marx 1958: 363). To see the world in terms of major transitions, such as those from ancient to feudal, has its limitations especially when this progression represents a purely Western sequence. Of

---

[1] In embarking on this broad discussion, I would like to thank the editor (R. Blackburn) and readers of Verso (J. Stallybrass and S. Budgen) who stimulated me to tackle questions that I too often take for granted, and on which my comments are scattered through different works over many years. In particular I was grateful for the suggestion that I discuss the work of Jared Diamond (1997) *Guns, Germs and Steel: a short history of everybody for the last 13,000 years.*

course the fall of the Roman empire was of immense importance to Europe and the adjoining Near Eastern and North African territories. But from a world perspective can the shift to feudalism be seen as a 'progressive' transition of a revolutionary kind, as suggested by Marx, either in terms of modes of production or of communication? How was this transition effected? Wickham sees the fall of the Roman empire as not leading directly to feudalism but to a 'peasant mode' which was weakly stratified and in which 'big men' gave out as much as they received and therefore did not amass a sufficient surplus to enter into the 'luxury' trade. England until Offa (d. 796) was one such society which he compares with Iceland and perhaps Brittany. The peasants, he concludes, were better off than under a feudal regime as they paid no rent to landlords nor tax to the state. In other words, the state and local forms of domination had virtually disappeared, leaving only the peasant base.

The reconstruction of local and more inclusive forms of domination followed slowly, always held in some kind of check by the Church, which had meanwhile established itself as 'a great organisation'. But it is difficult to see that process as 'progressive' in a general sense, since it largely involved re-establishing in a different form the structure of centralised and above all local domination that had existed earlier. In many ways, on the contrary, it represented a falling back in city life, in forms of agricultural exploitation, in trade and in knowledge systems and the uses of literacy. That is broadly the conclusion of Needham in his comparison of Western and Eastern science in the period after Aristotle. Of course there were 'advances' in Europe later during the medieval period, but much of this was a question of making headway against the earlier post-Roman decline. While the social relations of production certainly changed with the fall of empire, its colonies and its standing armies, feudalism brought few changes in the means of production; the realm of communication, at least in the secular sense, suffered badly.

Feudalism is widely seen nowadays not as a distinct mode of production or social formation but as the decentralised Western version of a political system found throughout Europe and Asia and recognised as a 'tributary state' (Amin 1980; Wolf 1982). Such a conception does away with what we may equally regard as the early European exceptionalism inherent in Marx's scheme. Discussions on whether feudalism was to be found outside Europe, as argued by Coulbourn (1956) and others, become redundant when it is seen as a variation of the type of state formation following on the urban revolution: the Eastern version became more centralised, the Western less so. This was due partly to the 'barbarian' invasions, partly to the dominance of the Christian Church as a 'great organisation' with its own alternative focus of wealth and power, and partly to the collapse of the wider economy (Goody 1971: chapter 1).

The basic problem with most Western commentators is that in concentrating on the undoubted advances that Europe made in the eighteenth and nineteenth centuries, they were prompted to ask why it was that Asia had not made the same progress. That is a valid question but it neglects the fact that during the Middle Ages, in a social, cultural and economic sense, it was in many ways Europe that was behind. In other words, instead of looking for deep-seated reasons for Europe's advance, we have to seek more short-term ones, especially as it was until recently Asia that was displaying the highest rates of economic and related social growth.

Europe began to catch up and expand at the Renaissance. Even earlier there was a development of mercantile, commercial cultures beginning in Italy that was accompanied by achievements in the artistic, scientific and technological spheres. Part of these achievements lay in the field of guns and ships that enabled the Atlantic coastal nations of south-west Europe to expand, both militarily and by trade, into the Indies, East and West, as well as the Americas.

What then happened in Europe in the sixteenth century? Turning back to ancient models and to some extent away from Catholic ones, that continent took up in a systematic way the search for knowledge, especially scientific knowledge, the accumulation of which was helped by or led to the 'invention' of printing, by the extension of education and by the organisation of learned societies, which took over the kind of scholarly communication that existed between monks and other members of the ecclesiastical establishment, including the staff of the early universities. The development of a vigorous urban, mercantile culture opened all that up. But it did so too in China and, to a lesser extent, in India and the Muslim countries. Differences were a matter of degree rather than of kind until the eighteenth century, when its greater development of knowledge systems, of artistic activity and its prolegomena to the Industrial Revolution created a real (but temporary) divide in terms of modes of production and indeed of ways of life more generally.

So we can speak of the success of mercantile capitalism from the third millennium BCE in Mesopotamia onwards; in my view that was necessarily accompanied by a measure of rural capitalism. We can also speak of the development of industrial capitalism in late eighteenth-century Europe. But is there any justification for talking of an abstract capitalism that emerged in Europe in the sixteenth century, as Marx, Weber, world system theorists and many other Europeanists suggest? At that time the bourgeoisie became increasingly dominant in social life, necessarily so as mercantile, commercial, manufacturing and bureaucratic activity grew. But in Italy that growth happened earlier, for instance with the rule of the Medici moneylenders in Florence and all the accompanying artistic and economic achievements. And there were similar, if less spectacular, examples of the growth of the bourgeoisie in other urban civilisations.

Had Marx taken in the developments of the Bronze Age, which affected both Asia and Europe, he might have been less inclined to posit a long-standing Asiatic mode of production and to differentiate this from the ancient. It is true that the classical societies of Greece and Rome employed substantial bodies of slave labour, while the Asiatic societies (and of course Egypt) increased their production through irrigation. But the results were less different than might appear, partly because both East and West were grounded in similar Bronze Age achievements, including literacy and artisanal production. So the nature of urban life, of bourgeois, mercantile, religious and intellectual activity – together with the systems of stratification, based largely upon differential access to arable land for plough or other forms of intensive cultivation – bore substantial resemblances one to another. And while the West was at times more firmly committed to slavery, other states too had reserves of servile labour, whether landless rural or urban proletariat, to work on their behalf.

Let me turn back to Marx's own argument. What precisely is meant by the advent of capitalism? Marx referred to the end of the feudal and the beginning of the bourgeois mode, which involved the dominance of mercantile (capitalist) exchange (Money–Commodities–Money in his formula) and subsequently of wage labour. Mercantile exchange had existed as long as merchants themselves, while wage labour of different kinds (including out-work) was found with many types of proto-industrial production as well as among rural workers in all post-Bronze Age societies. The utilisation of capital was an intrinsic part of such activities, though obviously it played a greater role with the gradual growth of commerce. Such commerce was already at high levels in China and India but increasingly so in the West after the considerable set-back in the post-Roman period, with recovery picking up from the twelfth century in Mediterranean countries until the European voyages of the sixteenth. That is when Marx saw the beginning of capitalism. According to him, 'The modern history of capital dates from the creation in the sixteenth century of a world-embracing commerce and a world-embracing market' (Marx 1970: 146). The formation of capital is based on the type of exchange (M–C–M) in which money is transferred into commodities and back again to money.

The particular formula is somewhat restricting, since any transaction may involve more elements and end up with commodities rather than with money. But in any case such transactions have long characterised mercantile cultures. Yet Marx's account formally identifies 'the modern history of capitalism' with the 'world system' established by European expansion. That is highly Eurocentric. It neglects the huge markets, internal and external, of China and India in the Pacific and the Indian Oceans, existing long before Europe's irruption into the East, and it neglects too the extensive Arab commerce described by Abu-Lughod (1989). While European commerce developed into a world system, and was combined with the widespread establishment of overseas colonies (some of settlement, others not), it started out in a way comparable to the trade of the other great powers and did not represent an entirely new activity which one can designate as 'capitalism'.

For Marx, then, modern capitalism began in the sixteenth century with the creation of a world market. That development paved the way for the industrialisation that took off during the later eighteenth century in England. Looking backwards from this point, many have seen England on that very account as having been the original home of capitalism in the broader sense, the active centre of particular market conditions into which fitted the victory of Protestantism, overseas trade and the English Revolution.

The attribution of the beginning of capitalism to England in the sixteenth century resembles the attribution to that same place and time of 'civilisation' by Elias, or of the emergence of modern attitudes to nature by Thomas, or of the invention of childhood, the start of feminism, or the beginning of modern Europe by historians generally. While important cultural changes took place at this period, as well as later at the Enlightenment, to talk about the beginning of those features in any exclusive way is to quite overlook the situation in other civilisations. It is true that Europe was accumulating capital – booty from South America – and that this income was used to finance Asian imports as well as government and other local expenditures.

But that process increased the volume of capitalistic activity; it did not represent the beginning even of (modern) capitalism in the broad sense.

Marx's account is more acceptable on industrialisation; he wrote of the 'industrial revolution' as beginning in 1735 when 'John Wyatt brought out his spinning machine' (Marx 1970: 372), though in fact imperfect ones existed already, and Italy was probably the country of their first appearance. This revolution was connected to the invention of machines, making water or steam power necessary to run them. For the machine is 'the starting-point of the industrial revolution' (pp. 375–6). In this England was acknowledged as pre-eminent. 'The English working men are the first born sons of modern industry' (Marx 1958: 360). Owing 'to steam power which only then began to impart value to its coal and iron deposits', England 'attained the foremost position in modern bourgeois development'. The reasoning here is much more specific than in the case of capitalism in the broad sense.

Marx's thesis has been taken up by many since that time, but I want to turn to two especially valuable discussions by Perry Anderson and Robert Brenner, who concentrate on the transition from feudalism to capitalism. As a historical category feudalism was an outcome of the Western Enlightenment, and it is clearly possible to define this and any other category in a manner that confines the notion to one country or to one continent. Equally we can specify other forms of landlordism by means of locally appropriate terms. However, many have tried to look at feudalism in a more analytic way, both Marxist and non-Marxist (for example Coulbourn 1956). But Marx's usage is not neutral. Feudalism was seen as a progressive phase found in Europe leading to the development of capitalism, a development that was impossible starting from other points of departure. In this sense feudalism is incorporated in later developments, as was, according to Anderson (and this is critical to his argument), classical civilisation.

From one standpoint the historical embodiment of previous events is necessarily true. The question is whether the features of these earlier forms were uniquely capable of generating capitalism. Here we come to a problem of whether we mean capitalism in the broader or narrower sense, for the argument swings between the broad definition relating to forms of wage labour (which, as Brenner argues, may have begun in Europe in the rural sector), or whether we refer to the specific form of industrial capitalism. I have suggested that while Europe saw a strong development of wage labour in the early modern period, in both rural and urban sectors, it was not unique in that feature. And mercantile capitalism certainly developed not only with Western feudalism but to a greater degree in some earlier and in some Eastern societies.

With industrial capitalism – which as all insist, occurred in one specific region, western Europe, indeed firstly in England – the situation is quite different. A certain development of bourgeois culture, in Marx's phase, was necessary. But that took place in other areas. Western society was of course marked by specific features, although I argue that this line of enquiry has led to the gross exaggeration of difference, about the family for example. But even when we make allowance for these misinterpretations, the relation between the remaining differences (for example later marriage) and the development of industrial capitalism remains obscure. There are other possible approaches. Marx himself charted the genealogy of inventions that led to the system of the factory production of textiles in Britain, which of course demanded capital involvement by entrepreneurs, as well as inventions by scientists, technologists and manufacturers. But the factors leading to this outcome seem much more specific than any theory of progressive development from classical times would allow. Moreover such discussions of long-term European progression fail to recognise the trough into which feudal Europe had fallen in so many respects, including knowledge systems. In some general ways China was as poised for the take-off as Europe. That the latter's pre-eminence in the late eighteenth and nineteenth centuries, and even before, was related to the particular developments of bourgeois culture in those knowledge systems and other spheres, is without contention. The explanation for this situation, however, cannot be that European feudalism was 'the gateway to capitalism' (Anderson 1974: 414). Or rather, it was only so because it constituted the chronological precedent in the same geographic area that industrial capitalism developed, not because of any intrinsic features. Those that were 'necessary' to industrial capitalism (since capitalist activity itself developed in other areas) were outcomes of the bourgeois transformations within and following feudalism rather than feudalism itself. Anderson argues that it was the economic dynamic of feudalism that 'released the elements for the primitive accumulation of capital on a continental scale' (p. 415). But was that not rather proto-industrial activity (in the wool trade), commerce and overseas expansion (and hence booty production)? There was little 'feudal' about these activities.

Marx was also critical of attempts to discuss feudalism outside Europe and stressed its European nature; he warns, in Anderson's words, of 'the dangers of a promiscuous extension of the fabric of feudalism beyond Europe' (Anderson 1974: 407). There were significant differences in India, for instance: 'By Indian law political power was not subject to division between the sons; thereby an important source of European feudalism was blocked up' (quoted p. 407). In other words, the succession of all the sons to high office, the absence of primogeniture, was a mechanism whereby power was dispersed; in India that was concentrated, differentiating its regimes from feudalism proper.

Anderson sees the universalisation of the concept of feudalism as being a feature of many recent Marxist analysts who wish to play down the differences between Europe and Asia, in contrast to earlier eighteenth- and nineteenth-century views. This merging, he argues, arises from a 'colour-blind materialism' that concentrates on similarities in the means of production but neglects the dissimilarities in the extractive mechanisms in class formation – embodied in the laws and government of Western feudalism. For if feudalism 'can be defined independently of the variant judicial and political superstructures which accompany it', 'how is the unique dynamism of the European theatre of international feudalism to be explained?' (Anderson 1974: 402). For no one has suggested that industrial capitalism developed spontaneously anywhere else except in Europe and its American extension. Moreover, while in capitalism the means of extracting surplus is purely economic, in earlier social formations exploitation operated through extra-economic sanctions, namely kin, religious, legal and political. There are several problems in this analysis. Firstly, industrial capitalism did not follow directly on after feudalism but after a phase of vigorous mercantile capitalism in which landlordism played a more limited role than in its hey-day. It was not differences in feudalism that were significant in the background of industrial capitalism but differences in the achievements of the bourgeoisie who later developed and established the system. Secondly, the differences in state and legal organisations were certainly much exaggerated by travellers like Bernier and others on whom Montesquieu and Hegel based their judgements. The reach of the state may have been greater in Asian empires but the peasantry nevertheless had a measure of independence, not only as bandits – primitive rebels as Hobsbawm called them – and so too did the urban bourgeoisie (and even the nobility). Recent studies have shown the legal underpinnings of commercial law and the degree of political representation that existed. The contrast is much less harsh than Marx and Anderson make it. Thirdly, Anderson's objection to a comparison of possible 'feudal' systems based only on the means of production rather than the mode is well taken. But the onset of industrial capitalism is frequently described by Marx and others in those very terms – the coming of the machine, the harnessing of steam, the establishment of factory production – so that it becomes reasonable to look for precedents on the same level, especially as the potential role of the bourgeoisie and of mercantile capital was present in other parts of Eurasia.

When Marx speaks of capitalism as being the first social formation to operate its exploitation through 'purely' economic means in the wage contract, he is referring to all kinds of paid employment, not only to that of industrial capitalism, but in the manufacturing and agricultural sectors as well. It is sometimes held, and it is a thesis vigorously maintained by Robert Brenner, that capitalism in Europe first took root in agriculture rather than manufacture or trade. That capital entered into agriculture at an early stage in many post-Bronze Age states is undoubtedly true. Europe and in particular England had its own particular forms of agriculture, but if capitalism can be said to have started there in the rural sector, that only goes to illustrate the relatively backward nature of the earlier economy. There is no sense in which in the sixteenth century or earlier Europe displayed a capitalist economy while India – with its huge output of manufactures exported to Indonesia and Indo-China – did not. The means of production were not then substantially different; what about the social relations of production? People had to sell their labour in India or China as they did in Europe. In no post-Bronze Age society did everyone have direct access to the means of production, so they had to work for others. Labour became a commodity and money was exchanged for commodities which were turned again into money, as in the extensive manufacture of cloth for sale, often abroad.

The sharp dichotomies between economic and non-economic, between the means and relations of production, are hard to maintain in concrete situations. The economic can be seen as an aspect of all social action as well as a specific sub-system of society, and there is often some confusion between the two. Equally, relations of production are closely intertwined with the means of production, as I have long argued for Africa. Another source of difficulty is the constant switch between capitalism as a form of surplus extraction (i.e. the employment of wage labour) and industrial (or even mercantile) capitalism, as a more specific area of socio-economic activity. It is true that Anderson sees this problem about the origins of industrial capitalism as being related to the nature of the social relations of production under feudalism. The existence of wage-labour in agriculture might make it easier to shift to the same system of employment in industrial or proto-industrial production. But that is only marginally the case. In Africa the movement of labour from farm to mine or factory has never been a major problem in achieving change. In northern Ghana workers in hoe agriculture went off to wage labour at least during the dry season, initially pushed at times by the demands of taxation and the pressures of officials. Within three decades the migration of young men was an accepted feature of many cultures. The problems of transition lay not so much in the recruitment of labour as in the social organisation of production.

In Asia Anderson sees Japan as being an exception in effecting a transition. 'Japan was ultimately to achieve a tempo of industrialisation more rapid than that of any capitalist country in Europe or North America' (Anderson 1974: 415), partly because its earlier feudalism did resemble that of the West. While it was possible to talk of Japanese exceptionalism in 1974 when Anderson was writing, that is no longer the case a quarter of a century later when we find that China as well as Taiwan and Hong Kong, Malaysia and Thailand have experienced similar trajectories. Nevertheless Anderson sees the fundamental factors as essentially *exogenous* (p. 415) – but the same is true of European countries, including some parts of Britain itself. And Britain too accepted elements of the transition from elsewhere; industrial capitalism did not emerge as a fully-formed embryo but employed some exogenous features, whether at the narrower technological level (machine designs from Italy or America) or in terms of broader social factors (knowledge systems, means of communication – the printing press). The common argument that capitalism emerged at one time and at one place, and was everywhere else 'exogenous', adopted under radically different conditions, has to be looked at with more than a grain of salt; capitalism was not an entity like the wheel or the alphabet.

The main reason that this discussion has taken place is because 'capitalism' has been treated as a single entity that arose in Europe because of 'the concatenation of antiquity and feudalism' (Anderson 1974: 420). For Anderson, unlike Marx, feudalism existed at both extremes of Eurasia. The feudal order made possible a dynamic opposition between town and country, in which the town was the centre of production in a quite different way, he argues, from the administrative cities of most of Asia. Feudalism thus promoted urban vitality more vigorously than other civilisations, and was incorporated into subsequent social systems. However, 'the advantage of

Europe over Japan lay in its classical antecedence' (p. 421). Classical society too re-emerged in the new social formation. To this point I will return.

What are the features Anderson sees as similar in Japanese and European feudalism? They are the fusion of vassalage, benefice and immunity into a fief system which constituted the basic politico-legal framework in which surplus labour was extracted from the direct producer (Anderson 1974: 413). It was the extraction of wealth by political means together with the feudal relationship that was significant. 'The links between military, conditional landownership and seigneurial jurisdiction were faithfully reproduced in Japan' (p. 413). However, Japan was more tilted towards inequality (as distinct from reciprocity), with legalism being very limited and the Estates system being absent. But that assessment seems biased towards Europe in that there are perfectly valid alternatives to 'legal' norms in the narrow sense, and to checks and balances other than those provided by the Estates system. And even if we can agree with the comparison, how significant were those similarities for the growth of mercantile, agricultural and industrial capitalism? How do they distinguish these countries with respect to that growth from other pseudo-feudalisms or forms of landlordism?

If one starts from the assumption that the uniqueness of European (English) industrialism was rooted in its long-term history, social structure or mentality, the search for Western advantage is almost bound to take an ethnocentric turn. The problem is that the chosen features are often far from unique and their role as predisposing factors unclear. If one makes other assumptions about industrialisation as a result of later developments, the growth of scientific and technical knowledge systems following the Renaissance (with the development of printing), the competition from Indian and Chinese manufacturers of consumer goods (printed cottons, silks and porcelain), and the accumulation of capital through overseas trade, plunder and local proto-industrialisation, then reference to the earlier politico-legal system, while not entirely irrelevant, is less compelling. For such circumstances, one may argue, gave rise to a commercial law and to appropriate political accommodations whenever they arose. One can discuss such a view as 'colour-blind materialism', and it certainly sees 'the relations of production' as largely dependent (in this specific context, not as a universal rule). In any case 'non-material' factors (how valuable is the dichotomy?) were obviously important. To view the higher level of capitalist productive activity – which contributed to the end of 'socialism' in

China and the Soviet Union – as if it were unrelated to the systems of knowledge is unsustainable.

The notion of progressive development being characteristic only of the European past is flawed. The 'profound economic, political and cultural regression' of the European Dark Ages is recognised by Anderson but he regards it positively as clearing the way 'for the dynamic subsequent advance of the new mode of production born of their dissolution' (Anderson 1974: 418). He refers here to the dissolution of the classical slave mode and the primitive communal one followed by the emergence of the feudal system. Regression is seen as a feature of the Dark Ages, which were succeeded by a more progressive feudalism. But in many respects the regression continued until the full Renaissance, despite the contributions from the twelfth century, including the founding of the universities, the developments of commercial institutions in Italy and the beginnings of an active secular tradition of arts and sciences. Anderson's concern with the Renaissance and with knowledge systems is extremely valuable. But his view of Antiquity as providing critical and rational components without any equivalent 'in the past or in other continents' (so Europe was 'intrinsically more advanced') (Anderson 1974: 420) is at least questionable. Europe's 'advantage' over Japan was what he calls the *remanence* of the classical mode which was still available to 'concatenate' with the feudal to produce capitalism. Here he refers to 'the rebirth of antiquity' at the time of the Renaissance which remains 'the crux of European history' and which had no parallel in Japan. That was partly because in the East there had not been the same regression, so less need of a rebirth. But in any case what happened in later Europe had little to do with the classical mode of production or to its civilisation more generally, except in a very broad sense. Rather, it called upon certain limited features of the earlier achievements, including the growth of knowledge, the secularisation of the arts and a clearer separation of the sacred from the profane – what Weber called the demystification of the world – not for the first time in human existence but for the occasion with arguably the most far-reaching consequences for cultural history. Contemporary Rome was rejected as a religious model for the Protestant reformers but historical Rome became a model in other spheres. For Anderson the combination of these two modes of production gave rise to absolutism with the expansion of mercantile capitalism (Anderson 1974: 429). And at that point, paradoxically, the rights of private property became consolidated.

This concatenation of different modes of production in one specific social formation is not to be interpreted as the articulation of contemporaneous modes in the way that Althusser posited. Anderson denies any 'purely linear notion of historical time' but rather a 'remanence' and a reactivation that defy 'an evolutionary chronology', with the classical mode awakening again within the feudal present (Anderson 1974: 421). As an account of the revival of Roman law, of the rediscovery of the classics and of a return to classical themes in art, this seems expressed in somewhat mystical, or at least over-complex fashion. The point can surely be more comprehensively discussed from a narrative perspective that recognises the reconstitution of knowledge systems under both internal pressures and the stimulation of Arabic learning. Essentially one could have a rebirth because the written word, art and architecture gave classical civilisations the potential of continuing to be present. 'The *cities* of Europe – communes, republics, tyrannies – were', argues Anderson, 'the unique product of the combined development that marked the continent' (p. 424). And they were based on Roman experience. The argument resembles that of Weber and others about the specific advantages of the commune of northern Italy, from whence it spread into transalpine Europe. That Roman experience was obviously unique but cities were not. Recent scholarship on towns such as Ahmadabad in India or Hangchow in China have done much to discount those supposed differences (see Goody 1976).

For law too there is an over-evaluation of the uniqueness of the Roman contribution to European norms, especially with regard to trade and land. 'Chinese law', according to Anderson, 'was single-mindedly punitive and repressive: it was scarcely concerned with civil relations at all, and provided no stable ground for economic activity' (Anderson 1974: 425). If so, how did China develop such a wide-ranging market system for its manufactures, within and without the Empire? The kind of commercial activity that Marco Polo described could not exist without effective social sanctions; whether or not these were incorporated in an empire-wide written law is neither here nor there if other forms of jural sanction existed, as they clearly did. Islamic law may have been 'inextricably religious', as was Judaic law and up to a certain point Christian law, but that did not prevent the development of extensive trading systems in the Indian Ocean and the China Seas described by Abu-Lughod (1939) and more particularly by Goitein for Cairo (1967). That misconception arises from too close and exclusive an attachment to a secular written code that neglects alternative law-making, dispute-settling practices.

Marx placed a great importance, which is echoed by subsequent writers, on the contrast between the private and individual nature of land ownership under European feudalism as compared with the other systems, especially with a formal state monopoly of land. According to this account Europe developed absolute private property in land under the influence of Roman law. But in fact Roman law was not that different from other early written legal systems. In any case a hierarchy of estates in land existed in later Europe, as the Roman lawyer Maine explained, just as they did under so-called state ownership; the radical contrast between individual and collective rights is not warranted by an analysis of the actual situation. My own freehold in a suburban Cambridge house is qualified by many obligations (the rights of other parties) that modify my individual ownership. The supposedly radical transformation in rights over land, seen as one from conditional to absolute private property, is described as an essential preliminary to capitalism. But it is a transformation, however described, that has taken place in many parts of the world under pressure of changing circumstances, for example the increase in the man–land ratio among the Ibo of eastern Nigeria (Jones 1949) or the introduction of mechanised farming and land registration in northern Ghana (Goody 1980). European conditions were not so unique as has been commonly supposed.

At this point let me return to another approach altogether to long-term history which is taken by Jared Diamond. Essentially this is an attempt, by an evolutionary biologist, to apply his own methods (comparative and the natural experiment) to human history over the long term. Like Marx and Engels, Diamond has a major aim to promote history as a science on the lines of those historical sciences in which he himself is engaged, namely ecology and evolutionary biology. Given that he cannot adopt experimental methods, he advocates 'what have proved useful elsewhere, the comparative method and so-called natural experiments' (Diamond 1997: 424). He looks at human history in relation to proximate and ultimate causes, the latter being environmental factors that discriminate between continents and regions regarding the potentialities for food production.

Diamond begins with the interesting example of the development of diversity in Polynesian societies and argues that the 'categories of difference within Polynesia are essentially the same categories that emerged everywhere else in the world' (p. 65). Differences in economic specialisation, social complexity, political organisation and material products are related to differences in population size and diversity, which are related in turn to environmental variables. Polynesia did not develop the full range of world variation, the use of iron for example, because 'no Polynesian island except New Zealand had significant metal deposits' (p. 66). Time was also a factor. 'Given a few more millennia, perhaps Tonga and Hawaii would have reached the level of full-fledged empires battling each other for control of the Pacific, with indigenously developed writing . . .'.

Time is obviously a consideration in any developmental process, but we have here the notion that it is in itself a causal factor when what seems to be at stake is the build-up of systems of cultural knowledge, which is never simply a matter of endurance, of longevity, of automatic evolution.

Comparing this area with the central region for the development of early agriculture in West Asia, Diamond argues that the Fertile Crescent's advantages for food production do not include any supposed advantages of the peoples themselves, but rather that the many distinctive features of the 'climate, environment, wild plants, and animals together provide a convincing explanation' (p. 143). The limitations on the development of food production in New Guinea and the eastern United States had nothing to do with the nature of the people but depended entirely on the local 'biota and environment'. The inhabitants domesticated all that was available.

That is too facile a conclusion. It excludes the long period when they domesticated nothing and neglects the role of culture in the acquisition and development of information. People rarely know all there is to know about their environment, nor do they exploit all possibilities. Many mistakes were made, many restrictions introduced. Why did the Near Easterners not consume pigs nor the Indians the cow?

Diamond has a geographical explanation for most questions, for example why Europe took the lead from the Fertile Crescent. One can, he claims, point to proximate factors behind Europe's rise: its development of a merchant class, capitalism, and patent protection for inventions; its failure to develop absolute despots and crushing taxation; and its Greco-Judeo-Christian tradition of critical empirical enquiry (Diamond 1997: 410). But technological superiority 'stemmed ultimately from Europe's much larger history of densely populated, economically specialized, politically centralized, interacting and competing societies dependent on local protection' (p. 358). There is much to be explained in this choice of features (which in my view is as questionable as most Western notions), but for Diamond the ultimate cause lies elsewhere. The Fertile Crescent enjoyed a head start because of its range of domesticable wild plants and animals, but after their domestication it possessed 'no further geographic advantages' (p. 418). So with the Greek conquests, power shifted westwards, then to Rome, finally to west and northern Europe. That shift was erosion-led because of low rainfall and the destruction of forests; the eastern Mediterranean was 'an ecologically fragile environment' (p. 411). The west had a more robust one with higher rainfall. China also lost its early advantage. Europe had many states and an 'ingrained commitment to disunity' (p. 413) because of its indented coastline and high mountains. Columbus could seek support for his explorations from different governments, whereas China suffered from a (despotic) unity.

The selection of pros and cons seems quite arbitrary. There may be some advantages in disunity, although a significant proportion of Europeans no longer think so. In fact the Roman empire did constitute a unifying factor, as did the Holy Roman Empire and the unity of Christendom that followed. There were a lot of advantages in large-scale unity, which Diamond at this point chooses to disregard. In China it meant fewer external wars, less wasteful competition, a wider, more integrated market for consumer goods (which the US and others are consistently trying to promote), more accumulated knowledge. Indeed Diamond elsewhere regards the size of 'societies' as being a critical factor in their development. But not here. China's 'despots' could certainly 'turn off the tap' but they could also turn it on, as with the encouragement of the production of silk and other exports or the extension of new varieties of rice in Southern China (Bray 1986; Diamond 1997: 416).

On Africa, Diamond concludes that 'Europe's colonisation had nothing to do with differences between European and African peoples themselves, as white racists assume. Rather, it was due to accidents of geography and biogeography, in particular to the continents' different areas, axes, and suites of wild plants and animal species' (Diamond 1997: 401).

Africa, of course, did initially 'colonise' Europe, since it produced the first human species, which emerged in the context of its favourable climatic and biological conditions. Diamond sees any differences in people's achievements as being either biological (giving rise to racism, not only white) or geographical. But he neglects the fact that after the emergence of differences humans become cultured, as a result of which differences in the 'peoples themselves' may occur since many of these cultural elements (for example natural language) are internalised. The problem is not simply innate differences versus environment, at least when the latter is interpreted in purely physical terms (Diamond 1997: 405). Accidents of geography alone cannot account for the colonisation of Africa, as Diamond accepts when he deals with proximate causes in the form of guns, steel, etc.; such factors cannot be reduced to geographical accidents in any meaningful way. Indeed he recognises the role of 'human inventiveness' when discussing 'geographical determinism' but he is unable to bring such considerations into the forefront of his conceptual scheme, and that is necessary if we are to pursue his aim of establishing history as a science on a par with evolutionary biology (p. 408).[2]

It is again these geographic factors that are seen to account for Europe's superiority over the Americas. 'That's an enormous set of differences between Eurasian and Native American societies [the absence of domesticable mammal species] – due largely to the Late Pleistocene extinction (extermination?) of most of North and South America's former big wild mammal species' (Diamond 1997: 355). Otherwise, the Aztecs might have ravaged Europe.

Most of the Americas was not occupied by food-producers but by hunters and gatherers, a fact attributed entirely to the local paucity of domesticable wild animals and plants, and to geographic and ecological barriers that prevented the existing crops and the few domestic animal species of other parts of the Americas from arriving. These were 'the sole missing ingredients'. However, did the former inhabitants of California and Oregon remain hunter-gatherers 'merely because they lacked appropriate domesticates' (Diamond 1997: 367)? From one standpoint, the argument is both obvious and circular, but the climatic difficulties are no ultimate explanation when we see what happened across the Sahara or the Taklamakan deserts.

For Diamond culture seems to be regarded as a purely dependent variable. Yet we have many examples of 'backward' peoples deliberately hanging on to their way of life even when alternatives are offered them. Among the LoDagaa of West Africa, my friend Bonyiri rejected plough agriculture because with the plough, cows would be farming, not men. A similar story occurred with water-mills in Ethiopia. We see what happened in China and the Soviet Union until very recently, and today in a number of Islamic

---

[2] I believe Diamond to be wrong when he discusses African achievements in the production of steel. African furnaces did not produce high temperatures and they were consistently unable to manufacture the barrels of guns and therefore, unlike Arabia, India and Japan, duplicate European firearms and start their own armaments industry.

countries, as a consequence of the deliberate rejection of what is seen as the American way of life. There may be more positive reasons why people may wish to preserve their existing way of life which they rightly see as threatened by the import of 'foreign' crops or animals.

Cultural factors, Diamond acknowledges, are relevant, as are the influences of individuals, but their historical role is very limited (Diamond 1997: 417). Some cultural variation is a product of the environment but minor cultural factors are among history's wild cards, unpredictable. Culture is always a residual for Diamond after 'the effects of major environmental factors have been taken into account' (p. 419). It is this view of culture that leads to his account of state formation being unsophisticated and inadequate. That account is based upon the classification adopted by some American anthropologists of a division into bands, tribes, chiefdoms and states. On state formation it is claimed that smaller units do not merge voluntarily into larger ones; they do so only by conquest, or under external duress (p. 283). This view appears to ignore experiences such as that of the Alur of East Africa who invited chiefs to come and take charge (Southall 1956). The discussion of the hydraulic thesis is equally inadequate; no one supposes that all states were based on irrigation, but some were, and the evidence about whether irrigation preceded or followed state formation is hard to resolve.

His suggestion concerning state formation is that 'the size of the regional population is the strongest single predictor of societal complexity', which seems difficult to prove or falsify for West Africa, and is in any case circular in argument (Goody 1980; Diamond 1997: 284). Diamond's calculations are often basically of this numerical kind. 'With a mere 1,000,000 people, New Guinea could not develop the technology, writing and political systems that arose among populations of tens of millions in China, the Fertile Crescent, the Andes, and Meso-america' (p. 306). The reason for its limited population was that food crops supplied little protein and the production of pigs and chickens was low (why?); the area of Highland New Guinea was small and intensive cultivation had to be confined to the mid-montane zone between 4,000 and 9,000 feet. Hence the population was too small for complex political development.

Diamond's geographical bias is often too earth-bound. He makes much of the difficulties of North–South communication across climate zones, as distinct from the case of East–West links within them. He acknowledges that the Chinese overcame this problem, partly because of south-flowing rivers and man-made canals, though he says nothing of India. But in those cases North–South links were also possible because of the exchange of products from different climate zones via sea transport. That form of exchange could have happened in the Americas, for the narrow Panamanian isthmus would have been an advantage, as it was later for the Spaniards; boats also did exist in the Pacific North-West, the Maya built coastal trading stations on the Caribbean coast, and claims have been made for long journeys from South America to the Pacific Islands (not to mention more speculative contacts between Asia and Mexico). Why are these factors relevant in one case and not the other? Geography in itself hardly provides the answer.

While geographical factors were certainly important in the shift from hunting and gathering to agriculture, those factors were present during the previous hundreds of thousands of years of the Old Stone Age. The end of the Ice Ages (and their corresponding pluvials) does not seem in itself a strong enough factor to account for the emergence of food production in these favoured areas that Diamond indicates provided botanically and climatically the proper environment. As I have noted, part of the environment consisted in the 'culture', the behaviour patterns handed down from one speaking animal to the next; at first those traditions developed very slowly over time and changes only gradually became more frequent. The world cultures of humans were remarkably similar in their material aspects, whatever the physical environment, until the Upper Palaeolithic. They became more diversified with the advent of food production and increasingly so with the coming of the Urban Revolution of the Bronze Age and its burgeoning craft manufactures, including the production of scribes. And the speedier the pace of change, the accumulation of cultural 'inventions', the less significance is to be given to geography, since its physical limitations are precisely those which culture, learned behaviour, assists humans to modify or overcome. Diamond, however, maintains that the 'persistence of Chinese writing in Japan and Korea is the visual twentieth century legacy of plant and animal domestication in China nearly 10,000 years ago'. Thanks to the achievements of east Asia's first farmers, China became Chinese. The notion of ultimate causes seems very ultimate and neglects too many intervening factors to be very convincing.

We need to look at long-term history from a cultural as well as geographic perspective, especially after the Bronze Age. Why was it that the paths of Africa and Eurasia diverged in the way I have suggested?

Sub-Saharan Africa had adapted to the production of food, and later on accepted the technology of iron from the Mediterranean. But it never adopted the plough and animal traction, the wheel, and only in limited ways the control of water for farming. Even with the advent of Islam a millennium ago, the uses of literacy were minimal. It might be assumed that the Sahara barred the way but in fact we find wells in desert areas which made use of the rotary principle, while rock engravings of wheeled vehicles appear right across the sand-sea. It is true that the forest environment did present problems for large animals in the form of the tse-tse fly, and the plough is less useful in that environment and for the cultivation of tubers such as yams. But there is a great deal of savannah land in the Sahel region of the West and in East Africa which did not give rise to these problems. However, any change to intensive agriculture and to urban society would have entailed considerable investment, a great differentiation of rich and poor and a completely new and complex social organisation of production which Africa was not prepared to accept. The initial disadvantages of adopting a new system outweighed any possible, unpredictable and invisible long-term gain. However this may be, the paths of these two continental areas did diverge in ways that affected conceptual systems, property, kinship and marriage, religion, politics and most spheres of human activity.

Bronze Age cultures certainly developed in locations that were especially suitable to intensive cultivation and the control of water. River valleys in warm climates were obviously candidates for these advances in production and in culture more generally. However, what happened was of course the result of human ingenuity, which manifested itself in varied ways. The wheel was invented once in the Old World and its use spread from a single centre, which thereby gained immense advantages. It spread from there to other societies where the craft technology was sufficiently advanced and the possible applications for transport or raising water were apparent. In this way culture fed upon itself and heralded the next step in a cumulative process, each contribution to which depended upon human agency.

The socio-cultural systems of Africa and Eurasia differed in substantial ways which made it much more difficult for the former to take off in an economic or political sense. World religions and later world education were imported rapidly and successfully to Africa; but with economics and politics it has been another story. Whereas Asia on the other hand has found it much easier to establish stable regimes and developing trade and industries.

There are of course differences in the family systems of Europe and Asia, especially after the advent of Christianity (as I discuss in chapters 2 and 3), but they are not of the kind to inhibit such developments; nor yet are any differences in property relations, which have been wrongly polarised in terms of individual and collective forms of tenure.

My account concentrates on the two major 'revolutions', the Urban Revolution of the Bronze Age and the Industrial Revolution of the late eighteenth century, but that is of course in no sense to deny the existence of other major changes. However, these particular shifts had far-reaching implications for the world that the intermediary ones did not have. And they were indeed based on more material factors than in Marx's sequence, on basic changes in the means of production, of destruction and communication, which were sometimes accompanied by but which in many cases preceded fundamental changes in social relations. The first 'revolution' gave rise to complex strata ('classes') based on differential access to the means of production, especially to land; this had extensive repercussions on social life, on people's perception of difference and on their doubts about the system (chapter 10). The second dramatically altered family relationships and working conditions as well as access to material and immaterial possessions. Moreover, both were associated with technological changes that affected cognition, people's understanding of the world, often through education. In the first revolution there was writing itself, in the second there was the mechanisation (begun earlier) of literate production through the printing press and the eventual application of steam power, as in the late eighteenth century factory.

The notion of the 'unity' of Asia and the Mediterranean at the time of the Bronze Age derives of course from the work of Gordon Childe, who saw Oriental power and knowledge as transforming Europe in later prehistoric times 'much as European power and knowledge had transformed the world under capitalism' (Gilman 1981: 1).[3] We do not need to see that 'unity' as being caused either by active borrowing or by parallel innovation, as Renfrew and others have insisted; no doubt both processes were at work. Nor do we need to decide between so-called evolutionary and functionalist arguments about whether or not capital-intensive agriculture preceded or followed elite formation; we need simply note for the moment

---

[3] Gilman discusses the updating of Childe, giving recognition to Europe's own innovative role, a modification that (in my view) should be reciprocal.

that agricultural production did intensify and that as Coles and Harding (1979: 535) observe, the most obvious consequence for the Bronze Age is 'the rise of the privileged'. Gilman sees social stratification as related to a 'capital-intensive subsistence technology', a view that has received broad support. It is certainly confirmed by my own observations in northern Ghana, where the acquisition of a tractor then made possible larger claims on 'communal' lands and produced a greater surplus. It is true that we have to account for the initial investment in the tractor, by personally accumulated funds or by government 'loan', but having obtained the tractor, superior achievement and status (not yet class) were almost immediately consolidated.

Nor yet do we need to decide whether the Bronze Age constituted one world system or more. Nevertheless all those discussions about 'unity' bear upon the general thesis about the uniqueness of the West. For the notion of a world system beginning in about 1450 CE in Europe is inevitably challenged by those who understand the extent of Asian trade after the Bronze Age (for example Schneider 1977; Frank 1993, with comments by Eden and Kohl). Whether or not we can speak of early 'world systems' with some similar characteristics to later ones (in terms of centre–periphery relations, interlocking economic cycles and trade in high value luxury items) does not affect my argument; except if we say, following Frank and Gelb, that 'our now single world system has historical continuity for at least 5000 years', that consideration must modify any view of East–West differences. We certainly cannot agree with the early emergence of different modes of production in Asia of the kind that are implied in the Soviet prehistorian, Diakonoff's, account of 'the rise of the despotic state in ancient Mesopotamia' which assumes the birth of Asiatic despotisms as early as the third millennium (Diakonoff 1969). It also sets aside Polanyi's notions of earlier 'pre-capitalist' economics, and of Finley's associated views of the Ancient Economy.

The objections to refutations of European exceptionalism are always countered, as by Gellner, with the question, Why England? Why Europe? That is a proper question, though the answer does not altogether lie within my competence, but has to do with competitive advantage. On industrialisation Marx (and many economic historians) was basically correct. In the sixteenth century, England, like much of western Europe (and in the centuries before that, southern Europe), had a successful mercantile economy, emerging from the relatively stagnant Middle Ages and eventually catching up with its Asian counterparts. Part of Europe's success lay in the ability promoted by guns and ships, by maps and adventure, by knowledge and inventions, to penetrate the semi-world system of Arab, Indian and Asian commerce and to import, with the aid of bullion looted from the New World and acquired by exchange from West Africa, large quantities of Asian goods, mainly Indian cottons, Chinese porcelain and Indonesian spices. Because of their quality and their colours, the manufactured cottons and porcelain were immensely popular on the European market, especially with women, and severely challenged existing local products. Towards the end of the seventeenth century western European producers of cloth attempted to exclude Indian cottons. As a result there was enormous pressure to provide equivalents at home. Raw cotton was therefore imported and Europe gained a commercial advantage over the East by reproducing more cheaply at home by machines the handmade commodities from abroad. That happened both with coloured cotton cloth and with coloured porcelain. But it required a large number of inventions, which Marx outlines for textiles, before this could be accomplished. Those inventions were offshoots of the scientific developments that emerged in the West with the decline of religious restrictions on man's curiosity, with the forming of large societies for the advancement of knowledge and with changes in the mode of communication, mainly the printing press, that facilitated the transfer and growth of information. And there was the ingenuity of human minds attempting to solve the problems that faced them.

In conclusion, Marx neglects the Urban Revolution of the Bronze Age and its important contribution to the achievements of the major Eurasian states, which were heavily stratified societies with a complex division of labour. Looking backward from a nineteenth-century European standpoint he was concerned to account for achievements of Western industrialised capitalism by tracing out a unique series of 'progressive' developments in that continent. In this he has been followed by many, including Anderson, Brenner and others, who radically distinguish between achievements in Europe and Asia, in a sense from the beginning of 'civilisation', concentrating too much on politico-legal differences and too little on similarities at the level of the means of production and of communication. It is true that Anderson's sensitive discussion, at the same time as giving more stress to the Renaissance, recognises the parallels with Japan, which only lacked the classical background, but he too fails to give sufficient weight to Chinese and Indian developments.

Diamond on the other hand starts from the animal kingdom and sees the greatest shift as being that from collecting food (hunting and gathering) to producing it, in other words the earlier Neolithic Revolution. For him the continental distribution of domesticable plants and animals structures future history in determinable and continuing ways. He even claims that the modern world is still dominated by the two earliest cultures of food production, the Fertile Crescent and China, through their offshoots (for example Europe and the US) (Diamond 1977: 417). That causal sequence is again of an 'ultimate' kind, a highly diffuse link which seems to downplay subsequent cultural developments, especially the Urban Revolution which so dramatically differentiated the food-producing societies of Africa and of Eurasia, namely the extensive against the intensive working of the land.

From their different viewpoints, both Marx and Diamond underplay the importance of the Urban Revolution of the Bronze Age, the first in favour of what he saw as the main developmental sequence based on the history of Europe, the second in favour of a geographically determined Neolithic Revolution, after which socio-cultural influences are heavily discounted.

Part I

FAMILY

This first section begins by summarising earlier works on the possible uniqueness of the West in relation to 'modernisation', 'capitalism' and 'industrialisation'. Chapter 2 goes on to suggest that a number of the 'unique' features of the European family are linked to the advent of Christianity and its establishment in a 'great organisation' by means of the acquisition of formerly 'family' property through gifts and legacies. In the third chapter I question more specifically some demographic accounts of the differences between the West and the Rest, and their relation to socioeconomic development. Chapter 4 constitutes a review of the history of the European, largely English, family centred on the work of Wally Seccombe. Once again his interesting Marxist account gives too much weight to 'the Uniqueness of the West' and specifically to 'the peculiarities of the English'. In my view the author, like many others, does not fully recognise the particular position of women in the major European states as recipients of conjugal funds, in the shape of the dowry and of inheritance, in comparison, for example, with African cultures. That fact strongly affects their situation, especially their class situation, as well as influencing strategies of marriage and heirship.

That theme is continued in the discussion of love, which attempts to break its association with modernisation (in many sociological and historical debates) as well as with Europe, seeing the expansion of love discourse as relative to changes in the mode of communications, specifically the advent of literacy and the development of printing and the novel.

Chapter 1

THE EAST IN THE WEST

Since the eighteenth century the social thought of the West has consistently sought out reasons why 'modernisation' should have taken place in Europe rather than the East. That problematic was later taken up by Karl Marx, as it was by Max Weber. For the former, Asiatic exceptionalism put Asia out of the general line of development to modern society. For the latter, a whole array of fundamental features – caste, clan, economic ethic – made the East an unfavourable seedbed for capitalism. Those ideas have held sway in much historical and sociological thought, for example in work on the family which sees Europe, or north-west Europe, or sometimes even England, as having a family system ('a nuclear family') that favoured modernisation whereas in other parts of the world different family structures inhibited such developments.

It has been suggested by some that I am tilting at ideas that have passed into the history of the social sciences, though others (including Sen 1996) profoundly disagree. It is true that when dealing with this general problem of the Uniqueness of the West, directly one feature has been shown to be more widespread, some authors come up with another Eurocentric suggestion. The discussion becomes hydra-headed. But the specific features I have dealt with previously still seem to be widely used as ways of accounting for the socio-economic development of Europe, and in any case the general problem remains, as we see from a recent thoughtful piece by Wallerstein. In an article in the *New Left Review* he looks at what he sees as the attack on Eurocentrism, arguing that while we should be aware of the European foundations of the social sciences (setting on one side the contributions of Ibn Khaldoun and the separate traditions in Asia), we should recognise that over the last two centuries Europeans have been 'on top of the world' and have controlled 'the wealthiest and militarily most powerful countries' (Wallerstein 1997: 94). This being the case we should hesitate before throwing out existing hypotheses. However, that does not seem to me to follow if these hypotheses can be shown to be wrongly based: we should not hesitate whether or not we have a viable alternative.

In his paper Wallerstein seeks to protect himself against the accusation of Eurocentricism, claiming he even believes that it was to their 'historic credit' that China, India and the Arab world did not 'go forward to capitalism' (p. 105). He takes the view that there has always been a degree of commodification and commercialisation, some entrepreneurs, merchants or 'capitalists'. But he sees a difference between that situation and one in which 'the capitalist ethos and practice is dominant'. 'Prior to the modern world system . . . whenever capitalist strata got too wealthy or too successful or too intrusive on existing institutions, other institutional groups – cultural, religious, political – attacked them, utilizing both their substantial power and their value-systems to assert the need to restrain and contain the profit-oriented strata' (p. 105).

Here Wallerstein seems to be talking about several different processes, that of world domination made possible (as Cipolla suggested, with guns and sails), the advent of science and of mass factory production (industrial capitalism), and the dominance of the bourgeoisie. Clearly these features are inter-related but are they best described in terms of the coming of 'capitalism'? Wallerstein does not give up the claim that 'something special was indeed done by Europe in the sixteenth to the eighteenth centuries that did transform the world'. He concentrates on the value aspects and sees capitalist developments as toxic but counsels against trying to deprive Europe of its specificity on the grounds that we are depriving it of an illegitimate credit. Morally he may believe it was a backward step; I find it difficult to understand that he sees a *realistic* alternative. In any case what I want to try to query are some aspects of that claim.

Let us begin by insisting that there does exist a problem to be explained, namely, how did the West come to be so successful, firstly in the development of artistic and knowledge systems from the Renaissance onwards (for example in the development of experimental science) and secondly, how did the West come to develop industrial capitalism? The two aspects are not independent – the first depending on developments in mercantile capitalism – but they are separated in time and do not constitute a single event.

I have recently been considering this problem in a book that has appeared in English, under the title *The East in the West* (1996a). Its aim is simple. In Europe in sociological, political, historical and much anthropological theory, and in most everyday thought, the West is taken as the model for the process of social development leading to industrial capitalism and to modernisation more generally. Let me take for granted that notion of 'everyday thought', since this is almost by definition ethnocentric in whatever culture, certainly in advanced societies. Regarding anthropological discussions, there has been a constant attempt to see Indian and Chinese societies as following quite a different track from the West, one that does not and could not lead to modernisation, capitalism and industrialisation because of persisting cultural features. The sociologists, Durkheim and Mauss, include China in their essay on 'Primitive Classification'; they classified the world in fundamentally different ways from us. The anthropologist, Lévi-Strauss, compares the Chinese kinship system with that of the Australian aborigines; they had basically different ('elementary') family structures from us. Chinese time concepts too have been seen by the orientalist, Needham, as circular, primitive in comparison with the linear concepts of advanced societies. Equally the south Indian systems of marriage have been compared by the anthropologist, Dumont, with those of the Kariera in Australia. Of course there are differences between the East and the West, but are they ones that make the development of modern institutions impossible and lead us to group the Asiatics with so-called 'primitives'? Or at least see them as so completely different from ourselves? For Dumont has also seen the Indian sub-continent as marked by hierarchy in opposition to the Christian West's individualism, a hierarchy that is characterised by allocating superiority to the other-worldly, to the Brahman, and hence ill-prepared for a modern economy.

Historians have tended to go even further in privileging the West; indeed many of them, especially English historians, privilege their own country because of its introduction of industrialisation. To explain this development they look for deep-seated causes of a cultural kind, seeing for example English (or in some cases Anglo-Saxon) individualism as critical to the development of the modern world. That is a topic to which I will return, though I would wish to point to some fundamental disagreements about the historical record. The anthropologist-historian, Alan Macfarlane, sees individualism as a peculiarly English quality which was instrumental in that country becoming the First Industrial Nation. That view has been challenged by a number of scholars, for example by the historian, Chris Wickham, in his account of early medieval Italy (1981).

The other major category of scholar involved in this discussion has been the sociologists, among whom I include Marx and Weber. Marx elaborated his sequence of development on the basis of Western European history, drawing a line from Germanic (or 'primitive'), to ancient, to feudal, to capitalist forms of society. Weber accepted a similar sequence but looked in the East for more specific factors, often non-economic ones such as caste and kin groups, that may have blocked the developmental process, as well as ones that promoted that process in northern Europe. While there has been some criticisms of these ideas, by and large they still hold sway among the vast majority of Western social scientists.

The notion of Western advantage was bolstered by looking at the religious ethic and giving value in the modernising process to the Protestant variety in its approach to economic matters. Demographic historians have seized on the family as constituting an important difference, the nuclear family or household of the West as opposed to more extended varieties, which are seen as collectivities that suppressed individualism and inhibited capitalism. Note that in these two respects, it was not only Europe that was being distinguished from Asia, but Protestant north-west Europe from the Catholic south, which in the analyses of Laslett and the successful Cambridge group of demographic historians was thought to have larger households, earlier marriage of women, and fewer extra-household servants (all three of which factors may be linked together). What these authors were concerned with at this point was the development of industrial capitalism, the factory system rather than mercantile capitalism which had of course a much wider distribution, and they interpreted modernisation in this highly specific way. So that all the many achievements of Italy, for example, leading up to the Renaissance – which on the commercial level business historians like de Roover see as creating many of the institutions (banking, bills of exchange) that were basic to capitalism – were neglected. It is clear that capitalism in its mercantile variety, which for modern Europe developed largely in Italy, did not depend upon those demographic and social features that have been seen as distinguishing north-west Europe; Italy was much more advanced in Renaissance times than the area in which industrial capitalism later developed. That fact leads one to suspect the nature of the terms in which the discussion has taken place.

Let me be clear. I do not wish to deny that from 1780 on, possibly earlier, the economies as well as the knowledge systems of north-western Europe outstripped the rest of the world in certain important respects. It is the nature of the explanation that troubles me. In looking for the causes of these developments sociologists and others have tended to seek out permanent, deep-seated cultural variables, forgetting that what they need to explain is a temporary state of affairs. For not only did southern Europe outdo the north at an earlier period, but I argue that before the Renaissance China was in some ways more advanced than the West. What these long-term cultural explanations of 'modernisation' tend to do is to primitivise the East on a permanent basis, by making it more despotic almost by nature, or by seeing it as having elementary ('primitive') forms of kinship, time-reckoning, social relations and conceptual rules generally. In this and other ways scholarship has taken a wrong turn which I argue has influenced not only our understanding of the East but our understanding of ourselves.

One specific way it went wrong was in terms of 'rationality', modes of reasoning. Max Weber argued that capitalism required a special form of Western rationality, the rationality of world mastery, which others did not have. I begin with an examination of forms of logic, which are formal procedures for reasoning, arguing that while as (Evans-Pritchard maintained) all societies have their own logical systems (none is pre-logical in the philosopher Lévy-Bruhl's sense), there is certainly something different about the formal procedures developed by Aristotle and the Greeks which defined logic for many centuries to come. I argue that the development of formal logic, especially in the shape of the syllogism which Aristotle favoured as a means of proof, as a procedure for sequential reasoning, was made possible by writing, which enables one to make explicit and formalise the implicit procedures of oral cultures.

However, we find the syllogism not only in Greece but in other literate cultures, in an embryonic form in Mesopotamia (as Bottéro has argued) and well beyond the Near East in India as well as in the Buddhist logic of China and Japan, where there are a variety of forms of syllogistic reasoning, some of which sound very much like children's games.

My conclusion is that forms of logic and sequential reasoning are no strangers to Eastern cultures and there is no need to assume a special form of Western rationality that permits *us* rather than *them* to modernise. Indeed, when we look around the world today (as distinct from the time of Marx and Weber), we see that there is something important lacking in any discussion which seizes on a supposedly deep-rooted cultural feature to explain a temporary state of affairs. If you attribute developments to the Protestant ethic, how are you going to explain what has happened more recently in Japan or China without perceiving the equivalent of the Protestant ethic in Buddhism or in Confucianism? Similarly with so-called Western rationality.

Interestingly for my argument, there was no continuous Aristotelian tradition in the West. The works of Aristotle were in fact partly mediated by the East, at least the Near East. Andalusia in the south of the Iberian peninsula remained in Arab hands until 1492, long after the Christians had re-established themselves in the north of Spain. It became the channel for much to pass from the Arab and the Near Eastern world to the 'West', especially by way of the Muslim-Jewish element of the population. Of particular significance was the work of the Muslim-Jewish scholar Ibn Rughd (1126–1198), known in the West as Averroës, who produced perhaps the most important scholarly work of the Middle Ages and contributed to the rise of Scholastic philosophy (Libéra 1991: 13). He commented upon virtually all the works of Aristotle at a time when the West knew few of them. His *Commentaries* were translated into Latin at the beginning of the thirteenth century and became well known in European universities; for four centuries, from 1230 to 1600, it was he who 'incarnated philosophical rationality in the Christian West'. In this perspective the philosophical rationality of the West owed its genesis to a Muslim-Jewish scholar from Moorish Spain. What he did was to lead the West to a return to the works of Aristotle, written some 1500 years earlier and now resurrected, reborn. No clearer demonstration could be given of the devastating loss in knowledge that struck the post-Roman, Christian West and that it required the help of the Muslim world to revive. For me the important point is that we cannot take the Western model as leading in a teleological manner from ancient society to the modern ('capitalist') world as is often assumed. Progression was blocked; the Middle Ages suffered from a loss of knowledge. Moreover it is an error to see the East as a case of a failed progression (Asiatic stagnation) and then to look round at Oriental societies to search out the blocking factors in their cultures and at the Occident to uncover the favourable ones. The East was well ahead of the West in many spheres, as has been shown over the last few years by Needham's monumental study of science in China.

From rationality I turned to book-keeping, partly because of the play of words with *ragioneria* in Italian, *livres de raison* in French, partly because literacy was involved in both, and partly because Weber and other German scholars saw one of the foremost examples of Western rationality as being the double-entry book-keeping that first emerged in Italy in the fourteenth century. That was described by Weber and others as a rational, scientific form of keeping accounts, essential to the development of capitalism and the modern world.

There were certainly advantages for some operations in a double-entry system. But it is difficult to see this as making the difference between 'scientific', 'rational' forms of book-keeping and others. The line is drawn too heavily to the exclusive advantage of Europe. The facts must make us modify our view. Firstly, many commercial and even industrial firms in Europe continued to use single-entry right into the nineteenth century. So it could not have been that essential.

Secondly, book-keeping had started with the keeping of books, in other words with writing itself. It was certainly an important innovation for commerce, as anyone will appreciate who has seen traders in an oral culture trying to cope with a multitude of credit transactions. Literacy made it possible to extend the numbers of transactors and the number of transactions without having the well-nigh impossible burden of trying to store these in memory. In Mesopotamia writing was used very early for such commercial purposes. Indeed, a French scholar Schmandt-Besserat has argued that the shapes of tokens used in neolithic markets in the Near East were the real precursors of writing. Merchants would later place these tokens in a clay envelope to send along with goods to a distant purchaser in order to act as a kind of bill of lading, to certify the number and nature of the goods being sent. Later still the tokens were actually impressed upon the wet clay to show what was in the envelope; finally the tokens themselves were omitted, leaving only the representation of the tokens, in a form of writing.

Accounts were also kept of trading expeditions in which a number of individuals took part to raise capital and share the risks. The profit and loss could be worked out and shared among the participants in the joint venture. Once again this institution was a precursor of the Mediterranean *commenda*, whereby merchants took shares in an enterprise, sometimes seen as critical to the development of early capitalism in Europe with its joint stock companies, but in fact a feature of all complex literate trading systems, sometimes using family members, sometimes unrelated traders.

Such record keeping continued throughout the Near East. In his discussion of Goitein's description (1967) of accounting fragments of the eleventh and thirteenth century in the Jewish community of Cairo, pre-sumed to have been made by bankers, Scorgie shows that they have a bilat-eral form akin to a modern T account, pre-dating the known usage of such a form in Italy (Scorgie 1994a: 140). In that country the *paragraph form*, with revenue written above expenditure, was used until the bilateral form was generally adopted in the fourteenth century or later (de Roover 1956). The Egyptian accounts used certain conventions that have also been found in the Indian Bahi-Khata system (the zero sign denoting the posting of an entry) as well as in Florentine book-keeping (striking through with a slant-ing stroke to indicate settlement) (Scorgie 1994b). The bilateral form does not appear to have been used in Roman accounting except in one example on a papyrus roll from Fayyum in Upper Egypt from the years 191–2. That finding supports the suggestion I have made concerning accounting sys-tems; once a particular point has been reached, subsequent advances in complexity and efficiency may appear in a variety of contexts.

More radical claims have been made. The precedence of the Near East (specifically 'Arabia') in 'the method of arranging and adjusting accounts' was recognised in an early textbook of 1765 by Gordon, who saw the art as subsequently 'communicated to all the cities on the Mediterranean' (Gordon 1765: 13–14, quoted Scorgie 1994b: 31). A later writer, Colt, sug-gested that the Italians most likely picked up, among other things, all they ever knew of double entry book-keeping at Constantinople, Alexandria, or some other eastern city (Colt 1844: 230, quoted Scorgie 1994b: 31). While there is no evidence for this, a recent writer has argued that the influ-ence of the Muslim empire and its Jewish traders on accounting in Italy was 'through their earlier development of the antecedents of accounting' (Parker 1989: 112, quoted Scorgie 1994b: 31). Others have claimed an Indian origin for double-entry in the Bahi-Khata system; there was cer-tainly a great deal of early trading by Jewish and Muslim merchants between India and Egypt as the Geniza fragments record (Goitein 1973; Lall Nigam 1986; Ghosh 1992).

There was clearly much communication. The Greeks took over from the Romans and were superseded by the Arabs. Cairo was in steady com-munication with India as well as with Venice. So that it is quite possible for accounting practices in those areas to have been transmitted to Italy before the fourteenth century. Such possible transfers did not appear to extend to double-entry itself but did include the bilateral forms which were its predecessors.

These early accounts were then in single-entry, but they developed complex forms. In order to try to find out what could be done with single-entry, I spent a short time in a traditional *pedhi*, accounts office, of a firm in Ahmadabad in western India that managed a number of cotton mills. These were modern enterprises, exporting to Europe and employing modern machinery on a completely industrialised basis. Yet by using a number of ledgers (just as we find in the early Italian records), they could keep track of their accounts and work out a balance sheet.

The method was in some ways less efficient than double-entry (which on the other hand is more complex to manage) but it served its purpose and did not prevent the development of mercantile and indeed industrial capitalism. There was certainly nothing irrational or non-rational about this form of book-keeping.

Thirdly, while double-entry is associated with the name of the Italian monk, Pacioli (his work is dated 1494), Europe is not the only place to have invented the system. Something very similar was developed for commercial purposes, apparently independently, in southern China. We do not know the date, but in a rather similar commercial environment to Renaissance Italy we find continual improvements made in the forms of accounting.

Improvements they are. We should not look upon them as quantum leaps of which only the West was capable because of its superior rationality, but as particular advances made against a similar background of commercial activity in literate societies.

For at that period, when Italy was making significant cultural advances in Europe, the leading commercial powers in the world were in fact China and to some extent India. When the Portuguese arrived in India, their ships were smaller than the local variety, their traders were less important; they were amazed at some of the towns they encountered and at the productivity of the handloom cloth industry which provided the bulk of their exports to Europe. It was the same with China. Marco Polo wondered at the size and significance of the southern Sung capital, which he called 'the greatest town on earth', far and away bigger than Rome.

Like India, China had developed considerable proto-industrial activity, especially in silk and above all in ceramics. Just as the French get the word *indiennes* for coloured cotton textiles from India, so the English derive their word 'china' from the porcelain of that country, indicating the dominance of the East for these two highly important commodities for which the West could at first offer only gold and other bullion in exchange (as in the Roman period for spices, silks and perfumes, about which the moralists loudly complained). Just as large quantities of hand-painted cottons came to Europe after the opening of the sea route, so did similar quantities of porcelain, transforming the domestic environment and the tastes of the inhabitants. Significantly, factory production of consumer products in Europe began with the copying of Indian textiles in Manchester and of Chinese porcelain in Delft in Holland and the Potteries in England.

Until the advent of the Portuguese with their superior armaments, Chinese and Indian merchants dominated the South Seas and the Indian Ocean, which formed an eastern world system of its own. We find Chinese pottery on the East Coast of Africa, and Indian cloth was traded there in pre-Portuguese times, just as it had been with Indonesia and Indo-China. These Easterners were then the great voyagers, traders and explorers of the major part of the world, to whom Europe, during the Middle Ages (especially Western Europe) was a backward appendage. We are used to seeing the Mediterranean as the centre of the commercial and intellectual worlds. But in the Middle Ages and before that was not at all the case. After the fall of the Roman empire, Europe suffered a great decline in trade, in the production of goods and especially in the production of knowledge. The view of Europe as the sole centre of the entrepreneur, the pioneer, the individualist, the thinker, needs radical revision, and not only for this earlier period.

Let me turn to the question of the individual and individualism which plays so important a part in sociological discussions of the rise of capitalism and the world expansion of the West. When the term 'individualism' came into the vocabulary of European languages (c. 1830) in England, it was used in a pejorative way, by the Right to describe the atomisation of contemporary society, by the Left as antithetic to socialism. It was de Tocqueville who gave it a more favourable tone in his treatment of democracy in America: 'Individualism ... disposes each member of the community to sever himself from the mass of his fellows and to draw apart with his family and his friends' (de Tocqueville 1945: Book 2, chapter 2). That was what capitalism, modernisation, entrepreneurship needed.

The genealogy of this supposed quality is subject to major disagreements. The British anthropologist Macfarlane sees it as essentially English (or rather, Anglo-Saxon), a product of the German woods. The French anthropologist Dumont argues that it was Christian. While Indians, constrained by family, caste and religion, can be seen as individuals-in-the-world, it is only in Christianity, a society based on the equality of all believers, that we find the true institutionalisation of individualism, 'individuals-in-relation-to-God'. What Protestantism did was to apply this religious concept to secular life, to the world of capitalist individualism (Dumont 1983. For a criticism see Morris 1987). For Dumont this quality distinguishes Europe from India and China, and from Islam too, and paves the way for capitalism. Medieval historians like Morris (1972) have seen the notion of individualist structures as already established in Europe in the eleventh and twelfth century. The art historian Burckhardt, who developed the idea in his *The Civilization of the Renaissance in Italy* (1860), saw individuality as something emerging from the flowering of the 'free personality' in Renaissance Italy, especially Florence, whereas in earlier societies man was conscious of himself only through some general category (Watt 1996: 120). For the literary critic Ian Watt, individualism has nothing peculiarly English or Italian about it; Don Quixote and Don Juan were Spanish, Faust German; all three adopted a posture of *ego contra mundum* (Watt 1996: 122). All were Europeans, from the south as well as the north.

In north-west Europe others tended to see the matter differently. The theologian, Troelsch, claimed that 'the really permanent attainment of individualism was due to religious, and not to a secular movement, to the Reformation and not the Renaissance' (Watt 1996: 163, quoting Troelsch 1931: 119). The distinctive note of puritan teaching was individual responsibility, not social obligation.

One major reason for this lack of consensus is that the concept of individualism is a very broad one which has to be interpreted in a contextual sense. What is one being individualistic about? Experience in other cultures does not lead to the impression that Indians or Chinese are overpowered by caste or kin in the way that Dumont and before him Weber (and numerous others) assumed, that is, in a way that would prevent them becoming entrepreneurs. Indeed the streets of European cities today give the lie to such notions. It is true that what we might well regard as the institutions of civil society are easier to escape from in a pioneering or mercantile economy such as we find in the early modern West; there was more scope for personal freedom. But similar opportunities existed elsewhere and threw up individuals, especially 'on the margins' of other societies, including Eastern ones. That is true of the North-west Frontier of India and it is true of the Water Margins in China, the home of bandits who are by calling strongly individualistic.

There is a good case for seeing a type of individualism as a characteristic feature of literate societies (writing is more individualistic than talking)

and especially of their literary products, such as the major myths of Western society, as Watt has maintained in a recent account. We get that impression partly because of the nature of literary invention after the Renaissance,
with its cultivation of the novel and the drama, which often require heroic
characters who stand up against the world.

In any case the critical question for world history is whether or not this
characteristic can emerge in a society when it is presented with a new challenge, such as capitalist activity, mercantile or industrial. And today we see
that it can do so in many places, in Hong Kong and in Ahmadabad, as in
Senegal and in Hausaland.

However, anyone who has worked with another culture knows very
well that the notion of the individual is not confined to the West. Evans-
Pritchard spoke of the spirit of individualism among the Nuer of the Sudan,
and the experience of any serious fieldworker tells the same story. Ideas to
the contrary belong to the kind of highly ethnocentric vision that cannot
differentiate one Chinese from another. They all look the same, part of a
collective horde with fixed customs, as distinct from us, who are all different, everyone an individual, acting rationally. That ethnocentric notion,
decked out in scholarly garb, lies behind many developmental schemata
that see the world as shifting from collective to individual institutions, for
example, in land tenure or in the family. Such general assumptions ignore
context. It is true that some collective rights to land disappear with
advanced agricultural systems, but our methods of production in manufacture are in many ways much more collective than those of simpler societies,
as are other aspects of our social environment, including the notion of
social welfare and pensions.

The sequence of development, from collective to individual, lay at the
back of some of Marx's thinking and it has dominated much historical work
on the family, where the extended families of peasant societies are seen as
giving way to the nuclear families, with their individualism, of modern
ones. When the Cambridge Group of demographic historians started to
examine parish records in England, they discovered that as far back as they
went (to the sixteenth century), there was no evidence of extended households (they were dealing in size of *households* rather than of families). This
led some to argue that England was therefore particularly prepared for the
Industrial Revolution, which sociologists like Parsons have seen as requir-
ing (ideologically and practically) a small nuclear family. Later historical
demographers extended this privileged area from England to north-west

Europe, the cradle of capitalism, drawing a contrast with southern and eastern Europe which were never seen as having made it in the same way (even though clearly the south had done so earlier on).

The argument is misconceived in several ways. It is true that by the Middle Ages Europe had lost most of the wider unilineal descent groups (clans and lineages) which were characteristic of much of the Mediterranean region in pre-Christian times. Not entirely. Klapisch has spoken of lineages in Florence, others among the Grimaldi of Genova, while Couroucli has found them in Corfu. And they were present until recently in mountainous areas such as Scotland and parts of the Balkans. But Germanic peoples do not seem to have had clans of this kind, organising kinship in bilateral kindreds instead, tracing relationships through both mother and father. Gradually these kindreds too became less significant as the state took over some of their functions (for example, vengeance) and as the Church organised its own form of spiritual kinship.

But while the range of kinship ties shrank, they were never restricted to the nuclear family alone. In any case, although sociological and folk wisdom in the West suggested that the small family, the nearest thing to the individual, was central to the development of capitalism, favouring as it did the entrepreneur, the evidence from contemporary Japan and especially from China and India shows that capitalism, industrial now, mercantile then, can take root perfectly well in societies with more inclusive types of family structure. Indeed, some observers have suggested that these societies display a kind of 'collective capitalism' (as distinct from the 'individual' variety of the West) precisely because kinsfolk are very much to the fore in the business arena. Yet according to Weber, Parsons and many others, that activity should be dominated by bureaucratic criteria, by non-family recruitment, favouring the family in any way being seen as nepotic, that is, sinful and inefficient. However, not only at the wider family level but even at the yet more inclusive one of corporate lineages and castes, these groups could become heavily involved in business and did not simply block development as Weber and others suggested. Faure's (1989) analysis of the southern Chinese lineages as business corporations shows this very well; they accumulated money from members and they invested in a variety of activities, including business transactions, hoping to make a profit for the benefit of members, rather like other charitable bodies.

We find the same spirit in a caste of bankers, the Chettiars of south India, studied by Rudner (1992). These moneylenders operated very successfully at home and abroad in south-east Asia. In the Chinese case the lineage served as a means of accumulating investment capital; in the Indian situation, the Chettiars could borrow money at better rates among caste members because of the element of trust that existed between them and, no doubt, because of the control exercised by the caste council; they could then lend this money to outsiders at a higher rate of interest. In other words there were certainly some advantages in collective groups as far as raising money and getting advantageous rates were concerned. Trust entered in as a commercial factor.

However, the radical contrast of so-called collective capitalism with Europe's individualistic approach is quite misleading. The latter notion is part of our mythology, represented most clearly in Daniel Defoe's Robinson Crusoe, who, marooned upon a desert island, managed to maintain life and eventually escape, by devoting himself all alone to hard work. In fact early mercantile capitalism, in whatever country, depended heavily, if not on collective groups, at least on ties within the extended family for similar reasons that we have seen in Asia. The Italian bankers in Tudor England who organised much of the export of wool and cloth on which the prosperity of the country largely depended, were cousins of bankers in Tuscany or Lombardy; one of the main streets of the City of London is still known as Lombard street. Bankers did not work as individuals so much as in family groups, like the Rothschilds, the Fuggers or Barclays, with people whom they could trust (rather than bureaucratically recruited outsiders who were more of a risk) and with those from whom they could raise money. They did not always operate on an individualistic or even a nuclear family basis, though they often did that. The fact that the business was a family one meant their planning was based on the longer term, rather than the short-term interest of shareholders, more concerned with the annual profit and loss.

That is particularly true of banking but is also the case with trading and manufacturing. Even where firms were set up by individuals, they may utilise inherited capital (or the wife's dowry), and they obviously soon become family businesses when sons and daughters get involved; the business is what sustains the family, like a farm, while the family sustains the business. Indeed, the most successful commercial enterprises in Britain today, found prominently in every High Street, namely Marks and Spencer and Sainsbury's, consistently have family members on the board as well as among the managers. Even though they have public shares issued on the Stock Exchange to raise cash, many shares are owned by the family who retain a measure of control. What is true of commerce is also true of industry. Far from there being any incompatibility between family ties, even extended ones, most firms contain a strong family component. It has been estimated that 90 per cent of firms in that very successful manufacturing economy, Taiwan, are based on the family. What is perhaps more surprising is that even in the most prominent capitalist power in the West, America, the figure is not very different, and includes not only small firms but large ones like Ford, Seagrams, IBM, which are marked by family participation at various levels. Participation also brings conflict and feuds of course. It is just this double-edged family participation in business that forms the basic plot of soap operas the world over, of *Dallas* in the USA, Galsworthy's *Man of Property* (1922) in England, and I have seen much the same not only in France but also in India.

My argument here is that in making a radical contrast between the collective East and the individualised West we have blinded ourselves to the operation not only of Eastern societies but also of our own, not only in the past but in the present too. In the past we have tended to neglect the role that ties of kinship can and have played in the development of mercantile and industrial production and exchange. Although de Tocqueville included the family within his notion of individualism, others do not, but aim at an absolute Crusoe-like individualism, seeing a depersonalised bureaucracy as the model for modernisation. In the present we have moved to systems of welfare that stress the direct relationship between the single individual and the state, leaning towards an atomisation of social life. Every person has rights to welfare. As a result of the increasing demands from the old and from single parents, even the role of the state in such matters has now tended to become reduced because of the spiralling costs. The problem is that when state support is insufficient because others object to high taxation, which is a form of social sharing, the responsibility for maintaining the old – and in many cases the young (or anyone in a crisis, for example through unemployment) – falls inevitably on the family who are being encouraged, in Britain for example, to fill the gap and take up roles that earlier were standard within it but have subsequently been devalued. There is a complete contradiction here with the insistence on absolute individualism. Under these changing conditions it is likely to be those southern societies in Europe, the ones who were considered malplaced to meet the Industrial Revolution because of their wider family ties, that are likely to come off best. The so-called amoral familism of Italy, so frowned upon among others by the American observer, Banfield, is likely to prove an asset rather than a disadvantage. For obvious reasons, the family has always been an important factor in social organisation, remained so under earlier capitalism and continues to be, in changing forms, today.

We can look at the history of the landmass of Europe and Asia in two ways. We can lay stress upon the division into two continents with two substantially different tracks of development, the Occidental and the Oriental. The Occidental derives from the classical tradition of the Mediterranean societies of Greece and Rome, culminating in the Renaissance, the Reformation, the Enlightenment and the Industrial Revolution of Western Europe. The Oriental on the other hand is seen to derive from quite 'other' sources and to have quite 'other' characteristics. Alternatively, we can place the emphasis on the common heritage of both parts of Eurasia from the Urban Revolution of the Bronze Age, with its introduction of new means of communication (the written word), of new means of production (of advanced agriculture and crafts, including metallurgy, the plough, the wheel, etc.) and of new forms of knowledge. The former account is embodied in much Western sociological theory; history and the humanities stress that account and the resulting division of the continents into West and East. Without wishing to deny the specificity of cultural traditions, including that of Europe, it is easy to exaggerate these claims to long-standing differences, especially when our own society (very successful in these latter centuries) is involved. That is what I maintain has happened in much of Western thought and scholarship. The distinctiveness has been blown up at the expense of the similarities, distorting not only the understanding of the Orient but of the Occident too.

Chapter 2

THE UNIQUENESS OF THE EUROPEAN FAMILY?

As we saw in the last chapter, the question of the uniqueness of the European family has become of especial importance in historical and sociological studies because of a possible relationship with the growth of industrialisation, capitalism and modernisation. The question has been linked to notions of the Uniqueness of the West in relation to the so-called European miracle. That is to say, it is often assumed by sociologists and historians that the Western family is not simply different but is so in ways that are associated with the development of industrial capitalism either as causes or as effects. In both cases there is what Weber called an elective affinity.

I want to deal with three sets of 'family' variables that have been suggested as being distinctive of Europe. Firstly, there are a number of partly psychological variables associated with the work of historians of mentalities, like Stone, Ariès, Shorter and others, which has subsequently played a part in discussions of modernisation, especially by the sociologist Giddens. Secondly, there are the numeric variables associated with the analyses of historians and demographers like Laslett, the Cambridge Group and the statistician, Hajnal. Thirdly, I have myself suggested a number of what I may call 'ecclesiastical' variables linked to the establishment of the Catholic Church as a major social institution.

There is clearly a danger in discussing any hypothesis of uniqueness about one's own continent or even country. A common folk view sees *our* institutions as different from *theirs* in ways that are related to our superiority in modernising, in taking the lead in world events. So that a great deal of the discussion (by English historians) has centred on the English family because of that country being the First Industrial Nation. That priority has been discussed in general terms by writers such as Marx and Weber, writing in the heyday of the development of European capitalism. And the concern with family variables has been accepted by many English historians and indeed vigorously promoted by some, because of this priority. Since sociology and history are largely non-comparative in their approach, at least not on a cross-cultural scale, they may assume difference between European and non-European (or modern and traditional) societies without carefully examining the situation.

So too does much work in my own field of anthropology, sometimes defined as the study of other cultures. Two well-known French anthropologists have drawn just such a line between East and West. Lévi-Strauss (1949) included China along with the Australian aborigines in the category of 'structures élémentaires de la parenté' on account of its supposed practice of cross-cousin marriage, while Dumont draws a parallel contrast between the individualism of Europe and the hierarchy of India; that too touches upon family and kinship, the small family, restricted kin, descriptive kinterms, with the monogamy of Europe being contrasted with the collective institutions of the East. Just as both the historical and sociological lines of thinking link the European family with the development of capitalism (at least in its mercantile phase), so too does the work of Lévi-Strauss and Dumont, though in less direct ways.

My question has partly to do with the suggested features of Europe's uniqueness, some of which are difficult to establish, others definitely questionable, and partly to do with the question of whether these features can be directly related to the rise of capitalism. Before I consider these family variables, I want to look at the way the argument has turned not so much around the European family but its English counterpart. A recent book in honour of Lawrence Stone, the distinguished historian whose work I take as exemplary, is entitled *The First Modern Society* (Beier *et al.* 1989). It begins with a quotation from Stone that is the genesis of the title:

> how and why did Western Europe change itself during the sixteenth, seventeenth and eighteenth centuries so as to lay the social, economic, scientific, political, ideological and ethical foundations for the rationalist, democratic, individualistic, technological industrialised society in which we now live? England was the first country to travel this road . . .
>
> (Stone 1987: xi)

Virtually nothing more is said about this thesis during the following

650 pages. It is simply assumed, we presume by the editors as well as by Stone himself. The one exception is Robert Brenner's chapter on 'Bourgeois revolution and the transition to capitalism', in which the author perceives in England

> a virtually unique political evolution: unified national state via the elimination of bastard feudal regionally-based magnates and the monopolisation of the legitimate use of force by the government; the short-circuiting of all tendencies towards the growth of absolutism, of the tax/office state; the establishment of parliamentary rule; and, ultimately, by the eighteenth century, the creation of an extra-ordinary powerful centralised state, with higher levels of taxation and more advanced forms of bureaucratic administration than could be found perhaps anywhere else in Europe.
>
> (Brenner 1989: 303)

This situation constitutes a political uniqueness which was made possible, he asserts, by 'the parallel emergence of a similarly unique aristocracy'. We cannot doubt that all aristocracies, like all aristocrats, indeed all commoners, are unique. But were they unique in their influence on the process of modernisation?

Like many other historians of England (who according to his account of his own education were taught little about the history of anywhere else), Stone sees modern society as being born in his own country. Italians would undoubtedly point elsewhere, to the achievements of the city states and to their contribution to the development of trade, commerce and business, which was more immediately central to the growth of capitalism. The Dutch would have their own account, emphasising their early struggle for nationhood, their financial and commercial expertise and their overseas trade, not to speak of their many artistic, scientific and democratic achievements. The French might contend that modern rationalism had its home in that country, where contemporary democracy was really born with the French Revolution. But England becomes important not only for straightforward ethnocentric reasons but because of its priority in developing industrial production.

That fact does not justify the wider claims. What historical evidence has anyone brought for England travelling alone down the rationalist road in the fast lane? The notion of its advance to democracy is bolstered by popular credence in the idea of the 'Mother of Parliaments'. But parliaments existed in many other parts of Europe (Bordeaux and Toulouse, for example) and elsewhere. Moreover, the period of the Interregnum apart, the English example was only hesitantly modern until after the Great Reform Act, and even then limitations still persisted, especially in matters of gender.

The question of that country's, or indeed Europe's, advance along the individualistic path has been at the centre of discussion, since that quality is thought to be basic to the development of entrepreneurial capitalism. But any assessment is complex because individualism is a matter of context; one can hardly claim that factory production is more individualistic than running a smallholding.

The concentration upon the Uniqueness of the West, Europe and particularly England, in its contribution to modernisation is entirely in keeping with the work of sociologists, including that of the great German scholar, Max Weber. So it is not surprising to find Stone writing that, though a 'belated discovery' (Stone 1989: 585), Weber's works 'have probably influenced me more than those of any other single scholar' (p. 587), although his mind had already been opened to this line of thinking by his close contact with R. H. Tawney. It was from Tawney he learnt that in this early modern period

> there had taken place in England nearly all the greatest transformations in the history of the West: the shifts from feudalism to capitalism, and from monolithic Catholicism to Christian pluralism, and later to secularism; the rise and fall of puritanism; the aborted evolution of the all-powerful nation state; the first radical revolution in Western history; the first large-scale establishment of a relatively liberal polity with diffused power, religious toleration, and a bill of rights; and the creation of a society ruled by the landed elite unique in Europe for its entrepreneurship, paternalism, and nearmonopoly of political power.
>
> (Stone 1989: 579–80)

The recital of these firsts is calculated to overwhelm any doubts. Such pats on the English back are handed out by progressive and conservative alike. All join in the national claims. Nevertheless a number of these are distinctly dubious. Why locate the shift from feudalism to capitalism in England when we have the example of Florentine and other Italian merchants, who among many other commercial activities financed the export of English wool? Does the work of business historians like de Roover on early

Italy mean nothing? Was not the rule of 'monolithic' Catholicism broken by Cathars, Hussites and other heretics long before the coming of Luther? To arrogate the advent of secularism to England is to overlook French and other traditions. Puritanism rose and fell elsewhere in Europe, in France for example, before it did in England. Quite apart from such doubts about some of England's 'firsts', were there not other features to be found elsewhere in Europe that were equally significant in the modernising of that continent, such as the invention of printing in Germany (critical for scientific advance), the coming of Protestantism and puritanism in Germany and Switzerland, all that took place in Italy including the Renaissance itself with its artistic, humanistic and scientific achievements? The Stone/Tawney list is singularly anglocentric and one-sided.

In fact, Stone narrows Weber's emphasis on the West (Luther after all was German, Zwingli Swiss) to an English focus, without offering any very specific argument in support, which suggests that we may be dealing here with deeply embedded, ethnic attitudes on the unconscious level (which in setting aside Freud he tends to dismiss) as well as with the scholarship itself (in the conscious sphere, seen as the realm of the historian). England is part of the problem. The explanatory model he favours, 'a feedback model of mutually reinforcing trends' (Stone 1989: 592), takes English society rather than Europe, or even Western Europe, as the system boundary. The model inevitably leads him to locate in that country the foundations of modernisation in the 'social, economic, scientific, political, ideological and ethical fields'. That country certainly made some specific advances down the road but an assessment of what it did do can only be made in a comparative setting, firstly in relation to Europe and then to a wider range of world societies. Even so it would be difficult to know how to support such a judgement in the social, ideological and ethical fields at least; and for the others, including the scientific, we need to take a good deal wider span into account than England alone. Or even Europe.

PSYCHOLOGICAL VARIABLES

Let me turn to the family itself. Stone studied the family on his sick bed, reading 'all English collections of family letters, autobiographies, advice books, journals, etc. from the sixteenth, seventeenth and eighteenth centuries'. That is to say, his analysis was 'based almost entirely upon non-quantitative printed literary materials mainly from the elite class' (Stone 1989: 590). There are two immediate problems, one of sources, and the other of how we should evaluate this material of a 'psychological' sort and integrate it with the quantitative data collected by demographic historians. If there is no conjuncture between the two, that would say little for 'history' as a scholarly field, and little too for the respective practitioners of the two approaches.

His book on *Family, Sex and Marriage in England, 1500–1800* (1977) is based on his reading of these English sources, virtually exclusively on the elite. So, quite contrary to his usual awareness of class differences, the holistic feedback model encourages him (at least by implication) to generalise from the elite to the country as a whole, setting aside the largely numerical, demographic, material that provides us with evidence of another kind. He makes occasional reference to these other strata as well as to quantitative data, but by and large consideration of such internal differences, as well as of external similarities, is excluded by the nature of his thesis.

That thesis is 'simply' stated by the author at the outset:

> It is an attempt to chart and document, to analyse and explain, some massive shifts in world views and value systems that occurred in England over a period of some three hundred years, from 1500 to 1800. The vast and elusive cultural changes expressed themselves in changes in the ways members of the family related to each other, in terms of legal arrangements, structure, custom, power, affect and sex.
>
> (Stone 1977: 3)

They were English changes and the critical one was that 'from distance, deference and patriarchy to … "Affective Individualism"', which he sees as the most important change in *mentalité* to have occurred in the Early Modern period, indeed possibly in the last thousand years of Western history. These issues 'are central to the evolution of Western civilization'.

The mentality approach (Stone was an early admirer of the *Annales* school) is based not only on the notion of England as a distinct system with its own unique 'world views' and 'value systems' but also on the idea that the 'evolution of Western civilization' produced results that are at once internally holistic and chronologically layered. Successive states of existence (of the mind?) are held to follow one another in designated steps. The Open Lineage Family of 1450–1630 gives way to the Restricted Patriarchal

Nuclear Family 1550–1700, then to the Closed Domesticated Nuclear Family of 1620 to 1800, followed by the Nineteenth-century Reversal. If we criticise the analysis of these changes, it is not because we perceive an unchanging family, which was the accusation Stone levelled at Macfarlane (Stone 1986). There have been continuities; the nuclear or elementary family and small household has persisted throughout, as Laslett and the Cambridge Group made clear; indeed it is a feature of a very wide range of human societies. But change also took place. However, the interpretation of these changes as catastrophic shifts, as frequent 'revolutions' in 'family type', rarely seems to do justice to the complexity of family variables nor to the way they change over time, not by blocks but by degrees, in ways that are not easily dealt with by global notions of 'mentality', value systems or world views. That is a major problem in dealing with the 'psychological' variables involved in mentalities, which are almost impossible to assess from the historical data.

What is also debatable about Stone's thesis is, firstly, where the supposed changes occurred and, secondly, when. Let me first begin with the place. It is understandable that French and other European historians take a different view of the location of these changes in mentality and family structure. Ariès sees the major shift of sensibility as occurring earlier than Stone and in western Europe as a whole rather than in England. So too does Flandrin in his authoritative work on the history of the family, and the same is true of most continental historians. Indeed, even those as closely attached to the English thesis as the Cambridge Group have discovered similarities in the structure of families in north-western (and sometimes western) Europe. About timing, Shorter sees the changes as taking place later than Stone, Ariès as earlier. The lack of consensus, which must make us query the criteria, becomes more pronounced when we look at the analysis of the demographic material by the Cambridge Group, when a number of the family variables are seen as being in place before the socio-economic changes.

Demographic variables

That group's material is based on demographic data rather than on literary sources. They have isolated a number of features which they see as distinctive of England firstly but also of north-western Europe more generally. There is late marriage for both sexes, the setting up of small, independent households at marriage and the employment of unmarried persons as living-in, life-cycle servants. These features are inter-related, with many of the young going off to work outside the natal home, marrying late (sometimes not at all) and setting up independent households when they do so, a constellation that has been seen by Hajnal as characteristics of what he called a European marriage pattern but is in fact a western European one. More recently (1982) he has shifted attention from household size to differences in household formation.

What is not clear is how far late marriage and the absence of 'grand families' are unique to Europe. Hanley and Wolf have argued that Japan and China differed in much the same way as western and eastern Europe, and have also seen that fact as linked to the recent development of capitalism in Asia. Japan preceded China because it had smaller households (or families), primogeniture and partible inheritance. However, they were writing before the very rapid development of the Chinese economy in recent times, and it does not seem that the latter's family structure was much of a hindrance to these developments. Indeed, some have argued that both in the past and in the present a wider range of kin (household size was not markedly different from elsewhere in Eurasia) held out certain advantages in financial and economic affairs.[1] These demographic differences, while not as radical as they have often been assumed, are certainly more solidly based than the psychological differences announced by Stone, Ariès, Shorter and others. But not only are they not altogether unique (Tibet for example seems to display many of the Western features), their contributions to the development of capitalism are not immediately apparent. Or to put it in more general terms, recent developments in Asia and elsewhere have tended to dissolve the idea of a tight bond between capitalism and any specific pre-existing family form.

THE ECCLESIASTICAL VARIABLES

I want to shift the focus from developments in the early modern times, embedded in the psychological and demographic arguments of Weber, Stone, Laslett and others, and look at some characteristic features of the

---

[1] See my discussion of the work of Faure and others on earlier China and Rudner on colonial India in *The East in the West* (Goody 1996a).

European family before that date, in the post-Roman period. These are not in themselves necessarily unique but in their ensemble have important implications for the social system. Such early features have been looked at from two angles that have long marked approaches to many European institutions. Are their strengths 'native' to tribal cultures or are they Christian, coming from an imported ideology? Or in somewhat different, 'ethnic', terms, are they German or are they Roman? In recent times Macfarlane has seen certain features as of German origin; however, the ones I want to deal with derive from Christianity and were therefore largely unique to Europe.

I have elsewhere (Goody 1983) discussed the changes that the Christian Church (and I emphasise the Church rather than Christianity for reasons that will become apparent) brought about. Here I want to start with a different example to reinforce the thesis. Saint Aubin or Albin was born in the region of Vannes (Morbihan, Western Gaul) in 469 and died there in 550. According to accounts of the saint's life, at this period many lords of the area married their sister or their daughter. At a time when the bishops kept quiet about this practice out of fear for what it might cost them, Aubin did not cease to object. 'You will see that they'll have my head and I'll finish up like John the Baptist', he used to say. His prediction did not come true. What he did achieve in the end was to force the Church of Gaul to condemn these marriages as incestuous and to excommunicate all those who contracted them (Englebert 1984).[2]

The reference may not be to full sisters and actual daughters but to classificatory ones (since marriage to the former was as far as we know confined to some areas of the Near East). But what the document indicates was that the Christian Church was in the business of imposing specific norms on its converts, in this case a ban on close marriages. In addition the famous Letter of Pope Gregory to Augustine of Canterbury that had such a wide circulation in medieval Europe, also made clear that, in opposition to native practice, it banned the remarriage of widows to close affines, for example in leviratic marriage to the dead husband's brother. Moreover the Church forbade adoption (which to Salvianus, Bishop of Marseilles, gave rise to 'children of perjury'),[3] and encouraged a new form of spiritual kinship

---

[2] I am grateful to T. Schippers for this reference.
[3] These observations have not gone unchallenged, and in her review of my book (1985) Zemon Davies cited cases of adoption in medieval France. But it was rare, and as O'Rourke Boyle remarks (1997: 84), 'as a strategy for heir virtually vanished'.

(godparenthood) tied to the Church, so loosening the wider bonds of secular kinship.

These procedures were not enshrined in early Christian theology or texts, they ran counter to Roman practice, and meant that the Church gained significant control of family matters, many of which came under the jurisdiction of ecclesiastical courts until relatively recently. At the same time they touched upon questions of inheritance and heirship, restricting possible strategies of transmission (most clearly in the case of Salvianus and adoption), for only the transmission of property to one's own children was justifiable in the eyes of the Christian God. Property came from God and to God it should return – by way of his Church. The procedures were encouraged, at least unconsciously, by the Church with the result (not necessarily always the explicit intention) of accumulating property with which to construct great cathedrals and to support widows and orphans who otherwise might have been maintained by their relatives (but who were not necessarily Christian). Christians were expected to leave a portion of their wealth to the Church, and in the case of childless couples a much larger part, in order to ensure their salvation. And widows were especially vulnerable to the entreaties of the clergy.

As a result of what amounted to changes in practices affecting inheritance, the Church rapidly gained large tracts of land (a third of the arable in Gaul between the fifth and eighth centuries CE) which they used to build, to support personnel, to invest in liturgical paraphernalia and to aid the poor and needy.

Three interesting questions arise. What about other world religions which required and obtained support for their activities? Islam clearly encouraged people to give property to the 'Church', for example through the *waqf*, a gift for religious purposes. But Islam was not a monastic religion and hence did not require the same diversion of funds that Christianity came to demand. Gifts were in the main directed more locally. The 'family *waqf*' enabled money to be left for religious purposes but to members of the family to support its poorer members (rather like the corporate funds of Chinese lineages). That strengthened the corporate descent group. Hinduism too was more locally centred and non-monastic; Brahmins were supported by grants of land which they farmed (or had farmed on their behalf). Buddhism, however, did originally depend on a massive transfer of funds from the laity to the clergy in order to maintain monasteries and build temples. It is not clear whether this involved changes in the kinship system *per se* but it certainly led to changes in family life and in social structure, which was perhaps one reason why both in India and in China that religion was diluted to such an extent. Indeed, in China the threat to the state of accumulation of property by the Buddhist community at the expense of families was specifically recognised, leading to restrictions on its operations and the encouragement of local cults and of family solidarities (again reinforcing lineages and ancestor worship).

Secondly, as Speiser (1985) has pointed out, one dramatic result lay in the effects of such transfers to the Church on European towns. He maintains that while in Western Europe towns were still rich and active at the beginning of the fourth century, by the seventh decay had taken place to such an extent that some archaeologists and historians see an almost complete disappearance of urban life, apart from a few exceptional cases. This dramatic development took place during the period following the reign of Constantine, when the building of churches and then of monasteries was permitted and encouraged on a huge scale. Major resources were needed for their construction and for the subsequent maintenance of plant and personnel. Accounts of the early lives of saints give some idea of this process of accumulation, which represented a spiritual as well as a material investment on the part of individuals.[4] Such major material transfers to the Church were made partly at the expense of the towns whose endowments and commercial receipts suffered accordingly. In late antiquity rich individuals had gifted or lent money to municipalities, receiving in return interest which was partly financial, partly social. In the third century, inflation destroyed the value of the fixed incomes of the towns which depended upon rents from civic lands, interest on money endowments and the *munera* given by councillors to the places that had elected them – an obligation that came under increasing disfavour. But the main problem for the maintenance of public buildings in towns arose because in the last decade of his reign Constantine deliberately confiscated these rents and dues, as well as seizing temple treasures and estates. That expropriation, which was confirmed by his son Constantine II, had a disastrous effect on public buildings and on the nature of urban life, as archaeologists have noted. In general, endowments now went to the Church rather than to the municipality, leading to an impoverishment of civic culture in the form of baths, theatres and other services.

---

[4] For example the Life of St John the Almoner.

Thirdly, we have to see these changes as taking place against a certain level of resistance, since they affected people's strategies of heirship and prohibited practices that were widely used for these purposes in Asia and the Near East, as well as in pre-Christian Europe. The story of Saint Aubin (as well as the work of Salvianus and Gregory's letter) indicates that force, at least spiritual force in the shape of excommunication, was used to install these new norms. The trend of my argument in *Production and Reproduction* (1976) was that the pre-Christian norms were in a sense 'natural' to Bronze Age societies, adapted to them in a broad sense (close marriage, adoption, widow remarriage, etc.). The new practices that ran quite contrary to this trend would have had to be imposed. While in many cases these new Christian norms were internalised, for there were certain spiritual advantages in acceptance, there remained counter-currents that led the medieval nobles described by Duby to continue to try to revert to the older ones in order to consolidate their position. Such tendencies were also apparent among the peasantry. These largely subterranean trends became explicit in the ideologies of some 'heretical', breakaway groups such as the Lollards and later the Protestants who allowed much closer marriages than had been permitted in the Catholic Church, abolished dispensations, and relaxed other of the norms that had worked to the Church's advantage, even in some cases allowing divorce. But the 'reassertion' of native norms came only with the weakening of ecclesiastical influence on marriage, including Protestant control. With the secularisation of marriage, most of those taboos (except on *very* close, 'incestuous', unions) were finally broken. Divorce was re-established; it had been allowed in Rome, Islam and Israel but was prohibited in Christianity on the grounds that if you entered into a marriage blessed by God, it could never be broken. 'What God hath brought together, Let no man set asunder.'

The introduction of this prohibition constituted a staggering shift in the notion of marriage, as did its subsequent disappearance in recent times. The new-found freedom in marriage and divorce (a freedom for the partners, not necessarily for the children) has produced the most far-reaching changes in the structure of the European family since the coming of Christianity, which institutionalised the ban on divorce.

These ecclesiastical variables were unique to Europe, since they were Christian and ran against the widespread Eurasian strategies of heirship (which for example allowed an Arab husband to divorce a barren wife in order to produce an heir, a strategy not available to Henry VIII of England in the same way). I do not wish to assert that the European family was unique with respect to each of these variables that I have listed, but certainly the general trend was exceptional in the way the kinship system was influenced by a 'great organisation', the Church, influenced away from strategies of heirship that would have promoted the interests of the domestic group. But I do not see them as having any specific influence on the development of capitalism or modernisation. It is true that the Church tended to restrict the efficacy of wider kin ties and to promote bilateral reckoning, features which have been seen as compatible with industrial organisation. But in the latter case German tribes already appear to have been organised bilaterally rather than by unilineal clans and lineages. The last two centuries have experienced determined efforts to abandon the ecclesiastical norms, as Stone has documented in the case of divorce.

Of the other sets of variables, the psychological ones seem particularly dubious, especially in seeing as characteristic of Europe love between conjugal partners and affection between parents and children, a thesis espoused by both Ariès and Stone. Neither (as I will argue in chapter 5) are in any way confined to that continent, nor yet to 'modern' societies. In any case 'affective individualism' is as capable of undermining as of supporting these features.

Equally it is not clear that the structure of the earlier English family (as pointed out by demographic historians with its later marriage, small conjugal dwelling groups and living-in life-cycle servants) provided the advantages along the path to modernisation that some have claimed (see for example Seccombe 1992). Nor were smaller households uniquely European, although the other features were rare elsewhere. Even the 'grand families' of the East were constantly splitting residentially, have conjugal families at their core and have proved no great hindrance to economic and social development. Indeed, the insistence of European historians and sociologists on the role of the elementary family may have prevented them from recognising the part played by wider kinship ties in the rise of capitalism in the West, let alone in the East, where what has been misconceived as 'collective capitalism' has recently been recognised.

Of course the nature of work in advanced societies has had important convergent effects on family life. Some of the recent changes outside Europe have taken the form of imitating the institutions of that continent, the white wedding-dress (in Japan, Korea and China) as much as the stress on the mutual choice of spouse. The latter development would probably have followed necessarily from industrialisation and the individualisation of pay packets (the absence of a joint wage for the cooperating domestic group); the former not. Industrialisation certainly influenced the structure of family life but pre-existing differences have not prevented this development in other parts of the world. Moreover these differences are often less dramatic than is often thought. Following the vast socio-economic changes of the Bronze Age, peasant families everywhere in Eurasia have had some important features in common. A number of the early characteristics of the European family arose from the prescriptions of Christianity which were imposed upon those peasant families in the effort to build up the resources of the Church at the expense of those and other families. These prescriptions clearly made Christendom 'unique', but were they really necessary to the process of modernisation? That seems very doubtful.

Chapter 3

COMPARING FAMILY SYSTEMS IN EUROPE AND ASIA: ARE THERE DIFFERENT SETS OF RULES?

Seeing Europe as the forerunner both in the development of industrial capitalism and of lower fertility, demographic historians have looked at predisposing factors in the complex of family variables that may have led to this situation. We are not directly concerned here with matters to do with individualism, the propensity to save, conjugal love, care of children, or the nuclear family, but all of these have been isolated by one author or another as characteristic of Europe,[1] north-west Europe or England (the location varies, often depending upon the birthplace of the historian). As with Hajnal's well-known European marriage pattern (1965), these features are then contrasted with the rest of the world which never made it. Since this exercise began, Japan clearly has made it, enabling us to set aside certain aspects of the Weberian thesis, for example. Historians and other social scientists, however, have had a field day in pointing out the similarities in family structure between Japan and England/Europe, contrasting it with that of China. Wolf and Hanley (1985) draw a specific comparison of Japan and China with western and eastern Europe in terms of Hajnal's hypothesis. But now we find Taiwan, not to speak of other little dragons, joining the capitalist camp, so quite rightly these family systems are being re-examined from the standpoint of development of various kinds (Greenhalgh 1987; Greenhalgh and Winckler 1990). Confucianism is found to be just as important as Protestantism (Redding 1990).

I want to query some of the demographic and economic presuppositions on which these and other discussions are based as being overly

---

[1] See Ariès (1960); Laslett (1965: 170) (on the uniqueness of political ideas), 195 (on the uniqueness of education); Stone (1977); Macfarlane (1978).

dependent upon the works of European scholars, largely in this case historians and demographers. For looking back from their post-industrial vant-
age point, they have tended to privilege the path of development taken by
the West. Specifically, I want to discuss Hajnal's important paper on household formation systems (1982).

HOUSEHOLD FORMATION IN WEST AND EAST

When demographic historians started to work on the data from English
parish records, the assumption was that pre-industrial households consisted of large, extended families. When this was shown to be incorrect, and
England and much of north-west Europe were shown to have relatively
small mean size of households (Laslett and Wall 1972), the contrast was
then made with the 'joint family systems' of India and China. However, in
terms of average size of households these too turned out to have around five
persons (Hajnal 1982). This information had long been available (Goody
1972b) and had formed part of the lengthy discussion about the role of the
elementary or nuclear family in human societies at large (Malinowski 1914;
Westermarck 1926 [1968]). While their conclusions were not framed in
terms of mean size of households (MSH), the implications were very similar. Most human societies, at all stages of development, were built on the
basis of relatively small conjugal groups ('families'), which often constituted a household from the standpoint of production and consumption.

The search for major differences in the size of households between
West and East has now been abandoned; Russia, for example, has been
found to have a much larger MSH than India, 9.1 in Czap's figures (Czap
1982a, 1982b), fourteen in the nineteenth century, as compared with five in
the so-called joint family households of India, which approximates to the
figure for north-western Europe on which so much has been built (the
'small, isolated, nuclear family'). The focus has now shifted to the internal
structure of domestic groups, and specifically to the related process of
household formation. Hajnal distinguishes two main forms which again
emphasise an East–West divide: the 'joint household [formation] system' of
the major Eurasian societies on the one hand is contrasted with the north-
west European system on the other. The latter is based on late marriage for
men (over 26) and women (over 23), and on the move of those men and
women before marriage to work for others, often as in-living life-cycle

servants. In a Danish sample for 1645 over 50 per cent of those who survived past adolescence had been in service; servants normally constituted
between 6 per cent and 15 per cent of the total population at any one time.
In 'joint household systems', on the other hand, both men and women
marry early and live jointly with the husband's parents, so that two or more
couples inhabit the same unit. In fact the difference is by no means absolute
in terms of structure. In a contemporary Maharastran sample, 77 per cent of
households were not joint (that is, did not have two couples); in the Danish
sample the figure was 93.4 per cent.

In predominantly agricultural societies, if people marry early, marriages are more likely to be 'arranged', whereas with later marriage, men
and women going out in service can save to help set up their own households. They may endow themselves if endowment is prerequisite of finding
a marriage partner. In that case they are able to exercise more choice. At the
same time the labour of the young is held to be distributed more economically, since they go where they are needed, not where they were born.
Nevertheless there is little difference in household size, since fission still
usually occurs in both cases but at slightly different times. As Hajnal points
out, joint households of more than one married sibling tend to split before
or shortly after the father's death, whereas the others divide, in effect, at the
time of the later marriage itself. Each type of household undergoes fission,
so that in the two systems similarities exist in the ages of their heads: when
the split occurs, a new head of a joint household is generally about thirty
(Hajnal 1982: 468), not much older than the average marriage age for a man
in north-west Europe.

One critical feature of north-west Europe is that a couple frequently
established an independent household at marriage, with the husband as
head. When the young (or the 50 per cent of them who went off) had fin-
ished their period of service and got married, the parents went into retirement, often with a contract specifying what they would receive in return
for handing over control (on retirement, see Gaunt 1983). As a result the
majority of people were never members of a 'joint household', whereas in
the other type of society the majority belonged to such a unit at some
period of their lives. The corollary was that somewhat earlier independence
of a household head in north-west Europe meant greater measure of
dependence for young men and women in the work process itself, since
they were working outside their natal households. They were not necessarily working for strangers, for some would have gone to kin; to the extent

that their employers were not kin, the dependency is likely to have been more severe. That at least has been the experience in Africa and there is little reason to assume it is different elsewhere (E. Goody 1982).

However, in another sense, they were clearly more independent of kin, in that as individuals they undertook outside-work experience but as couples also set up separate households at marriage. The fission of the household, the housekeeping unit, is linked to the fission of other domestic groups. The new family may occupy a separate house or dwelling unit (houseful), it may start its own distinct productive unit ('farm family') or it may simply establish its own consumption or housekeeping unit (household). All these distinctions have to be graded. Closely related persons tend to live in adjacent houses, and they continue to enter into complex relationships even after residential fission has taken place. It is perfectly possible to describe the Tibetan domestic system as consisting of 'nuclear' housefuls because old people and siblings live in separate dwelling units, which for some purposes are separate households (Levine 1987). From another standpoint we are dealing with the interaction between individuals who formerly lived together but now occupy adjacent houses; what would make more of a difference is not so much fission into separate households or housefuls, as the intervention of spatial mobility, movement to another settlement, the scattering of kin.

The difficulty of defining the household (a unit of consumption or housekeeping) as an exclusive unit, which Hajnal discusses from the standpoint of listings, is that in rural communities it may be overlapping rather than exclusive. This problem arises with any kind of formal classification of domestic organisation (especially those involving numerical procedures which require binary decisions). Continuities are broken by having the template of the census-taker placed upon the village. A household shares a table and may include living-in servants who do not cook for themselves. But in many cases some meals are had in common, others not; raw and cooked food is passed to parents in adjacent cottages, apartments, even rooms. The boundaries vary with context, especially where food is not consumed together around a table (as in Europe) but in bowls in distinct groups (as in Africa). In that continent husbands, wives and young men often eat separately, while aged parents would be sent cooked food if they live nearby; in India today cooked food regularly travels outside the unit of food preparation. In neither case is the compact housekeeping group the same as that for food consumption, even if this is calculated on a daily basis.

In rural Europe houses (housefuls) sometimes contained more than one couple; if they were kin, much sharing would occur, joint meals on national holidays, family celebrations and on other occasions; in addition other ways exist of passing food, raw or cooked, between individuals and groups, including the retirement contract that provides for consumption from a common supply.[2]

The central problem here is the perpetual one of the *coupure*, the cutting point. For in many societies, especially those in India and China, housekeeping, and to some extent residence, are 'nested' features. To take an extreme example of large domestic groups from my own fieldwork, when a LoDagaa girl gets married, she moves into her husband's house (compound). But immediately she is allotted her own room, her own hearth, and her own food supply; otherwise she would soon leave. On the other hand cooking tasks are shared with her co-wife and possibly with her husband's mother, each with her own hearth of three stones; the wives provide food for the husband on a rotational basis. In China, where monogamous unions prevail, the new wife will cook jointly with her husband's brother's wives on the same stove until the brothers divide; signs of fission in the household usually begin to appear early on and gradually develop into a definitive split (Cohen 1976; Hsieh 1985).

Headship of the household is nested in similar ways. African fathers do not usually retire in quite the same way as many European and even some Chinese and Indian fathers do. But nevertheless decision-making on farming matters is increasingly taken over by their sons. (For India, see Epstein 1962.) Equally in Europe and Asia, the fact that division has taken place does not entirely exclude the senior generation from playing a part. But there is a difference. Why? Mainly because in Africa there is no handing over of the support systems, except in pastoral groups like the Fulani, where a man may gradually denude himself of cattle in favour of his children (Stenning 1958). But cattle constitute a different form of capital from land, one that is capable of directly reproducing itself. In most traditional

---

[2] It is almost impossible to gain an understanding of this material from the usual kind of historical records; it has normally to be done by observation. A notable exception is Sabean's careful analysis of the ample data from Neckarhausen. The material on the LoDagaa refers to Goody (1956, 1958, 1962a). The references to India are based on my limited fieldwork in Gujarat. For Europe the material is derived from my own observations in south-west France as well as from Collomp (1983), Arensberg and Kimball (1940) and other historical and ethnographic sources (see Goody 1983, 1990, 1996a).

African societies land was not a scarce resource, and except for land around the compound did not enter into the normal system of transfer. In any case there was no material way in which land could be sold to create an annuity or a pension; parents had to rely on more spiritual claims for support in their old age and continued to play a part in the domestic groups as long as they could (Goody 1971).

The question of headship is therefore more problematic in practice than a census return or formal legal document might suggest. That is especially true after the establishment of a new housekeeping unit. In his detailed study of Neckarhausen in Württemburg from the seventeenth century, Sabean (1990: 266) writes that 'Houses in Neckarhausen frequently contained more than one married pair . . . throughout the eighteenth and nineteenth centuries, they averaged about 1.4 "families"', a figure that approximates the size of 1.59 'households' in the Free Royal Cities under the Hungarian Crown (1784–87)[3] which Hajnal sees as falling in the joint family range (Hajnal 1982: 469, 482). These German households normally consisted of close relatives. Moreover they often shared a kitchen, even when they did not always eat together, for a son might well apply for his own *Meisterschaft* (to hold the 'purse strings') while using all his parents' facilities. Even after division the father still had a call on the labour of a son:

> although marriage marked a turning point and began a process of redistributing resources, the period of transition was a long one. Independence marked the first stage, but even then there was no sharp generational turnover, and it was a very long time before a young couple got their hands on the old people's property.
>
> (Sabean 1990: 267)

It is true that parents and children might pay each other for the labour involved, for the introduction of book-keeping encouraged very precise notions of exchange, but at the same time they cooperated in work or in shared living areas, storage, and tools. Sometimes they even advanced each other cash or covered each other's debts. The boundary question has important analytic repercussions which are raised in acute form when Hajnal suggests that 'In a system where the children move out of the parents' household, the consequences of ageing cannot be dealt with in this

[3] The Hungarian figures refer to the total population while the Neckarhausen pertain to the village.

way', that is, by taking over their work (Hajnal 1982: 477). That seems to place too much stress on who is in a household at one particular time. Why cannot a child help who has moved next door, or back into the house?

The problem of nesting and cross-cutting in north-west Europe is recognised by Hajnal, partly because the various lists seem to be in doubt about whether or not to include the elderly in the same household. But he firmly contrasts this feature with the joint household systems of India and China, which are seen as fully integrated units, giving little room for doubt as to who its members are. In north-west Europe, on the other hand, 'there were frequently to be found living in the same farm, house, or group of building groups of individuals not sharing fully in one integrated house-hold' (Hajnal 1982: 482); the residents included servants and lodgers.

The generational contrast does not seem altogether valid, or if valid all that important, except in terms of how you count. In Tibet households are similar in many respects to the north-west European type, while the boundaries of Taiwanese domestic groups are layered in even more com-plex ways: in some groups members participate concurrently in joint agri-cultural and industrial activities. Complex arrangements of this kind are not uncommon in India, now and in the past. The boundary problem is everywhere present except in the case of the property-holding unit, the 'joint or Hindu undivided family' (HUF) of India, which partly corres-ponds to the inheritance group ('the heirs') in Europe and which is usually far from undivided, either in terms of the preparation and consumption of food or of many other activities.[4] In the case of 'upper' families the bound-aries of the HUF are often defined in legal documents that bring about the partition, and hence as in the case of censuses, precise limits have to be set. The assumption of an overall contrast in the boundary situation, together with the opposition between systems with living-in servants and those without, leads to the drawing of a distinction between those that use family labour and those with hired labour (Hajnal 1982: 473), the first being asso-ciated with the retention of sons (and their wives) within the household, the other passing a proportion of them between households. The radical dis-tinction depends upon a merging of the boundary between household and farm, between consumption units and production units. In Asia, it was

---

[4] On Tibet see Carrasco (1959) and Levine (1987); on Taiwan see Cohen (1976); on India see Shah (1973), Epstein (1962), Mayer (1966); on the general point see the discussion in Goody (1990), especially on the HUF.

perfectly possible to 'hire' additional labour; production units were certainly not confined to family labour. Unlike servants, one did not usually take them on semi-permanently but by day, month, season, like industrial workers; they did not live in but usually came from the same village where they had a similar role to the landless (or insufficiently landed) labourers in Europe, a feature that is intrinsic to the stratified societies of Eurasia as a whole. Creating a radical opposition between the distribution of forms of labour tends to simplify notions of the rural economy in both regions, where artisanal-like agricultural work has long played an important part and represents work outside the house for which payment is made. Sometimes payment is 'non-monetary', as with the so-called *jajmani* system of harvest contributions, but 'payment' is still made, often in grain, if not for specific but for annual services; it is a type of reward that bears some structural resemblance to that for in-living as against day labourers, for here too individuals or groups are employed on a more permanent basis and rewarded partly in a non-monetary fashion by being provided with bed and board. The opposition simplifies the agricultural scene itself. In Neckarhausen fathers sometimes hired the labour even of their own sons, and vice versa. That may appear an extreme form of internal reckoning, but no more so than is embodied in the highly specific clauses of retirement contracts, or than the more general calculation of the profit and the loss which accompanied or was reflected by the introduction of book-keeping to the rural economy.[5]

The two systems of household formation are visualised by Hajnal as deriving from specific sets of rules. The joint household system is constituted by the fact that all the sons bring their brides to their father's house (rule 2/B). If only one son remained in the house and brought in his wife, then this would not constitute an example of a joint household system but rather of a stem household. There are two kinds of 'stem family' systems, one in which the son takes over the farm at marriage (as in north-west Europe) and one where he does not (that is, where he forms part of a stem household under the control of the senior generation, an arrangement which Hajnal claims is not found in north-western Europe). That distinction is rarely clearly marked in practice, since as we have seen, similar

---

[5] Such retirement contracts were found outside the limits of north-western Europe, in the Czech Republic and in Germany (Gaunt 1983; Goody 1990). They represent a formalisation of the obligation felt by children towards their elderly parents in most pre-industrial societies.

relations may exist where fathers and sons are living in adjacent households. According to Hajnal (1982: 486), 'no kind of stem family system can be classified as a joint household system in our sense', since the rule specifies that all sons remain. However, in many cases 'all' is only one when the time comes for handing over. So that by 'stem family' Hajnal refers not to the household as such but to systems of production in which only one son among several takes over from the parents. Even under rule 2/B a joint household will be created only in a limited number of cases where more than one son of a particular couple attains adulthood; and even where this occurs, the other brothers may stay at home and not marry, giving rise, by their abstinence, to a single (or stem) line of filiation; or they may go away and marry, leaving behind a stem household; or even the inheriting son may leave temporarily to work elsewhere, to return when his father retires. In many 'lower' families in China and India, where joint family systems are said to prevail, the early departure or absence of younger sons is required by the paucity of property and leads to the formation of stem households (Freedman 1962, 1963).[6] In other words, rule 2/B applies to the rich rather than to the poor, thus accounting for the larger households among upper groups. Hajnal recognises this fact but since his numerical analysis is linked to aggregate data, the implications regarding the class stratification of household systems, in particular their relation to resources, do not fully emerge. The other major theoretical problem has to do with the analysis in terms of rules which here seem to lead to a premature crystallisation of the situation, raising some of the problems that Bourdieu (1977) found in the influential kinship enquiries of Lévi-Strauss.

In speaking of joint families, I refer to kinship groups; but households are consumption units which in Europe may also include unrelated in-living servants, just as today they may include the au pair. That situation is found less frequently in China and India, where servants rarely if ever eat from the same table, although they do depend on the same supply of food. Once again, the contrast can be drawn too sharply. It is true that in caste societies different groups do not dine with one another; but that was also true in the great houses of medieval England and certainly with later servants in the towns, where upstairs and downstairs were two different worlds.

---

[6] It does not seem to be the case that under joint household systems 'even the poor' formed them (Hajnal 1982: 455), a fact that might account for the similarity of the household sizes in the two systems when averaged over the whole population.

In rural Europe living-in servants are often 'life-cycle servants' (in Laslett's phrase) from similar households, though again less commonly so in the towns. Servants existed in Asia but they tended to come from service groups even when they were living-in (and in most cases they were not). While the latter may have had a separate hearth, they drew their supplies from the same housekeeping unit. So too in a sense do out-living servants, including the specialist workers, who are not provided with food but are rewarded by being paid more for their labour than are the in-living. Both in Europe and Asia money was often involved, whether for specialist, farm or domestic services. Even in-living life-cycle servants may have been working in order to save money for marriage (the self-accumulated endowment) or for some similar expenditure.

Neither kind of domestic servant was at all common in Africa; if you wanted permanent help, you married or reproduced it since there was effectively no wage-labour. Assistance was reciprocal or hegemonic. For in state systems, people acquired slaves (Goody 1971, 1979). Assistance was also reciprocal among the poor in China and India, where domestic service, though not necessarily service in a more general sense, was a class phenomenon. In West Africa there is an analogous institution to the in-living servant in the shape of fosterage, by which younger children are sent at an earlier age to live with kin, sometimes for particular reasons to help in the house or farm, but often on the more general grounds of getting a good upbringing. Under changing conditions, such fostering practices have become orientated in more economic or pragmatic directions, merging into the widespread urban institution of 'housemaids', where they are found in the houses of both kin and strangers. The numbers of foster children in some rural Gonja samples in northern Ghana attained nearly 60 per cent of all children (E. Goody 1982: 39 ff.).[7] Is it possible that the European institution of in-living servants could also be connected with an earlier practice of fosterage, attested for the Anglo-Saxon period, that predisposed parents to send their children away, eventually to stay with non-parental kin? That form of alienation was already common in upper groups (and more widely) for the wet-nursing of infants, which seems to have led to a reduction of the post-partum period of abstinence (or infertility) and hence to increased

---

[7] The figure is derived from the percentage of adults reporting having been fostered. The children between the ages of four and eighteen went to be fostered either for 'voluntary' reasons or because of a crisis (death in the family).

fertility, exactly the opposite effect to service, although fosterage at this age also seems to have resulted (unintentionally) in increased mortality. The factors relating to population control, either subjectively or objectively, are not easy to isolate.[8]

I have suggested that one of the problems with aggregate data is that they may lead to a neglect of vertical differentiation (class or caste) which characterises the distribution of the stem family in China and of servant-hood in India. There is another problem with aggregation. If we view household formation systems as generated by a different set of 'rules' in north-west Europe on the one hand and in India and China on the other; that is, if we see these rules as characterising whole societies, we are led to make too radical a binary division, especially if we do not build into the model mechanisms for shifting from one set of 'rules' to another. Yet precisely this shift is said to have occurred in southern France and the Baltic countries (except for Finland) during the nineteenth century (Hajnal 1982: 450). Could such a change not have happened elsewhere (Hajnal 1982: 476)? And if so, what does this possibility (and the actual frequency) of the occurrence have to say about the relation between the two systems and their constituent rules?

To treat the north-west European household formation system as a distinct entity, rather than as a cluster of variables, is to direct questions to its origin rather than to the factors that maximise this or that element in the cluster. You may be led to presume, as Hajnal does, that this kind of household formation system 'arose only once in human history', although many societies independently developed the alternative set of rules. Such an assumption overlooks or over-rides the existence of internal differences in both areas. And once again it tends to privilege north-western Europe and to primitivise the Asian continent.

When is this invention seen as taking place? Hajnal's evidence relates to the seventeenth century. But legal and other records point to three features that suggest that this state of affairs existed earlier. Firstly, there was the established presence of large numbers of life-cycle servants (though these were also to be found not only in the north-west of Europe but some 'probably' in the south (Hajnal 1982: 476)); secondly, the same is true of retirement contracts (though in more recent times they appear to have been more

---

[8] On wet-nursing, see Flandrin (1979: 203); on the mortality of infants, see Lindemann (1981) and Goody (1983).

frequent in Finland, central Europe and southern France than in England); and finally there is the question of public provision for the poor, especially the elderly, who were not being cared for by co-resident kin. Smith (1979) finds traces of these three features four centuries prior to 1600, although evidence for the very critical factor of late marriage is less forthcoming. But if we may accept the early data for retirement contracts and servants (and perhaps of stem families too) discussed in Homans' (1941) analysis of thirteenth-century villagers in England, we should also note the similar evidence that exists for these institutions in other parts of the world, for life-cycle servants in the case of Jacob's marriage in ancient Israel (which has links with bride service, temporary filiacentric unions and even some cases of adoption), for retirement contracts in other areas of the Eurasian continent[9] and for the public provision for the poor under earlier Christianity outside north-west Europe (Patlagean 1977; Stock 1983), as well as under Jewish (Goitein 1978), Parsi, Jain, Muslim and Buddhist dispensations.[10] The idea that only north-west Europe was charitable to the aged poor outside the family is a myth that derives from ethnocentric preoccupations with the nature of the 'Uniqueness of the West' and of Christian *caritas*. So too is the notion that life-cycle service and early retirement, seen as promoting independence, individuality and mobility, were exclusive to that area (though the first was very common there); variations on these themes were spread much more widely.

I want to elaborate on the question of provision for the poor since mistaken implications for comparative (and indeed European) studies may be drawn from an enquiry that is not widely enough based. The provision of extra-familial care of the old in (north-west) Europe has been seen as a possible check on fertility because it would make individuals less concerned about their old age and thus reduce the propensity to have children to provide for that end. And it has been suggested that such provision existed even before the Elizabethan Poor Laws, and hence prepared the European family for what was to come. Charitable donations are interpreted as an indication of the reversal of the upward flow of wealth that supposedly characterises non-European societies, where adults were in the end dependent upon the production of their children. If the children do not form part of the same

---

[9] For both of these see the discussion in Goody (1990).
[10] Muslim provision is often made permanently through the *waqf* as well as by alms (*saddaq*); Parsi and Jain foundations are extensive not only in India but abroad.

household, then (the argument runs) they were less likely to help, and the slack would have to be taken up by private charity or state support.

There are three problems with this argument. Firstly, such institutions were directed largely at the poor, providing a safety net for those who had no other means of support. Not in every case, for the Church offered a refuge or support for some of the widows and daughters of the better-off (who brought their dowries with them), just as in their turn the rich helped to maintain the Church by means of their gifts. But by and large the demographic effects of charity would only be felt by the poorer elements of the population.

Secondly, such institutions were in no way unique to north-west Europe, nor yet to Europe itself; they existed in Buddhist societies, in the charitable giving associated with the Muslim *waqf* as well as with other types of funded corporation found in China at least since the medieval period (see Rowe 1984). One might go further and suggest that most if not all human societies make some such provision for their less fortunate members. Certainly as far as Eurasia is concerned there is no reason to regard extra-domestic provision of support for the elderly (since that is what would be involved if the practice were to act as a check on reproduction) as in any way unique to the West; in Parsonian terms charity is a structural-functional prerequisite of 'state agrarian societies', as well as a precipitation of the morality that goes 'beyond kinship' and characterises the 'ethical' world religions embedded in them. That is the case if only because highly stratified societies are inevitably characterised by relative deprivation ('poverty' as well as riches), which gives rise to an explicit or implicit perception among some of their members of the discrepancy between rich and poor that in turn may manifest itself in internal questioning or in open protest about this state of affairs; it offends against 'natural justice'. I have discussed this point in the context of the preparation and distribution of food (1982), a matter of very immediate and central concern, as well as with other manifestations of luxury cultures such as aesthetic horticulture and artistic activity (Goody 1982, 1993a, forthcoming). When such concerns get articulated in a written tradition, whether in political pamphlets, in secular ethics or in a religious credo, charity becomes generalised and may even be acknowledged as a duty to God. People no longer offer objects in sacrifice to God, they give them to his Church and through that to his people instead. Such notions are found in all the so-called 'ethical' religions and often lead to public provision for the less fortunate members of society.

Thirdly, if safety-net institutions were characteristic of north-west Europe, they cannot be said to have done all that good a job. Hufton has described the poverty that existed in France in the years before the Revolution. The situation in urban England in the 1840s has been vividly described by Engels (1887). In a recent study of the ample financial records from Neckarhausen in Germany from the seventeenth century onwards, the poor were comprised of the elderly and the unmarried (Sabean 1990: 456). The young acquired property very gradually by a process of devolution, not suddenly at marriage or even at the death of the father, for there was no abrupt handover. Individuals were largely excluded from its direct control until they reached the thirties, then slowly accumulated until forty-five or fifty, after which transmission began to be made to their own offspring (Sabean 1990: 257). Even widows held on to little property themselves, but either remarried or devolved what they had to the younger generation, in both cases in return for support. In other words, by the late nineteenth century the situation had taken a turn which suggests a different process from that implied by those theories that see the demographic transition to lower fertility as connected with the earlier independence of children and the cessation of the upward flows of wealth based on their labour contribution. Rather than a more-or-less abrupt change of status with the death of the father, the young married couple accumulated wealth more gradually and remained in the orbit of the property-holding father or the widowed mother over a long period of time (Sabean 1990: chapter 10). So that the establishment of a separate household did not break the bonds of dependency on the senior generation, who tended to retain more of their wealth for a longer stretch of time rather than to pass it over at the marriages of their children. The move has been towards the diminution of dowry and the retention of property. That does not mean parents did not support or train those children, but over the last hundred years they have progressively retained a larger proportion of wealth in their own hands, with the result that in Western countries today, the married children may be more impoverished than the elderly.

For social scientists the importance of the distribution of such practices lies in the claim that, since in north-west Europe 'the welfare of the indigent elderly was the province of public institutions rather than the family even in pre-industrial times' (McNicoll and Cain 1990: 19, following Smith 1979), fertility was potentially able to be held in check because such provisions remove the worry of financial support which might lead to the search for additional children. The implication once again, as with the institution of living-in life-cycle service, is that Western Europe had some specific key to population control that others lacked and that this key contributed to industrial development. We have seen that such institutions had a wider spread than this claim implies. But their specific incidence remains important and I have argued (1983) that it was in the process of cutting the family down 'to size' in a social rather than a numerical sense that the Christian Church, which benefited directly from the restriction in the range of heirs, took over some of the responsibility for the widows who poorer families found difficult to maintain. But under both types of system – that is, under what Cain and McNicoll (1988), following Hajnal (1982), call the nuclear and the joint – the bulk of individuals always had to rely in their old age, at least in sickness or decrepitude, upon their children. They did so not only for economic maintenance but for general care and emotional support. Nevertheless economic help was often critical. That is the meaning of the notion of *pension*, the contracts that exist in contemporary Finland (Abrahams 1986) and France (the *hypothèque*) as well as in pre-Communist Czechoslovakia and in Austria (Goody 1972c). Only when the *pension* gives way to the pension – that is, to interest from an accumulated fund that others, not the family, arrange and utilise – does the need for economic support from children in old age tend to decrease. That process eventually leads to many of the major industrial activities of society being dominated by the massive growth of pension funds and institutions. But even then such needs do not vanish, since material support is by no means the only component in this relationship of interdependency; still today the old tend to live near their children more for general reasons of support than for economic ones (Young and Wilmott 1957).

In the past the elderly were often poor, despite such safety nets (and in Germany the standards of welfare were high). Even if Europe had this way of preventing the high rise of fertility, from the standpoint of welfare it did not do very well with the lower population growth it had. In her account of the poor of France during the latter part of the eighteenth century to which reference has already been made, Hufton argues that by the 1770s the family economy was no longer viable for a large proportion of the inhabitants. Given the steadily mounting population, they had to piece together an 'economy of makeshift' (Hufton 1974: 69).

The hidden problem behind much of the argument of European historians and demographers who look for unique conditions in the West is the underlying question that faced Marx and Weber. Why did industrial society develop in that continent? Why did they alone invent capitalism and learn to control growth? These are questions that need to be brought to the surface in any general analyses of population growth and development, since the models of both are so firmly rooted in Western experience. Let us leave aside the crucial question of what was involved in the invention of capitalism and the extent to which it was a cause rather than a consequence of a rather late decline in fertility (Seccombe 1993; Szreter 1995). We may question whether the best approach is to propose another unique 'invention' in the shape of a 'household formation system', which stands in opposition to everything outside north-western Europe. Many variables enter into the definition of domestic systems of relationships, even from the standpoint of population and development. Even if we accept the housekeeping unit as the most important one for analysis, constituting so broad a dichotomous typology seems premature. Would we not be better off dealing with the rules as variables among a number of others, some shared with Asian societies, some not?

The factors with which Hajnal is dealing consist essentially of three inter-related ones, the lateness of the age of marriage, the employment of the unmarried outside the household (rather than within) and the fission of the household at marriage. This constellation of features is designated north-western European and contrasted with the joint household formation system of Asia (and in effect Africa). It is specifically seen as linked to fertility control, since the nature of in-living service is seen as making possible variation over time in the age at marriage and in the proportion remaining unmarried (Hajnal 1982: 478). In 'joint household systems', on the other hand, an increase in population led to the underemployment of married adults rather than to a temporary or permanent delay in marriage itself.

What are the precise contributions of the north-west European system of household formation to long-term development? Hajnal is careful to avoid grand generalisations. Nevertheless the thrust of his thinking is to link these aspects of family structure to the Uniqueness of the West, and this is how his analysis has been interpreted by historians, demographers, economists and others (see Wolf and Hanley 1985; Cain and McNicoll 1988; Seccombe 1992 and 1993). It is an argument especially sympathetic to some members of the Cambridge Group, to which he acknowledges his debt. We cannot divorce his discussion from a central theme behind the work of many sociologists and demographic historians (including the Cambridge Group in its earlier phases), which follows a line of argument that sees nuclear families or households as being not only compatible with, but as being causally involved in the initial rise of industrial capitalism. These assumptions tend to be generalised to other types of 'development', and it is significant that in trying to apply the line of thinking suggested by Hajnal, and in pursuing the logical tenor of his argument, Cain and McNicoll have turned his north-western household into a nuclear family (in opposition to the joint variety), seeing other forms of domestic organisations as inhibiting development.

Hajnal himself deals in more specific factors. In his earlier article (1965) he refers to the relation between delayed marriage and the accumulation of wealth, which he suggests contributed to the growth of savings (for capitalism). He sees the migration of young married adults as servants, especially to the American South, as having no parallel elsewhere. But many other groups became involved in the semi-voluntary transfer of population abroad, on similar terms, even from 'joint family systems': the Chinese to many parts of Asia, Indians to the Pacific and the Caribbean, Russians to central Asia, Africans to wherever they can now go. It is difficult to see one general form of domestic polity as having an advantage over another.

Since women were as frequently in service as men, it is felt they had 'greater independence', financially as well as in decision-making. Nevertheless even locally it was as servants they went and they were in a kind of servitude. It is difficult to see them as completely free compared with those who remained with their families.

One important feature of service is seen as its ability to affect fertility control. If economic conditions were difficult people might remain longer in service and hence delay marriage. In a carefully argued section Hajnal (1982: 461) finds evidence that the incidence of service varied inversely with marriage and fertility. As a result he suggests that the two systems of household formation must have reacted 'in fundamentally different ways' to adverse economic conditions. A central thrust of the paper is to show the relationship between variations in age of marriage, incidence of service, fertility and household composition (pp. 478–81). The author conducts a preliminary examination of three situations: Iceland in the early eighteenth century, England in the seventeenth and eighteenth centuries and rural Denmark at the end of the eighteenth. He perceives some important correlations. My comments do not touch upon this interesting point but only on the nature of the overall contrast. The institution of service was 'probably an essential part of the mechanism by which . . . population growth was under partial control'. Populations with joint household systems lack that mechanism (p. 481). True, but the implication that Europe was capable of controlling its population when others were not seems to lack substance. Hajnal claims a uniqueness for north-western Europe which because of service could probably operate 'with a balance between birth and death rates established at a lower level than prevailed in other pre-industrial societies' (p. 478). In Africa the population seems to have been traditionally much more in balance, though possibly through exogenous factors such as disease, warfare and hoe agriculture (Goody forthcoming). In Asia, people resorted to female infanticide, to less fertile forms of early marriage, to coitus reservatus, while delays in marriage were theoretically just as possible if the young stayed in the household as if they moved outside (see Wolf 1995). It must be recalled that the great expansion of population in China and India took place in the context of a highly productive economy.

Later marriage meant joining together 'two mature adults', usually preceded by courtship, whereas in joint household systems marriage was generally arranged by parents. When they married they were on their own. Certainly the timing of marriage makes a considerable difference to interpersonal relationships, but the difference can be exaggerated. Many European parents had a say in their children's marriages if only because of property considerations; Jane Austen's women could be quite independent without going into service. Moreover it is probable that early marriage under parental supervision could have some advantages for mothers and children, as well as for the fathers. Support needs to be valued as well as independence, even in commercial matters, as we see in the case of the German town of Neckarhausen, examined by Sabean, not to speak of the generation of much commercial and industrial activity (Goody 1996a). Indeed, whatever differences exist, it is difficult to see them as contributing in any unilineal way to economic or social development as is often implied. That is to take a too determinative view of the relationship between macro-economic and family variables and to fail to recognise the degree of structural autonomy of each set.

Again, life-cycle service is seen as contributing not only to the decline in fertility but also to the independence of the young (that is, to what others have called individuation), and to the mobility of the labour force, which in turn prepared the way for the coming of the industrial regime. In fact the

stimulation to labour migration has rarely been a great problem in economic change. In India the working masses travel from village or suburb to
centrally located factories with few inhibitions; and in the medieval period
the growth of export-orientated manufactures in the south and of cash-
crops in the north led to more extended movements which have their analo-
gies in the dry-season migration practised today by Mali gardeners from
Haryana to the river valley of the Sabarmati in Gujarat or in the trans-
humant movement of Rajasthani herders from the deserts of Kutch down
to the stubble fields of their agricultural neighbours to the south.[11] These
are types of largely cyclical movement that occur in many parts of the
world and provide models for the kind of labour migration that is promoted by industrialisation, or even by the process of 'bureaucratisation'
and commercialisation (of services as well as goods) that are the characteristic features of much contemporary African urbanisation.[12] It is doubtful if
Europe was any readier for industrialisation in this respect than Africa (it
was in other ways); and in this as in a number of other features, Asia shared
many of the prerequisites, including some family variables, that appear in
Europe.

Thirdly, the fission of the household is often seen as being linked to the
inheritance of property. If landed property is handed down to only one sibling (say, at his or her marriage), then the others may leave and fission
occurs. It is customary to regard Europe like Japan as marked by impartible
inheritance and the rest of the world by the partible variety. Impartible
inheritance equals stem households (or alternatively one couple succeeding
another, as in the Western system), which means independence (of the kind
seen as needed for individualistic capitalism), accumulation (to establish an
independent household), and the regulation of the age of marriage by
which European populations controlled their growth in accordance with
the social and economic circumstances.

There were in fact many areas of early partible inheritance in Europe,
and it has been present virtually throughout the continent since the
Napoleonic regime and its codes (see Yver 1966; Augustins 1989). In any
case the question of impartibility usually refers to the division of land, not

---

[11] I use this example from my own observation in India, but such movements occur in many
parts of the world, especially among pastoralists.
[12] I use the term 'bureaucratisation' to describe a set of processes associated with the build-up
of urban centres. Firstly, there is the growth of government itself, followed by the growth of
what are often initially government-related activities, schools and hospitals.

to the estate as a whole; other siblings normally have to be bought off with movables.

In wider discussions of demographic variables and their relation to socio-economic development, a sharp line is drawn, by different scholars, between the regimes of north-west Europe, western Europe, or Europe as a whole with the rest of the world, but in particular with Asia. The argument of Hajnal acknowledges that mean household size does not differ significantly but pins the difference on methods of family formation. He contrasts the 'joint households' of the East with the single-couple arrangements of the West and sees these as implicated in different demographic regimes and in economic change. The shift in emphasis is welcome but there are several objections. Firstly, the categorisation again overstresses the actual differences, not only in respect of internal structure but of the related problems of service, of household fission and of the public (rather than the familial) safety net for the aged poor. Secondly, the data do not altogether justify such a sharp dichotomy. Thirdly, though this is an issue that cannot be elaborated here, it is not clear how these differences, real or supposed, inhibited or advanced the development of 'capitalism, industrialisation or modernisation'. Is it then true that the differences between the systems were of 'great significance for economic development' (Hajnal 1982: 476)? Of some significance they undoubtedly were, but in the shape that economic development took rather than development *per se*. Many of the fundamental contributions to European capitalism were made in Italy where the alternative system prevailed. Nor would it be correct to underplay the important contributions to mercantile capitalism in India played by the 'Hindu undivided family', although it was often property that remained undivided. In terms of contemporary development, it is the area of 'joint household' regimes that seem now to be making much of the running in the contemporary East.[13]

---

[13] See the extended discussion in Goody (1996a).

Chapter 4

WOMEN, CLASS AND FAMILY

The problems with the study of the family by Europeanists are twofold. Firstly, the terms they use like 'family' are often vague and unsatisfactory for analytic purposes (though they may serve as general signposts) (Seccombe 1992: 343; 1993: 286). Secondly, there is little comparative perspective. Yet this is needed not only to define the technical vocabulary but, more importantly, because every statement about the relation of the 'nuclear family' to capitalism and modernisation or about the invention of childhood is making a claim that concerns not only Europe but the rest of the world.

The history of the family in Europe has become tied in with notions of that continent's unique achievements, especially in terms of 'capitalism' and 'modernisation'. The knot needs to be untied, not in order to weaken the relation between production and reproduction, which Seccombe stresses in these two volumes,[1] but to rationalise at least the pre-industrial situation by reassessing its uniqueness at all levels in relation to other regions of Eurasia. When we do that the strong association between certain 'family' variables and the development of mercantile capitalism (and of modern knowledge systems) in Europe becomes much more attenuated.[2] Later on, the rapidity and innovatory character of mass industrial production did dramatically change the domestic lives of the masses, although many of those changes had and have their parallels in other parts of the

---

[1] W. Seccombe (1992) *A Millennium of Family Change: feudalism to capitalism in Northwestern Europe* and (1993) *Weathering the Storm: working class families from the Industrial Revolution to the fertility decline.*

[2] This is a point I have developed in *The East in the West* (1996a) and earlier in *The Oriental, the Ancient and the Primitive* (1990).

world where there has been a sudden growth in urban living, with all the usual consequences of crowded accommodation, dependent production, the weakened role of extended kin groups (though not necessarily of extended domestic ties), relative anonymity, and looser community controls. However, here as always it is the nature of the link that is at stake. Was it the same for all classes, for both sexes? Were there not continuities as well as discontinuities that related to the different social domains of production and reproduction which allowed them a degree of autonomy? Did political and economic hegemony, both of which demand their own space, always dominate the family?

Wally Seccombe has written a comprehensive two-volume history of the family in north-western Europe from the early medieval period to the present, trying to link the systems of reproduction with those of production, and offering a critical perspective on much previous work in the field. It is the most valuable summary to date of the situation in this crucial part of the world. Some of Seccombe's basic assumptions about the role of the family are built into his overall Western models, but at another level his reassessment of the work of others is a signal success. Starting from a Marxist perspective he concentrates on the transitions from feudalism to mercantile capitalism, to proto-industrialisation and then to industrial capitalism, attempting in the process to do what Marxists have often signally avoided doing in the past, that is, to reconcile demographic with social history. This *de facto* division has tended to give us two kinds of family history: the harder variety centres upon numerical statements about the size of 'families' (in fact households), and the softer accounts on changes in *mentalités*. The history of the family must be built around both, the numerical material buried in parish registers, exploited by the Cambridge Group, as well as the diaries and legal documents that form the basis of the work of Stone, Ariès, and others. One feature that has been lacking has been a serious attempt at drawing together both these threads and their insertion, in any rigorous way, into the wider context of the major social changes through which the West has passed. These tasks Seccombe confronts head-on. In addition he claims to take account of women's history, though the force of this claim is not always so easy to detect.

Seccombe pursues this massive undertaking with very considerable scholarship and many insights. It is one of the great strengths of his survey of the history of the north-western European (mainly British) family that he consistently treats domestic groups not only as reproductive units (for the workforce as well as for kingroups) but as productive ones, both in pre-industrial societies where domestic groups usually work together and also in industrial ones, where he sees reproduction as linked to productive processes mainly through wage incomes. His study will remain a source of reference and debate for many years to come. While other historians have attempted to relate factors such as the age of marriage to the price of corn, or the 'modernisation' of the family to the conditions of the market, he tries to associate the economy and the family in a much more comprehensive manner. To this end he uses a version of the broadly Marxist concept of the mode of production, trying to link relations of kinship and marriage to productive relationships, though not in any absolutely deterministic way.

There is no doubt that such an exercise needed to be undertaken. Seccombe has done so in a way that summarises a great deal of research and throws much light on changes in the family. If I do not see this as entirely successful, that is partly because success is difficult to achieve on such a contentious topic and partly because in this field one needs to look outside Europe even to understand what happened within that continent. Seccombe's account does not always command immediate assent all around, but that is partly a comment upon the nature of a much disputed territory which conceals a minefield of hidden agendas and ethnocentric prejudice. The family has been seen as contributing to or the consequence of a transformation of the economy and society that is considered to have taken place only in England (by some), in north-western Europe, or possibly more widely in Europe. That is, the question of the structure of the family (demographically, developmentally, emotionally) is seen as part of the Uniqueness of the West and the European Miracle. Seccombe is less critical of some of those assertions than he might be, coming at the problem (like the sources he is dealing with) from a determinedly European standpoint.

Seccombe's approach is more innovative for the later period (in volume 2) than for the earlier one. Here he draws out the full importance of proletarianisation in the eighteenth century (with the changes in agricultural and proto-industrial production) and in the nineteenth (with the shift to industrial activity). The emphasis on change leads him into direct conflict with the demographic historians of the Cambridge Group, whom he sees as discounting change through concentrating on the formal structure of the household. Indirectly he is equally critical of family historians of the *mentalité* tendency, for his own general position leans towards a demographic approach whereas the 'psychological' or cultural approaches, whether continuist (for example, as in the work of Macfarlane) or discontinuist (for example, in that of Stone), are largely ignored. He is looking for harder demographic and economic data than they usually provide.

The neglect is perhaps carried too far, for although the results of the latter approach have been disappointing (at least in a comparative perspective), there is undoubtedly a social psychological element in kinship that needs to be linked to the prevailing socio-economic changes. It is this component that Seccombe sometimes tends to play down, for example, in his attempt (discussed later) to account for the 'obligation' which married children continue to feel when in early industrial conditions they expand their household to include 'destitute' parents. Such neglect makes some of his explanations too 'economistic', not because of what they include but because of what they omit.

In dealing with the family under feudalism, Seccombe stresses the significant role of the seigneurial system in commanding the labour-power of peasants and in encouraging primogeniture. That was often the case, especially under the open-field agriculture of the manorial system, where plots were organised for one man or family to work. But primogeniture is never absolute; it is always qualified by equity among kin, a kind of distributional ethic among those raised together, which requires allocations to other siblings. Moreover it is found elsewhere, especially where land is a scarce resource. Indeed, the notion of a single main heir may well be initiated from below, as in the rural France of today, where the code is equal division but the practice is very different. Nor is primogeniture the only system found with seigneurial domination. The diversity revealed in Yver's study of inheritance in sixteenth-century France would be incomprehensible from a more deterministic point of view, and the same could be said for the distribution of gavelkind, Borough French and Borough English in England.

The focus of Seccombe's account is farming families in the early period and the working class in the industrial one. Seigneurial families are excluded, as are those of entrepreneurs, merchants, and the bourgeoisie generally. While such a focus is entirely understandable, it does tend to overlook the vertical interaction of different layers of the society, at least outside the economic sphere. I take my examples from the period following the Industrial Revolution, but the principles are the same and embedded in earlier sumptuary legislation. Later too one finds the possible effects of class emulation (for example, in the disapproval of working wives in the latter half of the nineteenth century, the whole notion of 'moral motherhood' and, after the First World War, the use of contraception) as well as of the way in which some practices of the working class were subsequently adopted by other wage-earning groups (the abandonment of the dowry, common-law unions, the matrifocal family). At the same time, concentrating on the family among the employed leads to the neglect of the role of extended kinship and affinal networks among the entrepreneurial class who continue to have productive and financial property to pass down. The structure of their families was far less 'isolated nuclear' than that assumed to exist among the other classes. Here the 'men of property' may again have had some demonstration effect for other groups or for aspiring individuals in society.

A related problem of taking only a single element in the population (or alternatively of aggregating the lot) is that one loses the perspective of class differences, which may be radical. In China one finds complex households among the rich, simple ones (stem) among the poor; that is a pattern that repeats itself in many parts of Europe. To treat nuclear households as the norm because they are in the majority is to interpret norm in a purely statistical way. Its preponderance will depend upon the nature of the developmental cycle as well as the pattern of fission and (in some cases) fusion. If upper (and older) households are extended (or 'expanded'), it is difficult to see nuclear as the ideal at a societal level (perhaps even for a class); it is to lose sight of the importance of hegemony.

It follows from Seccombe's attempt to link the family with the political economy and to demonstrate the way that family forms are incorporated in modes of production that he rejects the view attributed to the Cambridge Group that the structure of the family did not change from the late medieval period. That is of course the force of his title. He notes firstly that this work takes a very narrow view of the family (in fact it concerns household size and age of marriage, neglecting for example the changes in interpersonal relationships that Protestantism undoubtedly encouraged), and secondly that this contention would deny any effect of the other major socio-economic changes on domestic life, which is equally improbable, suggesting the inadequacy of the measures used. But Laslett is obviously not wrong concerning the data with which he is dealing. Indeed, as I have tried to show, the household is virtually everywhere a relatively small group, as is the conjugal family. Certain areas of kinship, marriage and the family, of reproductive systems, operate relatively independently of the mode of production, which does not have it all its own way. There is a significant degree of structural autonomy.

Seccombe rightly criticises the limitations of using the household as the basic unit of analysis, although it has to be said that these data are often all we have. But he sometimes accepts the same terms of reference. He notes that the studies of the Cambridge Group have shown that 'the households of early modern villagers were overwhelmingly simple (that is, nuclear) in composition'; in one survey there were only eleven 'relatives' outside the conjugal family in 1000 households between 1150 and 1749 but in the nineteenth century there were many more, thirty-two by 1851. But the boundaries of a house are not the same as those of a 'family'. As I sit here in south-west France, an aged farmer walks up the hill to have his midday meal at the house of his already retired son and his wife (who has officially taken over the farm so that her husband can draw a pension). The dwelling groups are separate; the consumption groups are largely combined; kin relations are close. Whether they are living apart (as possibly in the English villages) or together is of limited significance; it is not enough to describe some as nuclear, others as complex families, when one is placing so much emphasis on the distinction in relation to events of global importance.

If Seccombe is critical of the Cambridge Group's ideas about the continuity of the 'nuclear family/household' in England, he accepts with open arms the thesis of the uniqueness of the (Western) European marriage pattern, even following Smith in seeing the genesis of this in England. He argues strongly that late marriage and life-cycle service in other households (of the late-marrying sons and daughters) contributed directly to the advent of capitalism and subsequently to the Industrial Revolution (Seccombe 1992: 230–41). He sees late marriage as increasing longevity, stimulating savings, raising the productivity of female labour and providing a number of other benefits. However, which affected which is a matter for discussion. Some have argued that it is domestic service (like husbandry and apprenticeship) that delayed marriage rather than vice versa (Anderson 1976; Hill 1989: 134). In the same vein others have suggested that proto-industrialisation was already responsible for reducing the average age at marriage in the eighteenth century. This too is a moot point. Not only did the relationship vary in different parts, but the whole calculation of the average age of marriage is in doubt given that 'church marriage may well have covered only a minority of those living as couples' in this period (Hill 1989: 144). In parts 'unmarried motherhood' was common (perhaps for economic reasons), with some handloom weaving families, as in the delayed marriage of southern China, wishing to retain producers at home for as long as possible.

In any case the assumption that Europe invented mercantile capitalism is unsustainable; and if we look at Europe, early developments of that kind took place in the Mediterranean rather than the North-west, the very area that often did not have late marriage. The Industrial Revolution is a different matter. Seccombe's most persuasive argument has to do with the capacity for the case of marriage to be modified in order to increase the labour power available for industrial purposes. Despite its interest, this proposal seems curious. One might also suggest that a higher fertility (with earlier marriage) could have already put pressure on the land, encouraging a transformation of the economy (according to the Boserup thesis) which would absorb the surplus rural labour force. All in all, these factors seem of marginal importance when one considers the alternative possibilities. In any case the late marriage system is not unique; Tibet displays very similar features (Carrasco 1959).

Seccombe points clearly to the fact that because it is largely dependent on census material the Laslett discussion of the family turns on household composition, largely ignoring extra-household kinship.[3] In fact he seems to use the concept in the same restricted way when talking of the relationship of the nuclear family to capitalism. It is because of the problems inherent in both 'household' and 'family' that I have previously advanced an analysis in terms of overlapping domestic groups and of wider kin relations (Fortes 1958; Goody 1958, 1972c).

Seccombe himself prefers the concept of the 'family cycle' to household analysis; the implications are revealed in the following claim:

> Despite its degree of co-resident extension, the family cycle of nineteenth-century proletarians was overwhelmingly nuclear, with households typically being established by the younger generation around the time of marriage and funded through income acquired independently of parental property and wealth.
>
> (Seccombe 1993: 65)

Here he seems to be referring to a process rather similar to Hajnal's 'household formation' (1982). Whereas in earlier times, extension of

---

[3] Attempts have subsequently been made by members of the Cambridge Group to rectify the situation (for example Smith 1979).

households had occurred through children staying in the parental homes, now parents came to join their children. The difference is important and related to the fact that the generations have different working environments, since there is no longer joint access to a productive enterprise. Equally important is the realisation that 'nuclear' applies not to overall family or household composition, nor yet to the diminishing significance of kin networks (as in other work on the family), but to the process of establishing a household at marriage, 'a nuclear household'. It is not simply a question of separation at marriage; discussions of the developmental cycle of the domestic groups (see Fortes in Goody 1958) have pointed out that there is always some degree of fission when a marriage takes place, irrespective of the composition of the dwelling group. What is characteristic here is that a separate conjugal residence (neolocal in one sense of the term) is set up when a couple marry; but they clearly do not sever ties with their families of birth nor with wider kin, as the later composition of their households attests. Such arrangements seem poorly characterised as a 'nuclear family cycle' typical of capitalism.

Seccombe's modifications of Marxism include the attempted introduction of a feminist perspective. It must always be advantageous, and not simply politically correct, to see history from the standpoint of women as well as men, of children as well as adults, of the lower as well as the upper classes. Nevertheless a valuable approach may also have its problems. After some complimentary words about my own analysis of kinship and family, he suggests that I have failed to understand the unequal position of women in medieval Europe. He suggests that my 'conceptual framework renders an unduly positive impression of women's position in medieval families', stressing dowry rights but making 'very little of their subsequent exclusion'. Seccombe sees my disagreement with Hughes' use of disinheritance to describe this exclusion as merely a quibble. Let me take the last point first. It is simply not the case that women were disinherited if one sees inheritance (as I argue one should) as part of the process of devolving relatively exclusive rights (over property, etc.) from one generation to the next. It makes no more sense to speak of women being excluded from inheritance than it does to speak of men being excluded from the dowry; both are aspects of the process of devolution in which there may be some advantages for the junior generation in receiving one's portion earlier rather than later. If I hand over some property to my daughters as dowry when they marry and leave my eldest son to take over the farm later on at my death, I may be

privileging my son as far as land is concerned but I am not in any constructive sense disinheriting the daughters.[4] And in some 20 per cent of cases in
Eurasia, daughters will take over the lot – that is no exclusion. Even when
they had brothers many observers of the dowry have concluded that it
'offered in the past significant power to women' (Friedl 1986; Sarris 1995:
24). The disappearance of dowry (certainly its absence) could mean a disempowerment of women if no new measures of empowerment were to
emerge.

Of course the notion of 'bilateral diverging devolution' does not at all
imply equality of treatment of sons and daughters, nor yet of sons. It
implies that property (movable and/or immovable) is inherited through
both males and females. I find Seccombe's alternative notion of 'a conjugal
patriline' more problematic. Does it describe the inheritance of property,
succession to office or the reckoning of kinship? The phrase is as confusing
as the use of 'patriarchy' to describe male headship of households in an
unqualified way. Are female-headed households or women heirs to be
regarded simply as deviants? Were Elizabeth I, Victoria and Elizabeth II
mere anomalies in terms of a dominant ideology (implied by the term patriline) or were they part of a system in which, under certain circumstances
property and power descended to women when they obviously could have
gone to more distant males (cousins)? Seccombe sees this 'patriline' system
as tied in with the feudal-seigneurial society which structures family life in
favour of reproduction within conjugal families. A broader look at domestic structures might have identified that mode of transmission with the kind
of stratified societies found throughout Eurasia since the Bronze Age, in
which it was necessary to maintain the class position of daughters as well as
of sons. It is important that a feminist analysis does not lead to the neglect of
the class perspective. A comparative approach that included for example
Japan would have pre-empted this possibility.

The concept of diverging devolution bears only marginally on a global
question of the equal treatment of men and women, which always has to
be dealt with sectorially (what does it mean regarding childbirth, for example?). No one is suggesting that women were treated equally to men, but
some were more equal than others and some aspects were more equal than
others. Diverging devolution describes systems of property transmission

---

[4] In southern Italy (Davis 1973), as in Sri Lanka (Leach 1961), daughters did inherit land, as
did the eldest child, male or female, in parts of the Pyrenees (Augustins 1989).

where male and female property (often in some form or other of a conjugal fund) devolves to both sexes, daughters as well as sons, not necessarily equally but substantially. It may come under the husband's management, but the final rights to disposition remain with the wife in the preponderant instances of dowry. In such societies women's common interests are cut across by differential access to property (that is, 'class' interests). As heiresses women may even dominate the domestic domain, leading to the husband taking up residence in the wife's household (uxorilocal, matrilocal or, for me, filiacentric unions) with a concomitant redistribution of the power relationship: stronger women, weaker husbands.

The earlier tendency for some husbands to go and reside with inheriting wives (heiresses) is mentioned by Seccombe, although he seems to resist the full implications. He is clear about the importance of women in determining residence after the Industrial Revolution, giving rise to a matrifocal situation that in my view has important continuities (as well as discontinuities), especially after what he refers to as the Second Industrial Revolution.

For Seccombe the Second Industrial Revolution arose with the extensive use of steampower, especially in the railways. It began around 1873, with 'a swarm of technological breakthroughs and rapid product developments in steel, chemicals, electricity and gas motors' (Seccombe 1993: 82). That was the period when Germany took over the earlier role of England in Europe and the United States did so on a world scale. He sees the Second Industrial Revolution as giving rise to a new production regime, with 'an intensive mode of consuming labour-power, based on a reduced workweek, and a quieter, steadier pace of work under closer supervision' (p. 82). To this situation working-class couples responded by forging an intensive family economy where 'husbands were designated as breadwinners while their wives concentrated on being full-time homemakers'. That change to moral motherhood took place when higher productivity meant higher wages, which could be considered a 'family wage', so that a woman could direct all her attention to the home following patterns earlier established in much of the middle class. But there was also a political element, which we do not hear much about. The changing situation owed something to women's efforts (like Norton in England, Anthony in America) in pressing for changes in divorce, custody and other aspects of their domestic status, as well as to the work of other middle-class reformers caught up in what they saw as the injustices of the situation. Even in Victorian England the hegemony of 'patriarchy' was never complete; there were always internal contradictions related to the bilaterality of kinship and the duality of sib-linghood and sexuality.

The earlier disorganisation of working-class districts in towns described by Engels was followed by the transformation of housing, the re-establishment of more stable working-class communities and the increas-ing tendency to marriage within the neighbourhood, and dominance of female-centred institutions of domestic sharing among neighbours, so well described by Ross (1983) and related to the dominance of mother-centred families. In Tosh's words, 'private patriarchy' had almost disappeared from the urban working-class world described by Ross:

> the husband was often made to feel a bull-in-a-china shop, excluded from the emotional currents of the family ... The wife ... was the one who maintained vital neighbourhood support, who negotiated with landlords and welfare workers, and who super-vised the children's schooling.
>
> (Tosh 1994: 189)

Even money could come under her control, and London magistrates sometimes spoke of the wife's 'headship of the home' (Tosh 1994: 189). The man meanwhile found his companionship in the public house, a fact not unconnected with domestic assault.

This tendency to matrilocality is recognised by Seccombe when he notes that in nineteenth-century England bilateral kin networks veered in a matrilocal direction, with 66 per cent of widows living with daughters and 57 per cent of married children with the wife. Such complex households have been viewed by Ruggles as reflecting the realisation of 'the stem family ideal', with the increased availability of relevant kin due to earlier marriage and a decrease in adult mortality. Seccombe rightly insists on differentiating 'stem co-residence' (when a child brings a spouse to join the nuclear house-hold) from the vertical extension of a nuclear household (when a parent comes to live with a married child). From a cyclical standpoint these are dif-ferent in ways not initially recognised by the Cambridge Group.

Was this pattern due to preference, to the couple striving 'to fulfil an extended family ideal', or did it arise out of an obligation not to leave the parent 'homeless and destitute'? Seccombe rejects the first and accepts the second. In rejecting the first he still clings to notions of fulfilling an ideal, which seems a superfluous, holistic and simplifying concept since surely individuals or relations can have different norms (or aims) at different points in the developmental cycle. The residential set-up is a compromise between the wishes and desires of different generations.

As for the second solution, Seccombe accepts the obligation of the junior generation but limits that to cases of destitution. That cannot be right, either then or now. Whatever the 'nuclear family ideal' (of newly-weds), many couples eventually end up living near or with their close kin. Such arrangements do not require homelessness but only a measure of 'filial piety' and parental affection or dependence.

I cannot see how one can make any statement about the invention of childhood (which Seccombe recognises for what it is worth) without look-ing at the situation in other cultures. That is equally true of other aspects of the family, which is why a history of the family in Western Europe is bound to be inadequate in the long run. Unlike many historians, Seccombe's sociological background makes him appreciate this point even if he does not always follow through its implications. Which are, as Marx and Weber recognised for the growth of capitalism, that we need to look elsewhere too if only for the counterfactual position, even if they themselves did so in too ethnocentric a fashion. That is the real criticism to be made of our distin-guished predecessors.

The thesis of the changing family of the nineteenth century under the impact of industrial capitalism was clearly stated by Frederick Engels (1887 [1884]: 3):

> The history of the proletariat in England begins with the second half of the last century, with the invention of the steam-engine and of machinery for working cotton. These inventions gave rise, as is well known, to an industrial revolution, a revolution which altered the whole civil society . . .

Seccombe's study excellently describes the growth of wage-labour under industrialisation and its effects upon domestic life, characterised as a process of proletarianisation within the capitalist mode of production but beginning with earlier proto-industrialisation in the eighteenth century. This was one major aspect of the development of a modern economy in the West. But wage-labour and its consequences did not only affect the work-ing class but also large elements of the bourgeoisie, who are today experi-encing some of the same problems following from the instability of paid work. It also affected many workers in socialist countries, where the isol-ation of the one-generation conjugal couple was even greater because of the confiscatory laws of inheritance and the difficulty of accumulating for one's children, thus depriving the workforce of an important incentive to production. The changes are surely closely linked to the process of industrialisation and modernisation in a broader sense that affects other groups and other 'non-capitalist' 'modes of production'.

The change is well described, but again the account sometimes places too great a reliance on vague terms like 'patriarchal', which have been used rather loosely in much recent analysis. For instance, in discussing the role of kin-networks in protecting women seeking employment, Seccombe (1993: 32–3) remarks that 'There was, in other words, a strong patriarchal aversion to their full proletarianisation.' But kin-networks (as opposed to descent groups) are by definition bilateral, and as we have seen there is plenty of evidence of the role mothers played in their daughters' welfare, including their place of residence. Studies of working-class relationships have stressed the continuing bond of mother and daughter in determining spatial proximity, allowing the mother's mother (in Eastern Europe as in the West) to play a part in looking after her grandchildren while the daughter is working or even shopping. That relationship is psychologically strong because of the identification of the two, especially after childbearing, when both will have gone through the same experience and the junior often depends upon the knowledge of the senior. The closeness in every sense is of course much greater than with the father's parents, who for the mother remain in-laws rather than real kin, a perception that is transferred to her daughter. That proximity has been emphasised in studies such as Young and Wilmott's (1957) on London's Bethnal Green and Madeleine Kerr's (1958) on Ship Street, Liverpool, while R. T. Smith (1956) has shown the prevalence of 'matrifocal families' not only in the Caribbean and among American Blacks but among 'lower-status' families in other parts of the world. In some parts such closeness is reflected in kinship terminology as when the term 'nanna' in southern England and *mémé* in France is reserved almost exclusively for the mother's mother rather than the paternal grandmother (Goody 1962b). Does this not, in Seccombe's terms, indicate a matriarchal rather than a patriarchal dimension? Certainly the role of women as household managers and as increasingly independent agents should not be underplayed in 'capitalist' societies, yet that is what is being done by the insistent use of the vague term 'patriarchy'.

In matrifocal as distinct from traditional matrilineal structures (involving a clan organisation, inheritance, etc.), men are marginalised, whereas in the latter they are usually significant as 'mother's brothers'. That 'marginality' can often equal 'irresponsibility'. How far is this 'irresponsibility of fathers' a characteristic of modern industrial society? Undoubtedly wage earning loosened the control of senior over junior generations. No longer did marriage involve the transmission of 'productive' property. What devolved was less immediately critical to one's existence, and the dowry became transmuted into parental assistance in other ways (education, house purchase) that involved a looser control of marriage. Education for the children, which full-time motherhood certainly promoted, meant that women as well as men were becoming better educated and were attracted to the new clerical work involved in running industry and the government bureaucracy as well as school teaching and nursing. Young men and women, as Seccombe stresses, were able to set up on their own and make independent choices of a partner, who was no longer necessarily a life-long companion. With increased mobility, men might get a woman pregnant and then leave for another job in another town (the quitting of jobs was more significant than getting the sack, except in crises). That development already got going in the eighteenth century. 'Paternal desertion appears to have been a major factor in German villages in the first half of the eighteenth century, the couple eventually married in two-thirds of the first births conceived out of wedlock; a century later, just over half did' (Seccombe 1993: 50–1). Is this the trend that continued in the phenomenon of 'dead-beat dads', of the male marginality in many working class and Black communities of the present day (Mitchell and Goody 1997)? While there is certainly a great difference between failing to marry a pregnant lover and failing to support children after a longer relationship, the effects may be similar in terms of lone-parent families and their offspring. Freedom to choose a marriage partner implies freedom to end the union. The shift of jurisdiction over divorce in England in 1857 from ecclesiastical to lay courts was initially of benefit only to middle-class couples. Working classes had long practised desertion, but the Christian Church had hitherto forbidden divorce and remarriage except in a very few circumstances. Inevitably the opportunities gradually widened to include the population at large, leading to the possibility of remarriage as well as cohabitation.

Extra-marital liaisons, including those leading to the birth of children, are not the only aspect of the modern family and marriage that are prefigured in earlier working-class marriages. There was the reluctance to enter into formal arrangements. Consensual unions had always been known but became much more common among the nineteenth-century working class, where they avoided expense, and at the same time, any permanent commitment. Church marriages were almost impossible to undo except for the very rich and powerful. But consensual unions could be dissolved by informal procedures, by 'wife sale' or by stepping backwards over the broomstick over which one had walked forward at marriage (Seccombe 1993: 52–3). There was also the disappearance of dowry (apart from the self-acquired dowry), which happened first among a proletariat who depended upon income rather than capital. By the beginning of this century it had virtually vanished among the British middle classes, although persisting in France among the middle class until more recently.

Seccombe is only marginally concerned with these issues, though they are of central importance to the contemporary situation. Where he concentrates his valuable contribution, as the subtitle of his second volume indicates, is on the rise and then decline of fertility that followed the Industrial Revolution. Indeed, there seems to have already been a rise under proto-industrialisation, as we have seen. Under full industrialisation Seccombe sees a relation between the demand of the economy for the labour of women and children and the encouragement of high fertility (1993: 74). Here he is following Adam Smith and Engels. The former wrote: 'The demand for men, like that for any other commodity, necessarily regulates the production of men' (*Wealth of Nations* I sect. 8, p. 36, quoted Engels 1887). To this Engels adds: 'If there are too few labourers at hand, prices, i.e. wages, rise, the workers are more prosperous, marriages multiply, more children are born and more live to grow up, until a sufficient number of labourers has been secured' (1887: 54). That higher fertility was partially counteracted by the involvement of women and children in industrial labour, which increased their mortality. What was new was not the involvement of women and children in labour; in rural England, none had sat at home and few had gone to school. The difference lay in the shift from domestic, agricultural or even proto-industrial production to the inflexible factory arrangements of wage labour, together with the accompanying housing conditions that Engels so vividly described. These conditions meant that in the first half of the century the death rates in cities averaged 20 to 25 per cent above those in the country.

Women's labour disappeared from various industrial sectors such as mining, partly through pressure from the men who saw their wages as being kept down, partly by outside reformers. It continued in a few areas such as textiles which experienced an earlier fertility decline among married women. From the 1880s more and more clerical work was being done by women – up to a quarter in some cities – and male clerks protested at this 'slur on their manhood' (Tosh 1994: 194). But beginning in the last decade of the nineteenth century, fertility declined across the whole of north-west Europe (though it had done so earlier in France). Between 1890 and 1920 it contracted by more than 10 per cent in over half the countries of Europe. While this was the period when contraceptive methods became more sophisticated and were adopted by upper-class couples, the working class only did so in the 1920s. Nevertheless the decline in their birthrates, even in consensual unions, had begun much earlier as a result of 'natural' methods.

While the reduction of fertility obviously has some 'elective affinity' with the growth of women's employment outside the home (as it does even more directly with the decline in child mortality, which is likely to lead to over-compensation), in fact it begins before the great rise in numbers of 'working women'. That followed rather than preceded, leading to the present situation where more women are employed in Britain (many part-time) than men, an extraordinary reversal in which Engels might have seen a disturbing disempowerment of men (especially of the middle class). While economic factors such as women's wage rates and the changing nature of 'work' are relevant, we must also consider that this development is linked to the education of women and to pressure from the women's movement as well as to considerations of equity embodied in the Sex Disqualification (Removal) Act of 1919. But to revert to my earlier theme, whatever the demands made upon the family by capitalism, there existed in the major Eurasian societies not merely 'patriarchal' tendencies but also a previous hierarchical system in which it was important to maintain the status of daughters as well as men, not necessarily equal to them but to distinguish them from daughters of lower groups and to enable them to make marriages in the same or higher ones. To insist on this factor is not to dwell upon the unchanging family (which Seccombe rightly rejects) but to recognise that such structural elements may continue to play a role over time. What I have called 'diverging devolution' adapts to new situations, perhaps providing a countervailing tendency within them that has its own logic of development as well as a measure of autonomy, urged on by human agents that stand to gain from the changing nature of domestic life.

The general problem in the history of the family is one of articulation. Yes, the economic and family systems are inter-related. But in what ways?

Much of the discussion has assumed a pre-existing affinity between the development of capitalism and the nature of the family in north-west Europe. In general that hypothesis suffers from a failure to enquire in a sufficiently comparative manner. And where comparison is made, with the East for example, it is done from too ethnocentric a point of view, as in the case of Marx and Weber. Other historians who look at what they see as the consequences of capitalism again take a limited European perspective, misattributing to their own continent aspects of family life like the invention of childhood or love or individuality that are found much more widely.[5] These claims Seccombe rightly ignores. Demographic historians who concentrate on the continuities necessarily tend to play down the other changes that have taken place at the domestic level. Seccombe rightly offers a critique of this approach. He sees a relationship between production and reproduction, and by bringing in a wider range of considerations insists upon change. What he does not sufficiently do, in my view, is to allow for the degree of structural autonomy that exists between production and reproduction. More forms of kinship can exist with capitalism than modernisation theory allowed; the same is true for earlier periods too. Male domination in the political or economic sphere may not simply be reflected in the family. Among the Asante of West Africa, the political system is staffed by males. The role of the Queen Mother alone reflects politically the fact that this is a matrilineal society in which women (and their brothers as distinct from their husbands) play an important part in determining the residence of men. Male (patriarchal?) authority at the political level is consistent with quite a different distribution of power in the domestic domain.

---

[5] I have discussed these features in more detail in *The East in the West* (1996a).

Chapter 5

LOVE, LUST AND LITERACY[1]

A number of historians especially of the French *mentalité* school, as well as many sociologists, see modern Europe as marked by a particular constellation of sentiments, including love, that characterised, even promoted, the contemporary world in ways that were more difficult for others to accomplish. As with other features of domestic and personal relations, there are those who see this European exceptionalism as going back to the eighteenth century, to the period of the Enlightenment, or sometimes to the Reformation or Renaissance; others regard it as going yet further back, not (as with some claims about rationality) to the Greeks, but at least to the troubadours and to medieval poetry. There is no doubt this perception exists, both at the level of folk concepts and of scholarship, sometimes on a European basis (for example, in the work of de Rougement), sometimes on a more nationalistic one. It is especially English historians who have considered love, between husband and wife, between parents and children, as well as romantic love, as being unique features of the modern affective family in which that country, the First Industrial Nation, is seen as leading the way in the process of 'modernisation'.[2] While that particular view is not likely to commend itself except to an Anglo-Saxon audience, there is a much more widespread belief that a unique attitude to love is characteristic of Europe, either ancient or modern.

---

[1] This chapter was originally written for Professor Louisa Passerini's seminar at the European University Institute, 1996–97, entitled Love in the Western Tradition. I am grateful to the Institute for having invited me to spend six months in Florence.
[2] Just as many Europeans see romantic love as having a European origin, so American sociologists like Ogburn and Nimkoff (1955) see it as more advanced in the US, anyhow in terms of choice of mate. On this phenomenon, see Hill (1989). On America, see Biegel (1951: 331).

Although the existence of this belief is indisputable, I want to question its basis. In doing so, I am not concerned to deny that contemporary (modern or post-modern) or European relationships may not have their identifiable profiles, connected in part to wider socio-economic features, but rather to suggest that the analytic descriptions are often unacceptable because they fail to take fully into account the comparative and longer-term historical dimensions. That questioning will lead to a criticism of certain sociological treatments of the concept of modernisation, which again seem to me too ego- and ethnocentric.

Some have even gone so far as to see other cultures, especially those of Black Africa, as being marked by lust or desire rather than love. Others, less obviously racist, see romantic love, if it exists at all in other parts, as being characteristic of relationships outside the family (in other words as 'adulterous') or as displaying a yearning for the unattainable. Questionable as these hypotheses are in their general form, I want to suggest that we may be able to discover some more acceptable way of accounting for differences and similarities.

By love I am here talking specifically about a quality of sexual relationships and the associated kind of intimacy. That is to say, I am not discussing the full semantic usage of the English word. In the writings of Augustine, that word covers both divine and earthly love, sexual and parental, as with *amor* in Latin. Rather, I am referring exclusively to earthly love of a sexual kind. There is often some interplay, as in the theological interpretations of *The Song of Songs*, but by and large secular and sacred love are clearly distinguishable. Of course even in the secular sense the word in English applies to parents and children, to ice creams and lollipops. It can be platonic (friendship) or intimate. Nor is that only the case in European languages. Among the LoDagaa of northern Ghana, the word *nɔne* can also be translated 'like' or 'love' in a more general sense. I doubt if there is anything analytically to be gained by conflating the general and the particular meanings. I do not mean that there is not some overlap between 'loving' or 'liking' men, ice creams and even God, in all of which sexuality may play its part, but the term would then refer to so general a cathectic disposition as to require a minimum of sociological or historical comment. At this level there is little about emotions or attitudes that is specific to any culture. I want to discuss the question of whether at the more particular level there is any analytically distinguishable form of love between the sexes that is characteristic of either European or modern societies, as distinct from an idea of the actors that there is something special in their own beliefs and practices.

Such love is usually treated as consisting of romantic and conjugal love, the latter being more widespread than the former, which is the type often seen by Europeans as specifically theirs. Others like the anthropologist Boas and the sociologist Giddens distinguish between passionate and romantic love (Giddens 1992; Freeman 1996: 188). Following Stone, the latter sees romantic love as associated with modernisation beginning in the late eighteenth century, although he regards what he calls congruent love as being yet more modern. Some have taken a more negative view of 'romantic love' as disruptive. Despite the aim of an unending relationship, the reality is that love of whatever kind suffers from decay, habituation or transformation.

I want to begin by discussing three representative accounts of love – especially romantic love, which I see as a quality of sexual relationships and the associated kind of intimacy – by a sociologist, Giddens, by a psychoanalyst, Person, and by a historian, Stone, each of whom addresses the topic in different ways. Then I look at some evidence from outside Europe, first from Asia, then from Africa. I conclude there are some major differences not so much between Europe and the rest but between Eurasia and Africa. In the final section I try to offer some non-racist explanation for this situation.

The discussion of Giddens is tied up with his view of 'modernisation'; romantic love is modern, modernity is European, hence love is European. So he assigns romantic love and 'the emergence of sexuality' to modern (post-eighteenth century) rather than to traditional societies.[3] He has a view of pre-modern Europe that distinctly biases his notion of modernity. 'Most marriages were contracted, not on the basis of mutual sexual attraction, but economic circumstance' (Giddens 1992: 38). The opposition is too hastily drawn; economic considerations do not exclude love, as Hufton (1995) has noted in a sensitive study. Marriage was often a mixture of both, but among the poor (where Giddens sees marriage as 'a means of organising labour'), most are agreed that there was considerable freedom of choice, especially when marriage was late and courting was often done 'in service'

---

[3] Regarding the emergence of sexuality in the context of marriage, he may have some justification in terms of the 'common man' (where the exploration of sex was restricted) but not for upper groups.

rather than at home. Even in the home, Duby (1997: 48) writes of the well-known 'exuberant sexuality of the period', that is, the twelfth century, insisting on the role of sex and love in elite marriages.

Giddens recognises that class was relevant here. By his account sexual licence was only openly permitted among aristocratic groups, since it followed power and was found where women were sufficiently liberated from the demands of reproduction. In other words, in an apparent paradox, licence was allowed in precisely those situations where marriage was most likely to be arranged. Nevertheless it is probably true that sexual freedom was more common among upper groups, not only in Europe but in Asia too.

Giddens distinguishes between passionate love, which is more or less universal, and romantic love, which is more 'culturally specific'. Romantic love was distinct from the *amour passion*, although it still depended upon the 'projective identification' of *amour passion* to attract and bind the partners together, creating a feeling of wholeness that relates to male–female differences. Romantic love he sees as making its presence felt from the late eighteenth century, drawing upon specifically European 'ideals of love closely connected to the moral values of Christianity'. We had it, the Asiatics did not. Devotion to God and the consequent achievement of self-knowledge became part of 'a mystical unity between man and woman'. The reference to Christianity omits any consideration of those aspects of that religion which are hostile to sexual unions of any kind, to marriage, to sex as well as to romantic love. The existence of these contrary elements makes more problematic the attribution of the emergence of romantic love to the Christian tradition, in which he follows Luhman. In romantic love Giddens sees the temporary idealisation of passionate love as supplemented by a certain reflexivity and 'a more permanent involvement with the love object' (Giddens 1992: 39). Romantic love introduces 'the idea of narrative into an individual's life', associating for the first time love with freedom and self-realisation, with sublime love predominating over sexual ardour. Indeed, in this complex 'love breaks with sexuality'. For romantic love is also associated by him with the idealisation of motherhood (that of maternal love); it was essentially 'feminised love', related to women's subordination in the home.

Giddens links the rise of the 'romantic love complex' with other facets of women's life, the creation of a home, changing relations between parents and children, and the 'invention of motherhood'. More questions arise. As

Hufton points out, and as should be clear from first principles, there was no such 'invention'; the notion of the 'creation' of a home is no more sustainable. If we were considering adaptations of home and motherhood, the ideas might be arguable, like that of the changing relations between parents and children, which are obviously involved in a partial freeing of the choice of partner in upper marriages from parental constraints. However, taking up Ariès' thesis, Giddens offers a more general account and sees a growing emotional shift, in Ryan's words, from 'patriarchal authority to maternal affection'. The reference in Ariès, the quote from Ryan, the reliance on Stone, places Giddens in the 'mentality' tradition that offers broad psychosocial generalisations to sustain the argument of an exclusive Western development of modernity. Hence the distinction between passionate (worldwide) and romantic (European) love. With this development is associated a formidable list of attributes which are but vaguely delineated and seem to have no clear-cut relationship one with another. All in all, the contrast between modern and other is drawn too sharply, as usual to the detriment of other and earlier societies. In specifying modernity, an attempt is made to group a whole array of features as associated with 'romantic love', when the link is far from clear. While smaller families and the non-working mother meant, for a period after the Second Industrial Revolution for the working class (and earlier in the eighteenth century for the bourgeoisie), withdrawal from work and the possibility of increased attention to children, 'moral motherhood' was a relatively late development and achieved its zenith when children were increasingly being despatched outside the home to spend their time in non-domestic, non-maternal institutions such as schools and even boarding schools.

There can be little consensus about these views, since the criteria are too questionable. That makes the comparison of its historial singularity with the Protestant ethic somewhat extravagant. The emergence of romantic love is connected with freedom and self-realisation, which is once again to take a very late and culture-bound view of both. Which society did not display these features in some contexts of social life? Are we really sure enough of the status of these concepts to make such an assertion? In romantic love, asserts Giddens, the element of sublime love tends to predominate over sexual ardour (lust?). Here we touch upon the mystically vague. 'Love breaks with sexuality while embracing it'; 'virtue' takes on a new sense for both sexes, referring to 'qualities of character which pick out the other person as "special"' (Giddens 1992: 40). In so far as these statements can be contextualised, could one not say the same of many attachments in the plays of Shakespeare, or even of those of the Indian playwright Kalidas?

The origin of romantic love in the late eighteenth century (which Christopher Hill among other historians has dismissed), its roots in the Christian tradition of devotion, and the link with 'the mystical unity between man and woman' place the phenomenon in the context of Europe, Christianity and modernisation. That association seems to neglect too much. The existence of notions of the mystical unity of male and female are found in many other traditions, earlier and elsewhere, especially India and China. Giddens characterises romantic love in terms of permanent idealisation, of the introduction of personal narrative, freedom, self-realisation, feminisation, and a break with sexuality. Elsewhere motherhood is thrown in. That is an apple-pie listing of an ethnocentric kind. Idealisation, even if quasi-permanent, seems much more widespread than he proposes, being found in much of the love poetry of Asia. And narrative, even the novel, is hardly to be associated exclusively with romantic love or with Europe; *le roman* is not to be identified with romance, but with vernacular languages (romance) from which love stories took their names.

Giddens does not stop there but goes on to define what he sees as the yet newer form of love, namely congruent love, that depends upon intimacy rather than projective identification; it 'is active, contingent love, and therefore jars with the "for-ever," "one-and-only" qualities of the romantic love complex' (Giddens 1992: 61). This love is seen as cause (rather than as effect) of the 'separating and divorcing' society of today, in which it is a special relationship rather than a special person that counts, a relationship that is at once equal emotionally and introduces ars erotica ('for the first time'!) into the core of the conjugal relationship, which is no longer necessarily monogamous or heterosexual. While romantic love is predicated on gender inequality, congruent love is based on equality. The changing position of women in employment and, to some extent, in the house, is certainly reflected in the relationships into which they enter, but to analyse this change in terms of differences caused by the nature of love seems to confuse rather than clarify the situation.

Despite his denial, congruent love looks like an adjustment to the turn-over of relationships rather than some kind of ideological replacement for the romantic variety. While the latter was often seen by the actors as permanent, like any attachment, that was rarely so in practice, as de

Rougement and others have noted; it was a time-specific sentiment that merged into conjugal love, though nowadays with frequent divorce it is as likely to be followed by a new romance.

Is it really the case that there are now two types of alternative relationship, romantic and congruent love, the second of which is superseding the first? If romantic love involves distance and idealisation, it is clearly a feature of the initial phase of a 'modern' relationship, something that is more or less bound to fade with time. Despite the ideal of perpetuity, total addiction to a notion of romantic love would mean one was changing one's partner every five years or less, as the romance faded; hence it is a recipe for the long-term instability of relationships, running contrary to the evident desirability of maintaining a steady framework during the childhood of one's offspring, that is, in Western societies until they are sixteen, giving a periodicity of twenty years for a socially adequate union. The doctrine of freedom of choice implies the ability to choose again if and when the first relationship falls flat, unless some other component, such as conjugal love, loyalty, habituation, is recognised. That component runs against the ideal of romance, which as many have observed is destructive as well as constructive of particular relationships.

Romantic love has less space to develop when marriages are arranged by the senior generation, or are organised by the kinship system (as in Lévi-Strauss' elementary systems), or when the courting phase is much reduced (as with early marriage). There is less room for absence or for idealisation, although the latter may form part of any process of sexual exploration. However, even in modern societies conjugal rather than romantic (or congruent) love is socially the predominant form of the relationship, since it is more stable over the long term and does not fade to the same extent – or any fading may merge into loyalty or habit(uation).

Giddens' exposition of love is profoundly ethnocentric; romantic love is here, passion or lust is for the other. However, in looking at the association of romantic love with European modernity Giddens points to a feature we regard as highly significant and which is neither European nor yet modern. 'Romantic love', he claims, 'introduced the idea of a narrative into an individual's life – a formula which radically extended the reflexivity of sublime love' (Giddens 1992: 39). Here he is playing upon the meaning of romance as a novel, when 'this story now became individualised, inserting self and other into a personal narrative'. We have to reject the claim that individual lives did not have a narrative before the end of the eighteenth century, when it was introduced by romantic love; life histories were certainly 'individualised' from the beginning of time, with notions of self, as Mauss discusses, being universal but taking different forms.[4] And of course the idea that romantic love was connected with the emergence of the novel and a 'newly discovered narrative form' applies only to *written* narrative. There is a strong case to be made for a connection between romantic love and literature, but not only in the West and not only in the novel; his more ethnocentric or Eurocentric view is part of the Westerner's myth of modernisation. Other societies are just as modern in a chronological sense (contemporary) as our own; we need always to remind ourselves that what Western sociologists and historians mean by modern is Western modern.

The specific nature of the relation between love and literacy in the wider sense is suggested by Giddens himself when he writes of reflexivity: 'Romantic love presumes some degree of self-interrogation. How do I feel about the other? How does the other feel about me? Are our feelings "profound" enough to support a long-term involvement?' (Giddens 1992: 45). It involves 'a meeting of souls', 'the capturing of the heart of the other'. This inflated discourse of love was certainly not confined to Europe. The self-interrogation seems to indicate the kind of questioning of feeling that is encouraged by reading about that relationship, in whatever part of the world and in whatever form, whether in the *Roman de la Rose*, later in eighteenth-century novels, or later still in the pulp fiction and stories of sexual encounters that flood the bookstalls following the invention of cheaper printing techniques in the nineteenth century. Nor is it only the novel. The incorporation of romance into films, above all from Hollywood, has dominated the viewing of a large part of the world, calling forth resistance as well as acceptance. Nor is it only narrative, since poetry and song are heavily involved. For reflexivity is part of the act of reading, which while it lacks the immediate *inter*action of conversation, of speech, it encourages a more contemplative mode of understanding. In my own formulation, it helps to make the implicit explicit, the unconscious conscious. Modernisation implies just such an updating of the technologies of the intellect and of the emotions.

In this spread of literacy, women played a considerable part. Their education became more common; excluded from many of the literate

---

[4] See for example Fortes' account of West African notions of self and individuality in *Oedipus and Job* (1959).

professions, they turned to romance and the novel as a means of achievement and distraction, providing a number of authors as well as the bulk of
readers. Romantic love was spread not so much by an abstract modernisation but by the literate woman.

A more usual sociological approach is taken by the American, Lantz.
In the first place he sees romantic love as disruptive of the family, following
Plutarch, who provides the first written comment (Lantz 1981: 352, 358).
Secondly, he sees romantic love (perhaps what Giddens calls passionate
love) as appearing much earlier but as spreading under the impact of modernisation. For him romantic love is deviant in its origin, involving a questioning of authority structures, part of 'destructive individualism' but
eventually becoming 'an integral part of society's norms'. He defines
romantic love as based on personal-emotional attraction, with a strong
erotic element (often repressed) and also characterised by idealisation, 'the
notion of a one and only' (albeit temporary) and 'the idea that true love
overcomes all obstacles' (Lantz 1981: 349). As such it is to be contrasted
with conjugal love. His discussion aims at taking romantic love out of the
purely modern context where it is sometimes placed and looking at it historically. The general disposition to romantic love can be developed in a
more focused way at particular times and places. But his focus is always on
the European context. Let us return to the notion of idealisation.

The argument about romantic love in the modern context – where it
doesn't take refuge in the plots of Hollywood films – often refers to the
freedom of choice of a partner. So that what happened recently in Europe
could perhaps be better regarded not as a change in mentalities (for Lantz
claims that romantic love is universal even if spread by modernisation) but,
since the reference is so often to mate selection, rather as a lifting of certain
of the restrictions on marriage due to the changing nature of individuals
to property, to a new occupational structure, to changes in literacy and
graphic communication, and to shifts in life courses more generally, the
latter partly as a result of education outside the family.

Psychologists make similar assumptions about love and the West to
those found among the sociologists. Psychoanalytic views are complicated.
Reik for example saw love, romantic love, not as he claimed psychoanalytic
theory would have it, as 'an attenuated and goal-inhibited form of the sex
drive', but as a cultural experience, 'an unknown psychical power', impossible before a certain stage has been reached among members of the group.
It is, in his view of the evolution of human societies, impossible among

'half-civilised people' (Reik 1949: 6). Once again vague mysticism and ethnocentricism are key features in the approach.

The American psychoanalyst, Person, comments on the subject: 'Whatever we may think of it, professionally or personally, romantic love is the single most powerful passion in many contemporary lives' (Person 1991: 383). However, contrary to Giddens and others, she identifies 'romantic love' with 'passionate love' and sees its core as neither carnal passion (lust) nor affectionate bonding but as 'the lover's idealization of and yearning for another' (p. 384). This seemingly 'primordial emotion' is not universal, she declares, though more available to moderns, but it is specific to individual cultures. Goode (1959) for example reports romantic love as occurring on a continuum, receiving a negative social sanction in China and Japan while in the West of today it is a disgrace to marry without it; like Stone and others he is talking essentially of mate selection, not of the kind of experiences related in the Japanese novel of the Heian period, *The Tale of Genji*. Even where it is negatively sanctioned, Person recognises that some examples nevertheless occur, as in the case of Abelard and Héloïse, Jacob's love for the younger sister Rachel, Michal's for David and Solomon's for Shulamith as depicted in *The Song of Songs*. Love, even romance, is therefore a universal psychological possibility.

However, as 'a large-scale phenomenon' Person sees romantic love as being a product 'mainly of the West', a cultural construct that first appeared in twelfth-century Languedoc, following the view taken by de Rougement (1956) and by many European historians. The truth of this statement of primacy is doubtful. Firstly, Provençal culture of the period owed much to Arabic models in which a similar idealisation took place. Secondly, the troubadours represented not 'a large-scale phenomenon' but elite practice.[5] In the modern period Person takes a similar view to Lantz and sees romantic love as spreading in Western culture with the 'increasing emphasis on individuality as a primary value' (Person 1991: 386).

---

[5] Duby follows de Rougement in thinking 'twelfth-century Europe discovered love', the truth of which is far from self-evident. However, he does not see the troubadours of Aquitaine as being the only discoverers. Similar songs were sung in Paris, by Abelard for example, who acts 'as a troubadour' (Duby 1997: 66, 61). Such activity also appeared at the Anglo-Norman courts under the Plantagenet Henry II, which constituted 'the most productive of the workshops of literary creation' and gave birth to the legend of Tristan and Isolde (Duby 1997: 73, 68). Changes in the orientation to love he regards as related to the 'feminisation of Christianity' and to the changing role of younger sons of knights as a result of the increasing wealth of that period.

Person points to another factor in the dominance of this relationship which touches upon my central theme. 'Love stories, the narratives that bind these impulses and wishes together and give voice to the surrounding culture's attitudes to love, are for the most part the product of the West, and it is through them that so many of us in the West have learned to seek romantic love' (Person 1991: 386–7). So narrative is again particularly important in establishing romantic discourse. Since the author is writing of the West, this necessarily refers to written narratives. She notes that there were relatively few love stories until the Middle Ages, which would fit with our view of the stimulus of literacy. However, poetry and song have played a similar role at other times and places.

The third account, by the historian, Stone (whose work served as a source for Giddens), sees the development of the cult of romantic love, on the other hand, as not beginning until the late eighteenth century (that is, with the Industrial Revolution), whereas it played little or no part in the daily lives of men or women of the later seventeenth and early eighteenth centuries. Like Trumbach (1978), he considers such love as first marking the professional or aristocratic classes, especially in the increasing freedom of an individual to choose his or her own spouse. That development is related to the emergence of 'affective individualism' within the family made possible by the spread of early capitalism. But as Hufton (and Lantz) points out, mate selection was never constrained in the same way among the lower classes, who had little or no property; indeed it could be argued that upper groups (who in fact were themselves never totally constrained) adopted what had already existed in the lower ones (Lantz 1981: 361; Hufton 1995). In any case the notion of individuality, if it is to be of any analytic value at all, has to be applied sectorially and is useless as a general concept.

Like others, Stone sees the growth of marriage for love (that is, by choice of the partner) in the eighteenth century as caused 'by the growing consumption of novels'. C. Hill queries both of these claims, regarding the contemporary assertions used by Stone as being no more than 'talking about'. But 'talking about' is certainly important and may well have affected not only the emergence of romantic love but its spread, popularity and expression, which is also its very presence. Instead of being faced with a theory placing the emphasis on aristocratic or upper inventions followed by downward diffusion, which Stone has proposed over the long term for courtly love and Ozouf over the shorter term for the eighteenth century, we can link its development (not its initial appearance) with changes in communicative techniques and practices, changes that differentially affect different groups at different times and places. It was the differences in property holding which left the lower classes freer to choose a partner if not to elaborate the notion.

In this context Stone (1977: 11) remarks on the possibility that 'What appears to be a growth of affect may in fact be no more than a growth in the capacity to express emotions on paper.' The phrase 'no more' is dismissive in the same way as Hill's 'talking about'. Expression on paper has important repercussions on people's emotions, not simply expressing already existing feelings but in creating or expanding those sentiments through a process of reflexivity. Is it also the case, as Stone argues, that literacy and printing created a great divergence between rich and poor? Or did it just exaggerate existing ones? In both cases one would expect patterns of love to be different in upper and lower groups, with the situation changing slowly as society became virtually completely literate. That, I suggest, is more or less what one does find. Working-class autobiographies of the nineteenth century for example show a bond 'based if not on romantic love then at least on a sense of shared experience' (Vincent 1981: 54). In many cases love was present at the start of the relationship, and certainly there was freedom to choose, though perhaps less so for girls.

Stone subsequently modified his earlier Eurocentric assumptions and recognised that cases of romantic love could be found everywhere. What is not universal is 'social approbation' and 'the actual experience'. It is not clear what is meant by the second phrase; if cases exist everywhere, they presumably form part of actual experience. By 'social approbation' he seems to imply something rather more specific. Following the traditional genealogy he sees the beginning of love in Europe (the very expresssion is ambiguous) as 'a socially approved artefact' among the troubadours of the twelfth century (the Arabs and classical world are left out of the picture) and as spreading in the medieval period. 'By the sixteenth and seventeenth centuries, our evidence for the first time becomes quite extensive, thanks to the spread of literacy and the printing press' (Stone 1988: 17). We then find love poems, love letters, pornography, with courts as 'hotbeds of passionate intrigues' and romantic love as familiar to society at large. However, he does not regard this love as completely 'approved', since every advice book rejected both romantic passion and lust as suitable bases for marriage, for parents were the most appropriate persons to arrange a partner for a son or a daughter. So 'Public admiration for marriage-for-love is thus a fairly recent occurrence in Western society, arising out of the romantic movement of the late eighteenth century, and only winning general acceptance in the twentieth' (Stone 1988: 18). In his later work Stone sees the role of passionate attachments (romantic love) as being obscured by sexuality (Stone 1988: 19). Consequently he perceives a blurring of the distinction between love and lust, which for other commentators constitute different forms of passionate attachment.

By social approbation of 'marriage-for-love' he refers to orthodox opinion shifting away from focusing on the interests of the group (in favour of individualism again) and away from economic and political considerations. In doing so he creates an opposition which does not seem to exist in that form. The group he refers to is essentially the parents as distinct from the couple; in fact we always have to differentiate the generational interests in marriage. 'Love' was frequently a concern of the couple, just as parents often had, and still have, different values in mind. What we see is a shift from the dominance of parental concerns among the higher classes; the lower ones were always freer, so that one has to think of normality and orthodoxy in terms of class. Property interests which were often significant in marriage transactions (female dowry, male endowment) – not only among the upper classes but for those in the rural population who had direct access to the means of production – necessarily ensured that parents were heavily involved. But with the proletarianisation of the rural worker following the enclosures of the eighteenth century and the subsequent recourse of many to wage-labour, both in agriculture and industry, marital transfers became of less importance for the purposes of establishing a household as a going concern, which became more dependent on help with training or apprenticeship.[6] Such changes, leading eventually to the disappearance of the dowry in the twentieth century and its replacement by help with education, as income replaced capital, were of course preceded by 'the rise of the novel' but also accompanied by the growth of 'pulp fiction' and the decline of parental influence in marital selection. That decline opened the way for the expansion of partner selection in which 'love', always an element, became dominant, as Stone implies in invoking individualism. The expression of such love was certainly encouraged by the novel, and indeed by earlier literate expressions, and given a further boost by the 'near-total literacy' at the end of the nineteenth century.

---

[6] See the autobiographical accounts in Vincent (1981).

On Stone's thesis Person comments:

The dissemination of the new ideology of love depended upon the unprecedented availability of the written word in the nineteenth century, courtesy of the institution of the lending library as well as the greater affordability of books and periodicals. Love stories came to constitute much of what was written about in both the novel and the popular press.

(Person 1991: 394)

That literary influence was already the case in the eighteenth century as Charlotte Lennox, herself a novelist, observed in *The Female Quixote* (1750 [1989]: 7): 'By them [Romances] she was taught to believe, that love was the ruling principle of the World; that every other Passion was subordinated to this; and that it caused all the Happiness and Miseries of Life.' In the nineteenth century that relationship became even closer. On his proposal that M. de Rênal in Stendhal's *Le Rouge et le Noir* take out a subscription to a library in the name of the lowest of the servants, Julien comments: 'it would have to be specified that the servant should not take out any novels. Once they were in the house, those dangerous works might disrupt Madame's maids, not to speak of the servant himself' (Stendhal 1830 [1938]: 53). Here love (which Julien feels so strongly for Madame) is linked to the novel and not only to writing but to printing. As Stendhal again comments, 'in Paris love is the child of the novel' (p. 58). Printing is of course loosely related to 'modernisation', and Lantz (1981: 365) remarks that 'the spread of romantic love among a populace is itself a result of growing rates of literacy and the spread of printed media, all aspects of modernisation'. The novels would have outlined the parts to be played, shown the model to copy. But what is not an aspect of modernity? In this context it seems helpful to concentrate on more immediate, less vague variables than modernisation. The great exemplar of the more specific relationship to literacy is of course Flaubert's Emma Bovary, whose desire for love is directly generated by her reading of literature.

All these commentators have seen the widespread development of the notion of romantic love as being essentially European, some considering the concept to have originated in Europe, either at the end of the eighteenth century or among the troubadours. However, there has been a hint that the phenomenon may be more widespread, especially in the Biblical references to ancient Israel, *The Song of Songs*. The troubadours also point in a Near

Eastern direction, since they were almost certainly influenced by the tradition of Arabic love poetry. Much earlier in the Near East Hopkins remarks upon the love letters passing between aristocratic brothers and sisters in Roman Egypt, where they were potential marriage partners, and he has also noted similar feelings in Heian Japan (Hopkins 1980). That list can be expanded to include examples from India, China and the Near East, all societies with writing.

I would suggest that this elaboration of the discourse of love, this idealisation of the beloved, occurs in societies with writing and is therefore not only earlier than the eighteenth century and even the troubadours, but is found in all cultures which developed literary traditions.

Let us first look at one example from the written poetry of romantic love, that of a trobaritz, one of the most famous of the female troubadours, Na Castelosa, from the Auvergne, wife of Turc de Meyronne, who loved Armand of Bréon and composed songs for him at the beginning of the thirteenth century. She wrote a poem of which the first line ran

Mout avètz fach long estatge.

The French translation of the first verse goes:

Vous avez laissé passer un bien long temps
depuis que vous m'avez quitté: et cela m'est
dur et douloureux car vous m'avez juré et
garanti que, de toute votre vie, vous
n'auriez pas d'autre dame que moi. Est si
c'est une autre qui vous préoccupe, moi,
vous m'avez tuée et trahie, car j'avais
en vous l'esperance que vous m'aimeriez
sans le moindre doute.

(Bec 1995: 86)

The lover and the loved one are separated in space; the poetry elaborates reflections about their situation, one of parting. This is not entirely Wordsworth's 'emotion recollected in tranquillity', but a parallel process, one that is encouraged by writing about rather than speaking to. Emotions are re-presented rather than presented; the written poem separates condition and reflection. I do not wish to assert that such separation is impossible in the spoken tongue; indeed, it is a feature of all or most language use, but it is definitely promoted by writing, which creates an object outside oneself in a way that speech cannot do, at least in the same clear-cut fashion.

This context seems to be one in which idealisation can flourish. As Lantz (1981: 354) notes, 'their wishes and fantasies about the man–woman relationships [were] expressed in romantic love-tales', that is, essentially as text. Indeed, the love of the troubadour may be a purely literary phenomenon, for some have queried whether it existed at all outside the text (Robertson 1966). These texts were also models. Writing of the twelfth-century romances, Duby (1997: 65) remarks that the 'men and women who were enthused with this literature tended to copy their ways of thinking, of feeling and of acting'.

That same element of distance and idealisation is found in the extensive tradition of love poetry which the Chinese developed dating back to *The Book of Songs* from the ninth to the seventh century BCE. Subsequently a corpus of erotic and elegiac rhapsodies known as *The Songs of Ch'u* was composed between the fourth century BCE and the second century CE. However, there was much ambivalence about this type of poetry, some believing it to be distinctly decadent. So that exegetical scholars were sometimes led to interpret the poems in a political or moralising way, just as Christian apologists did with *The Song of Songs*. In the years 534–45 a court poet, Hsü Ling, put together an anthology of love poems which he called *New Songs from a Jade Terrace*. This consisted largely of love poetry belonging to the aristocratic court tradition of southern China. The 'Palace Style Poetry' took on a standardised rhetorical form that bristled with conventions. One of those was that 'the woman's lover must be absent from the love scenario' (Birrell 1995: 8). As a consequence there is throughout a pervasive sense of obligatory melancholy, a frustration of desire. Once again love poetry is founded on absence. In the earlier poems an 'image of divine eroticism develops into an idealized portrayal of palace ladies' (Birrell 1995: 9), a claim similar to that made for Christianity (Giddens 1992: 39). Later the focus shifts more to unhappy love. It is usually a woman who is the subject of the poem, often a wife whose husband has gone off on a long journey, for the love expressed is mainly conjugal. Women are 'victims of love's desire' and inevitably remain behind while the man moves on. She looks back towards the past; 'nostalgia reigns in the boudoir poems'. The following poem by Fu Hsü is typical of the shorter poems.

Autumn orchid shades a jade pool,
Pool water clear and fragrant.
Lotus blooms to the wind unfold,
Among them is a pair of mandarin ducks.
And paired fish impulsive leap and dart,
And two birds capricious wheel and glide.
You promised nine autumns past
To share with me your robe in bed.

Or from a poem by the Emperor Wen of the Wei Dynasty:

Day to part so easy! day to meet so hard!
Mountains and rivers far away, the road is lost to sight.
My full cup of love for you I dare not confide.
I send words to floating clouds; they move on, never come back.
Tears fall, rain down my face, spoiling my appearance,
Who can endure despair alone with never a sigh?

This anthology of Hsü Ling consists of 656 poems; like others before and after, it bears ample witness to the cultivation of love, including romantic love, in China, especially within aristocratic conjugal relationships. As the current editor remarks, 'The idea that Chinese poetry does not deal with love is a myth' (Birrell 1995: 1).

We need to discount the division between Europe and Asia regarding love, especially 'romantic love'; indeed, there is even a counter-current in European thought that sees love (not just desire or lust) as being a feature of the East rather than the West (think for example of Scheherazade, of Antony and Cleopatra, of Omar Khayyám, even of the Kama Sutra). Such a notion is clear in eighteenth- and nineteenth-century discussions of the origin of the language of flowers, especially in the context of love relationships. That language was attributed to the undefined East, referring at times to an account of emblematic communication in the Topkapi palace of the Turkish rulers, where it was said to have been a means of conveying secret messages between members of the harem and attractive slave boys but may rather have served the same purpose between the women themselves (that is, romantic lesbian love) (Goody 1993a).

One constant element of love, romantic love, in the Western as in the Chinese perspective involves the idealisation of the loved object. The paradigmatic case is that of the troubadour poet and *la grand dame*, who is not only idealised but distant, superior in rank. That feature is held to differentiate courtly (*fin'amor*) within a more generalised concept of romantic love. Difference in rank was clearly not altogether essential either to romantic love or to marriage itself, since many unions were not in fact hypogamous in this way. In the imagination courtly love involved an unattainable hierarchical relationship, which is part of the idealisation. But idealisation, as Lantz suggests, may take other forms in these societies. In fact, Duby (1997: 62) notes that courtly love acted 'as a decoration, as a veil, but inadequately concealing the reality, that is the sexual appetite'. Bodily pleasure did not die, as in courtly love, with marriage.

Do we find this idealisation more widely, in Africa for example? I have earlier remarked that we need to reject that grossly racist view of Africans as having lust rather than love, which I now examine in the context of my own field material. Nevertheless I do not find the same idealisation in the oral cultures of Africa.

Among the LoDagaa of Birifu in northern Ghana, who were 'tribal', hoe agriculturists, local speakers of English translate certain words by 'love' and 'lover'. We have seen that there is a general word *nɔne* which can be translated as 'like', 'be fond of', and can be used of women or men, as well as of one's children. The neighbouring Gonja of northern Ghana use the word 'want' (*ʃa*) both for the male and the female affect; 'I love you' is the same as 'I want you'. I do not see much idealisation here. What one finds is attraction, and attraction involves desire and pleasure.

I have no entries in my field index for 'love' but many for 'lover', a term which I employ to translate the word *sen*, although the associated verb is better interpreted as 'to court'. *Sen* often designates a friend of the opposite sex and is the equivalent of *ba*, same-sex friend, male speaking. Both could be translated 'friend', but *sen* is used for women or men to whom you might possibly make love (L65).[7] If I went to a house where they were brewing beer and found there was none left, I might say to the brewer, if I knew her at all, 'Have you not got something for your *sen*?' She might then bring me a small pot saying, 'That's your lover's beer', meaning that I would not have to pay. Among the neighbouring LoDagaba of Nandom, a woman might gather together a number of her female friends and take them to her 'lover's' farm in *sen kob*, to harvest groundnuts or even to hoe between the rows.

---

[7] The textual references are to the pages of my LoDagaa (L) fieldnotes.

Whether a relationship known by this term has a specifically sexual conno-
tation is rarely clear (as appears to have been the case with the troubadours).
Sometimes such an implication is present, as when Naabiere ran off with a
girl without paying any bridewealth to her family. He wanted her to live in
his house as his 'lover' although the children would then be *sensenbie*,
attached to the mother's patrilineage (L705).

I did not collect many songs among the LoDagaa – that was before the
days of portable tape-recorders. But I have nothing in my notes that could
be called a love song. The public situations in which the xylophone is
played and songs are sung do not altogether lend themselves to such a
theme. A number of the songs I did write down are about food (or hunger),
others about death; in addition I recorded some praise songs. However,
when I was visiting Birifu much later in 1978, a young woman called Akwei
was staying with her baby at the bungalow attached to the chief's house,
with which she had a connection. She had been a pupil teacher at Nandom
before she became pregnant. Seeing my tape-recorder she asked to record
some 'love-songs' in English she had learnt at school. I tried to persuade her
to sing the local equivalent, but significantly that proved difficult. The first
two songs she sang in LoDagaa were about suffering and death, so too were
the last two. The middle one did refer to the search for a husband, incorporating a protest against plural marriages.

> I hear it is difficult to get a husband,
> I will share him with no one.
> If somebody wants to play,
> I will shut the door and beat her,
> I will shut the door and beat her.
> A husband is not for sharing.
> I will not share with anybody.

The sentiments in this song may have been influenced by the Christian
and modernising background of Nandom, a centre of the Roman Catholic
mission where she had been teaching. But the desire for attachment to one
man, which is perhaps one interpretation of Western 'love', is not foreign to
polygynous societies, any more than the opposite is to monogamous ones.
Both are part of the structure of the situation of desire. Women sometimes
sing of these matters as they undertake the arduous work of grinding the
hard bullrush millet (they also sing songs critical of men – one cannot say
that the inclusive ideology is entirely 'patriarchal') but men do not seem to

do the same. On the other hand, since polygyny is permitted (but polyandry only in the special case of twins) some married men are always 'legitimately' courting women, addressing them as *sen* and perhaps inviting a further sexual or marital relationship. Attachment in marriage and to some extent outside cannot be as exclusive for them as it is for women. Western observers, used to the perspective of monogamous marriage, often consider love an irrelevant concept in polygynous societies. That seems to me wrong, as the Biblical case of Rachel and Leah suggests. One partner may be chosen as the recipient of romantic love ('the favourite'), and the situation may change over time; however, the relationship certainly differs for men and women.

One reason for the relative absence of discussions of 'love' in my notes is that girls get married very early. These are the ones that usually sing songs, at work and at play. But they marry soon after puberty and there is no extended period of post-pubertal courtship for them to respond to. Courtship may occur later on, in the process of changing husbands, or getting remarried after a husband's death (though this transfer is often arranged semi-automatically). I certainly do not want to imply that there is no courtship at all, for dancing played that role non-verbally. But there is no extended period of adolescent attachment before marriage; late marriage encourages yearning (and idealisation), early marriage acceptance. For the girl there is little delay, no absent object, though this may exist for men who marry later. On the other hand, for them the alternative is male bonding, intensive farming, nowadays labour migration, youthful violence (for example among the Konkomba who 'seize' women as brides) or incestuous and adulterous desires.

The relationship of 'lover' (cross-sexual friend) is not in itself adulterous; as I have remarked, it may not imply sex or it may be a preliminary to marriage. Some husbands (and wives) even continue to call their partners *sen* after marriage, though this is rare. They do so because 'shame' prevents them from using the first name of their partner. Otherwise they will call her by the name of her natal settlement to avoid the personal appellation; or when she has given birth, she will be known by the name of her child, 'the mother of William'. In this sense, the use of *sen* would indicate an avoidance of familiarity, of the public recognition of sexual intimacy, rather than an expression of it. Conjugal intimacy requires distance. Generally there is a kind of opposition between wife (*pɔɔ*) or husband (*sire*) on the one hand and *sen* on the other. One day when my assistant, Timbume, was particularly annoyed with his wife, he declared, '*Sen nomena gõ pɔɔ*', 'a lover is sweeter than a wife', recalling some Roman and Greek pronouncements about the respective merits of wives, lovers and prostitutes. The reason for such statements are easy to fathom. The lover relationship depends upon continually pleasing the other person; otherwise one simply breaks off the relationship by handing back any gifts that were given (as often in the West). One day when Timbume met a former *sen*, he suggested they meet again but she refused. 'Then give me back my twenty cowries', he said, signifying the end of the affair; as long as she retained the gift (possibly an imaginary one), the relationship was potentially open.

I should add that, although the marriages of women were early and often influenced by parents ('arranged'), there was no question of them being united with no matter whom in a union in which lust was satisfied but not love. Marriage involves some choice – or at least the right to reject, especially as divorce is an ever-present possibility, even for the woman. Hence the notion of *sen*, of a lover, is of central significance, not only outside marriage but as a preliminary to marriage and even within it (despite Timbume's comment).

The lover relationship stands opposed not only to marriage but to adultery, although it could lead to both. It stands opposed to adultery precisely because the use of the term is vague about the implication of a sexual relationship. For example, you don't play with your sister but you might call her *n sen*, even when she is married, since you did so earlier on. However, sex is not inconceivable with a distant 'sibling'. 'If sisters are unmarried and still living in the house' (and here it is my strong impression that the reference to sisters and houses is 'classificatory'), 'you might sleep with them; it is like little children' (playing sexual games). Today, with the increase in monogamous marriage and the advent of Western schooling, women are marrying later, so their unmarried presence in the house is a possible temptation for adolescent males. But that would only (rarely) be the case with a full sister (L2041). That hardly constitutes a lover relationship, which is more open and more persistent.

Although lover relationships should in principle exclude lineage members and their wives, that is not always the case. For there is always some ambivalence about 'close' lovers. I heard Yingmaa of Tom calling the wife of his elder brother's son by this term. When I objected, he replied there are different kinds of *sen*: some are merely friends, women who help you find the slivers of wood to assist you roof a room or who put beer aside for you when they brew. At a woman's burial I have seen a man bring a pot of beer to the funeral stand and make a long speech saying how well she had looked after him whenever he came to drink at her house. Such a speech is a kind of 'taking out the dream', which is a constant theme throughout the funeral, attempting to acknowledge and dissolve the significant social relationships with the deceased (Goody 1962a).[8] But while the use of the term *sen* may refer to platonic friendship, the shadow of a double entendre is often present. When Timbume called the wife of Lendis (his mother's brother's son) *sen* and when I again objected that this was the wife of a close kinsman, he replied that in reality he had been addressing her daughter. But that was not at all the case and he only replied in this way because of the potential ambiguity.

In other words, a friend of this platonic kind may turn into a lover in a fuller sense. If a woman continues to buy you beer over a long time, her husband may call you aside and say 'I see that you and my wife get on well [*kpen ta*].' He may ask you to bring a fowl for him to kill to his ancestor shrines. Then you and she can sleep together (L2069, Timbume). If he did not make this sacrifice, such an action would amount to adultery (*pɔɔ sogna*, the spoiling of the woman) and you would have to produce a much more important sacrifice for the ancestors.[9] The wife too would have to report her action to the appropriate agencies, otherwise she would be in danger from that same source, or possibly from some other shrine associated with the household. That responsibility explains the incident at Tugu market when I was sitting with the Chief, Kayanni, drinking beer on his rooftop. A woman arrived in a state of considerable distress, saying that someone 'had touched her vagina' in the market place. When she would not be pacified with beer, the Chief sent for the Native Authority police, then thought better of it and called the alleged offender himself. That man was told on the spot to provide a fowl. Had this not been done, the woman

---

[8] Death of course is absence, and funerals among the LoDagaa are occasions for addresses to the dead person which take a 'literary' form (see Goody, *Death, Property and the Ancestors*, 1962a); they certainly involve praise, possibly idealisation. But I have never heard expressions of what could be regarded as the idealisation of love; in the usual physical sense at least the dead are not merely absent but have disappeared ('turned to maggots, burrowing underground', as the funeral Bagre has it).

[9] There is a significant gender difference in speaking of adultery. Of a woman it is said *a pɔɔ sogna*, she has committed adultery (spoils herself); of a man it is said *a deba soɣpɔɔ*, the man commits adultery with a woman, he spoils the woman. The woman is 'spoiled' in both cases but the man is guilty of doing so only with a married woman.

would have been 'spoiled' (by adultery) and that could bring danger both to herself and to her husband (there is no parallel concept of a man being spoiled). At a man's funeral the widow goes through a number of testing rites to prove that she has not endangered her husband's life by sleeping with someone else. But a lover relationship has been legitimated by the sacrifice and poses no threat; it is the opposite of adultery.

Drinking is often involved in lover relationships of all kinds. You 'love' the woman who provides beer. You always ask her to pour and to take the first calabash-full to ensure it is safe. You may also ask her to drink in a more intimate way by sharing a calabash and drinking out of it at the same time, cheeks pressed closely together; that is quite an art. If you are yet more intimate, you will let your leg rest on hers (*dɔl o gbɛr*); this is the stage at which your wife may complain about your attendance at the beer house and the husband of your *sen* may ask you to bring a chicken to sacrifice.

A proper *sen* may also make shea butter (*ka*), a complicated and oner-ous task, and send it to you as a pomade; then you know she wants you for herself. If a man is sent shea butter, he will later tell his friends he needs help as he has to 'return the pot'. So they may contribute some guinea corn (sorghum) to send her and he will put a guinea fowl on top; that bird is the customary gift to a female lover, like red roses or chocolates. The friends will then take all this to her house where they will be well entertained with beer.

'In the old days' such relationships are said to have been stronger than they are now, for in the Nandom area today they are frowned upon by the Catholic Church; elsewhere too they are felt not to be altogether 'modern'. Dakpaala of Tom reminisced to me about his father's lover (L3044). Every time she cooked porridge (*saab*) she would cut some to bring to his house to feed the children. That story was topped by the history of Teko, a bachelor. His lover crossed the river Volta to Diébougou in present-day Burkina Faso to fetch the daughter of her mother's brother who had been 'sold' there in a time of famine. She brought her back to be Teko's wife. Such rela-tionships, it was implied, are not so strong nowadays; nevertheless as we have seen in the Nandom area (LoDagaba) a woman will sometimes bring a team of her women friends to plant or harvest a ground-nut field. A wife should not object to such friendships. If she does, her husband may beat her. Of course she too may abandon a husband in favour of a lover. The ser-ious problem comes when a lover relationship produces a child, a *sensenbie*, that is, with a woman who is not at that time properly married, for if she

were married and the bridewealth had passed, the child would belong automatically to her husband, the pater, although rumours might still circulate
about the genitor. Such a child would be attached to the mother's lineage
and would gradually become absorbed over time. But it could be a difficult
process, for a lover's child is always bad news for the house, tending to produce a split within it (L2130).

In conclusion, lover relationships certainly exist among the LoDagaa.
But there is little elaboration of 'romantic love' in art, in discourse or in
actuality. That seems to be the case in oral cultures more generally. I can see
little expression in what I resist calling (because it seems to derive all oral
accomplishments from lettered ones) oral literature but refer to, rather, as
standard oral forms. Folk tales in cultures without writing have little about
this aspect of male–female relationships in them. Neither do most songs,
although there is some element in those that women sing when they are
grinding grain. In West African theatre, the playlets do treat of male–female
relationships, often in a rather bawdy way, but theatre in this sense is rare in
African cultures (Goody 1997).

In Black Africa generally one does not find much development of a discourse of love. As evidence for which I turn to two written sources, one by
the literary critic, C. M. Bowra, which he called *Primitive Song* (1962),
referring to the songs of hunting and gathering peoples; the other is by the
anthropologist, Ruth Finnegan, entitled *Oral Literature in Africa* (1970).
Bowra (1962: 185) writes that 'on the whole primitive songs about love are
in short supply'. The songs he collected were of course orally composed
and transmitted, having usually been written down by a literate visitor.
Bowra gives but one definite example of a composition expressing romantic love from Trebitsch's account of the Eskimo of West Greenland:

> My betrothed,
> My beloved,
> I leave you now.
> Do not sorrow too much for me.
> I cannot forget you.
> Your eyes full of tears
> Are the image of my heart.
> All who love one another
> Find it hard to part from one another.

This virtual absence among hunters and gatherers he contrasts with settled agriculturalists, and refers to the Aëta of the Philippines who have produced a number of love songs. That area was influenced by written cultures: lyrics of this kind are certainly not greatly developed in the oral cultures of African agriculturalists, except those affected by written Arabic traditions. Enough exists to suggest that those who view love, even romantic love, as a purely Western invention are certainly wrong. But there is little elaboration of a love discourse as compared with Eurasia.

Some love songs, lyrics, are known from that continent, especially among the Hausa, the Somali and the peoples of the East African coast who have been influenced by the Arabs, with their developed written tradition of love poetry. But like nature poetry, songs of this kind are not at all common. In her comprehensive survey of the oral arts in Africa, Finnegan (1970: 258) gives a number of examples and provides some references. It cannot be said that much deeply passionate love poetry emerges, nothing like Ovid or *The Song of Songs*. But a Somali poem does approach this type of sentiment:

> Woman, lovely as lightening at dawn,
> Speak to me, even once.
> I long for you, as one
> Whose dhow in summer winds
> Is blown adrift and lost,
> Longs for land, and finds –
> Again the compass tells –
> A grey and empty sea.
>
> (Laurence 1954: 31, quoted Finnegan 1970: 254)

Here there is both separation and idealisation. The Somali are of course literate, Muslim and much influenced by the Near East. I certainly found no equivalent among the LoDagaa who were distant from and rejected such currents.

My discussion of love in the cultures of Africa has been based on first-hand data. We find a different but consistent picture in the fictional writings of the 1960s published in the *African Writer Series*, edited by Chinua Achebe. For example the work of the Senegalese writer, Sembene Ousmane, and his short stories, *Voltaique* (1962, translated as *Tribal Scars*, 1974) tells the story of a young girl whose father shows her a photograph of an old migrant to France who is looking for a bride. She is attracted by the prospects of travel, by her father's sponsorship and by an old photograph of the migrant when young. When she arrives in France she realises she has made an appalling mistake and falls for a younger man. Another story, entitled *Love in Sandy Lane* tells of a young kora player and the daughter of an administrator who were clearly in love but gave each other few signs. She is whisked away by a minister in his large automobile. It is not that love does not exist. It does, but it does not necessarily form the basis of marriage, as recent Western ideology insists.

How would we account for this difference in the idealisation of the loved one? I have maintained that there is not the great gulf in sentiments, attitudes and structures between Europe and Asia, the West and the East, which many Eurocentred theories assume, except in relation to shifts of emphasis in the way that partners are chosen. That is particularly true of those notions that see the existence of romantic love as related to modernisation. On the other hand, there does seem to be a certain gap between Eurasia and Africa, the reasons for which have been partly indicated, namely differences in what we might call language use, between written and oral cultures. Connected with this difference is one of the nature of stratification, since the Bronze Age – that gave birth to writing and never reached Africa – also gave birth to a 'leisure class'. But let me concentrate upon literacy.

Few would dispute that the invention of language enabled human beings to acquire a measure of self-awareness, to advance oral communication (which is necessarily self-monitoring), to extend representation and to develop role-playing. Writing introduces a further technique for expanding this process, and one of its functions is precisely to make the implicit explicit. As we have seen, historians have discussed the relationship between love and literacy. We must distinguish the problem of expansion and elaboration from that of creation. The view that romantic love has been handed down from the affluent classes to the poor (Stone 1977) seems mistaken, as Thompson (1977: 500) has remarked. If we are looking at romantic love as a mechanism for the selection of a spouse, then there is evidence to suggest that in Europe 'free choice' rather than arranged marriage was always more important among the poor. But everywhere there was some element of choice, as Hufton has noted. On the other hand, if we are thinking of romantic love as a developed form of address and response, then there is a case for saying that we borrow our expressions from literature, which has in earlier times often been more closely associated with the upper (educated) classes. Lantz (1981: 362) claims it has been suggested that

'People have to be able to read and discuss feelings before feelings can become part of their experience.' Because of the reflexive nature of the process, writing and reading encourages an elaboration of sentiment, a heightening of emotion. In writing a love poem one is rarely addressing directly the loved object; she or he is almost by definition at a distance – again communication at a distance is one of the attributes of writing. For the troubadours, courtly love, in retrospect called 'romantic', was 'l'amoor de lonh', distant love in both a physical and a social sense. The object addressed, usually feminine, is absent at the moment of composition and hence liable to be idealised in words. One is more likely to say, 'My love is like a red, red rose' in her absence rather than in her presence, although these written phrases may subsequently become incorporated as words of immediate address in speech. In most Western societies, love discourse involves idealisation, often of a standardised kind, which one often borrows from expressions that others have developed, frequently in literature. One quotes rather than invents the discourse of love. It seems significant, as in the case of the troubadours, that such a developed discourse occurred in text rather than utterance, in written societies rather than in purely oral ones. That is not to say love discourse cannot take a spoken form in written societies; it can, but by way of feedback. Love poetry seems to me largely a development of writing. If the emotion of love is developed by the representation of a relationship, above all by a representation in written form, then it is understandable that 'love' should be different in literate Europe and Asia than in oral Africa, except where that continent has been influenced by Islam and by Arabic texts.

In conclusion I suggest then that one major factor in the differences between Europe and Africa, and in the similarities between Europe and Asia, is that of language use, related to the means and mode of communication, which of course has some relationship in turn with relationships of production. That suggestion clearly links with the development and in some cases the revival of secular literacy in twelfth-century Europe, epitomised in the work of the troubadours. The tradition was developed in later literary forms. Chaucer's *Roman de la Rose* 'purports to be a text based on love, an uncontrovertible vision of what happens in the garden of love' (Klassen 1995: 16). How does this relate – if at all – to the attributions of romantic love to the 'modern' period, that is, from the eighteenth century, and to the notion that this can be seen as a mark of (Western) modernity?

Literacy was the key to the mode of representation of love. Today modelling of love (and sex) in representation has been pushed much further with the huge expansion of the journals that fill the newsstands of airports and railway stations and, above all, with the advent of television and electronic media. Such representations encourage a certain reflexivity, a feedback on behaviour which occurs with any form of 'narrative' but is especially marked in its written form and, to a lesser extent, with graphic representation. Such representation in itself emphasises the distance from the loved object. In this sense the stress on love, especially romantic love and the elaboration of its discourse, is linked with what is loosely called modernity in no exclusive way and through the mediation of the growth of literacy and the circulation of print. Love, even romantic love, is neither exclusively European nor modern, but the discourse of love, and hence in a sense its practice, has been promoted by changes in communicative systems.

Part II

FOOD

My interest in food relates once again to the similarities in the structure of cooking and cuisine in Europe and Asia, and the difference from Africa, which is linked very closely to the different forms of stratification in those areas.

The sixth chapter represents a transition from the first section, in which I discuss the influence of France on English foodways and try to relate this continental domination firstly to the continuing transmission from prehistoric times of cultural features (such as differentiated cooking) from East (the continent) to West (Britain). That was particularly the case from the mid seventeenth century, when the elaboration of an *haute cuisine* in Paris and the great influence of the French court on the English royalty and aristocracy in exile during the Commonwealth led to the adoption of French models, especially in spheres associated with women, dress, toiletries and so forth. Women had a prominent position in the French court, and in Parisian society and in intellectual life more generally; they were favoured, argues Ozouf, by the strong monarchical regime (as distinct from the weak monarchy, almost a republic) in England.

The next chapter began by being a reply to commentators on the thesis in my book on *Cooking, Cuisine and Class* (1982). I have omitted the particular responses and selected only the aspects of my comments that had a more general significance, especially concerning the globalisation of cultures of food. Chapter 8 elaborates and develops my remarks about globalisation in the context of the expansion of Chinese restaurants in western Europe since the 1960s. But my reply also insisted upon the correctness of my view of African cooking and the absence of a strongly differentiated repertoire, which the major Eurasian states possess and which relates to the nature of their system of stratification, so very different from Africa. Finally in chapter 9, I turn to another feature of this system of stratification, namely the actual rejection of certain 'luxury' practices within some cultures, here specifically the rejection of the drinking of wine, which is a feature of some major religions. There is an ambivalence inherent in the use of wine, which may lead to restrictions on the intake of alcohol, especially in religious contexts.

Chapter 6

FOOD, FAMILY AND FEMINISM

The cultural dependence of England on France from the later seventeenth century was especially marked in the field of food, but also with regard to the culture of women more generally, including relations between the sexes. Of course, there were also reverse dependencies, but my focus is on the one-way traffic westwards across the Channel, a traffic that was markedly important ever since the Norman invasion.

In Antiquity European culinary practices were subject to a great divide. The major civilisations of the South enjoyed the products of the Mediterranean, the grape, the olive and wheat providing the bread and the wine for sacred and profane occasions. The Germanic peoples of the North cultivated other cereals less intensively, and consumed large quantities of beer and meat, of both wild animals and the pig (which also provided them with fat) that lived on the acorns of the forest (Montanari 1994).

French diet was fundamentally changed by the advent of the Romans from the Mediterranean, first as traders, then as conquerers, leading to a much greater differentiation of consumption. Wine was first introduced by the Greeks to Marseilles, from where it was traded, together with drinking vessels, to the tribal areas, mainly for chiefly consumption. In describing the political economy of that penetration, Dietler (1990) has spoken of being 'driven by drink'. The wine came from Italy, Spain and subsequently from Languedoc. However, these imports were not for all or sundry; they enforced and created hierarchy.

Olive oil, which displaced the earlier animal fats in the southern regions, was another index of romanisation (Dausse 1993: 81). In addition the Romans introduced shellfish, above all oysters, which were often preserved. Other conserves included anchovies and prunes, the first salted, the latter dried, but more typical were garum and the concentrated must of grapes. Sharper sauces using garum, spices and aromatic plants were added to the repertoire. The body of imports also included fruit trees such as the cherry and the peach. In return the South-east, for example, exported to Rome cheeses (possibly including a predecessor of Cantal and of Roquefort), salaisons and other agricultural products. These exchanges were facilitated by the adoption of Roman currency, and they reached a level not attained again for nearly ten centuries.

There was a further dimension in this North–South contrast. The South had a differentiated repertoire of cooked foods, with a higher cuisine among the upper groups, and lower, ordinary foods for the masses. The difference is well illustrated in cookbooks such as those of Apicius, which provide recipes for the elaborated cooking of elite households. Northern cooking, as it appears from Anglo-Saxon literature, was relatively undifferentiated, with the leaders having more of the good things of life but eating much the same foods prepared in much the same way as their followers. That was part of their egalitarian organisation. But they now acquired certain luxury items for consumption, especially Mediterranean wine, brought up the valley of the Rhine (Dietler 1990).

When the Germanic tribes broke out of the northern forests and came to dominate the lands of the Roman empire, they brought with them some of the features of their earlier life but they rapidly adapted those to southern practices, modifying at the same time some of the elaboration of the host cultures, not only regarding food but the whole socio-cultural system. That elaboration included a considerable degree of hierarchical differentiation; that was very strong in both Rome and Greece, as we see from the accounts of Roman feasts, of Heliogabalus serving 600 ostrich heads or of the grand banquets of Athenaeus. But this differentiation partly disappeared in the early Middle Ages with the collapse of the Roman empire and its economy. There were fewer differences in the culinary practices of social classes, which were again marked by variations in quantity rather than quality. In Anglo-Saxon England, and the same seems to be true of other areas dominated by the German tribes, chiefs ate the same foods as their followers, only more of them. That is a feature noted for Africa, where there is also little difference in tribal foods either hierarchically or regionally, apart from those ecologically determined, or apart from local taboos, rarely affecting everybody. The state of affairs began to be altered with the advent of Mediterranean foods and culture.

A possible index of the decline in complexity in early medieval Europe from classical times is the disappearance of new agronomic treatises. Presumably monks copied old works, but new studies only began slowly to reappear in the West, after centuries of absence, with the Arabic literature in Spain (Montanari 1994: 53; Ambrosogli 1996). Written knowledge even if neglected or unknown can be recovered; hence the importance of the transmission of classical texts through the Arabs. But nevertheless their temporary disappearance had meant that the written corpus was not added to, even though some changes in agricultural practice undoubtedly took place during this period.

Regional differentiation also occurred, and we find dishes taking on national labels, with references to 'English broth' or 'Catalan blancmange'. That does not mean there were no regional cuisines earlier – just that we do not know (Montanari 1994: 63). However, though we can see a major distinction between north and south Europe, there is necessarily little national cuisine until the creation of distinct nation-states in the early modern period. Before that the emergent differences were largely ones of class, as Stouff (1970) has pointed out for Provence and north Italy, though he may have underestimated local differences, especially in the lower classes (of whose cooking we know little).

The twelfth and thirteenth centuries saw the birth of a 'courtly' ideology of food parallel to that of courtly love (*fin'amor*) (Montanari 1994: 85). What one ate became seen as constitutive of the very quality of persons, giving rise to sumptuary legislation which saw to it that people consumed the foods appropriate to their status and not those of higher groups. Cookbooks appear once again in Europe in the thirteenth century, the first since the late Roman handbook of Apicius. Differentiation increased radically in the fifteenth and sixteenth centuries, with the less war-like aristocracy offering spectacularly lavish banquets. In Florence the dishes were sometimes taken round on display before the meal, not only in front of the guests but the general public too. Ostentation was of the greatest social importance, and the banquet was as much a *show* as a meal, with the idea and ideals of differentiated food being made known and communicated to the populace.

The major revival of cuisine in Europe came with the Renaissance. In Italy in the mid sixteenth century enormous quantities of expensive foods were prepared for high-ranking persons. In sixteenth- and early seventeenth-century England expenditure on food and entertainment was often crippling. At that time scholars of the new learning searched through classical sources to explore the food of the ancients for recipes, although the influence of the humanists on elite food can be exaggerated. However, these researches were incorporated in texts, beginning with Platina's *De honesta voluptate* of 1475, which heralded the revival of the salt-acid taste based on olives, capers, anchovies, etc., a real contrast to the sweetness, golden colour and fragrance of the High Middle Ages, all three features of which being associated with the sensual and luxurious dining of the Arab world. The use of butter in sauces, according to Flandrin, marks a break with the common tradition of medieval cookery. There was also a further advance in Martino's recipes which appeared as a sort of appendix to Platina, in Cristoforo di Messisbugo's *Banchetti* (1549) and in Scoppi's *Opera* (1570).

It is often suggested that after the break with medieval cookery in Renaissance Italy, the *nouvelle cuisine* was brought to France by the cooks who accompanied Cathérine de' Medici (1519–1589) on her journey from Florence in 1533 to marry the future Henry II. The notion that French *haute cuisine* went back to the Italian influences following this marriage has been denied by Revel and others (Pitte 1991: 120), who have seen French cuisine (like the Italian) as being essentially medieval until the mid seventeenth century (Boucher 1982). But there were certainly strong influences from Italy, as Flandrin has noted – the vogue for rare vegetables and fruits (especially artichokes, cardoons, asparagus, cucumbers, mushrooms), the introduction of American cultigens, table manners, cookbooks, the use of the fork, flowers on the table, perfumed water. Although most of their cookbooks were not translated, Italy had a great impact on northern Europe, as we see in many other cultural spheres. While we know little of the northward expansion of Italian cuisine, Montaigne (1533–1592) has left us an account of the Italian cook employed by Cardinal Caraffa, of whom he says 'He gave me a discourse on this science of supping with a grave and magisterial countenance, as if he were speaking of some grand point of theology'.

The individuality of French cuisine followed that of Italy (possibly earlier than has been suggested above) in the sixteenth century, and that of Spain in the second half of the sixteenth and the first half of the seventeenth century. It seems to have established itself even before the potential pre-eminence of the French king, Louis XIV (1643–1718), judging by the English translation of the *Cuisinier français* in 1653, two years after the original publication of this book that marked the real beginning of modern French cooking and a break with Italy (Flandrin and Montanari 1996: 567).

The publication of *Le Cuisinier français* by François Pierre de la Varenne in 1651, according to Peterson (1994: 163), saw the birth of modern cooking, although its originality may be exaggerated because no cookbooks had been published in France since 1542 (Flandrin, personal communication). In France the tastes of the Middle Ages finally gave way, and there developed a liking for vegetables, fruit and milk products, as well as the separation of the salted and the sugared (Flandrin and Montanari 1996: 563). All this was held to be more natural. Many of these changes took place first in France, following a relaxation of the link between cuisine and diet. The new style of French cooking did several things. Firstly, it all but eliminated sweet odours and the colour of gold. Secondly, it developed a range of new sauces.[1] Printing was now available and cookbooks proliferated as a means of transferring knowledge to the growing bourgeoisie; there was a remarkable increase in the numbers circulating in France in the second half of the seventeenth century. That knowledge was not confined to France. The *Cuisinier français* also appeared in Italian in 1680, as did some other French works on cooking. For whereas Italy, the home of the Renaissance, had earlier been the arbiter of taste, now France prevailed.

From then on the reputation of French cuisine grew around Europe and around the world; but its own history, it is claimed, often looked back to local cultural sources (Pitte 1991: 15). While Pitte treats the question of Italian influence more seriously than many, he also sees French cuisine as going back to Roman, Celtic, Germanic roots, leading eventually to its achieving a status as the greatest cuisine in the world, an opinion naturally held by Escoffier. We have to see such statements as partly ethnocentric in character, for not only are Asian repertoires, such as the Chinese, entitled to make similar claims, but even in Europe Italy had its own major cuisine; the fact that it never had a national court meant that it did not develop a single elaborated cuisine in the same way, but it had and has many related regional cuisines of considerable importance, though simpler in some ways.[2] But whether the global pre-eminence of French cuisine can be justified or not from a

---

[1] It has also been claimed that the French adopted a salt-acid taste from Italy, but French cooking had always been more marked by an acid flavour than others in Europe, although there was a slight decline between the sixteenth and eighteenth centuries, despite the arrival of capers. As regards salt, there was the arrival of anchovies as a seasoning, but France displayed less taste for salt than countries of the north and east of Europe (J.-L. Flandrin).
[2] On Florence see G. Alessi, *Alla Pentola dell'Oro* (1994) for a contemporary example that draws on its historical roots in the classical, medieval and Renaissance worlds.

culinary point of view, it has certainly been of overwhelming importance in Britain, which has, together with the United States, been partly responsible for its cultural dominance in the wider world, just as Britain has helped to create the wider taste for Bordeaux wines.[3] But important as this has been, English cooks have constantly reinterpreted French recipes.

It was the European aristocracy who were the amateurs of the culinary arts, but whereas in France these elites were open to the development of a national style, in other countries, especially England, the attractions of French cuisine hindered the dialogue with popular cooking which was necessary for an *haute cuisine* to develop (Mennell 1985; Flandrin and Montanari 1996: 569). French practice greatly influenced English food at this time, but it is important to recall that an impact had already been felt as a result of the Norman conquest and was evident in the cookbooks of the fourteenth and fifteenth centuries. That we see from the bizarre duplication of meaty words in English, with the Anglo-Saxon being used for the animal on the hoof and the French for the animal on the table: hence sheep and mutton, cow (or bull) and beef, etc. That duality in turn was associated with the English myth given literary form by Sir Walter Scott, in which the Anglo-Saxons looked after the animals while the Normans consumed them. Hence the dual usage.

The elaboration of cooking in England after 1066 took place largely in the houses of the Anglo-Norman nobility, at a court which owed its roots and many of its current interests to France, as well as in the establishments of the higher clergy whom William had imported from Normandy in considerable numbers to take over the positions of the ousted Anglo-Saxons. The Plantagenet courts of Henry II in England and France were not simply

---

[3] Pitte (1991: 34): the wines of Bordeaux 'seraient médiocres sans la marché anglais en vue duquel ils furent élaborés dès le Moyen Age'. Flandrin comments that Bordeaux wines were mediocre in the Middle Ages, and that in the modern period the English drank less than the Dutch and Scandinavians, preferring port wines. But from the end of the seventeenth century London was a valuable market, especially for the first of the new great wines of Bordeaux, château Haut-Brion. On the earlier wine trade between Bordeaux and Britain, see Postan (1987: 172 ff.). He notes that England became 'one of Europe's chief importers of wine (she imported over four million gallons in 1415); the clarets of Gascony went mostly to England'. England also brought Rhenish wine from Cologne merchants who came at the end of the eleventh century, while 'there was a regular flow of sweet wine from Spain and the eastern Mediterranean to the countries of northern Europe'; a thirteenth-century *fabliau* narrates a combat of wines and reviews some thirty or forty regional vintages, mentioning Bordeaux, but the 'prize goes to what were undeniably the most highly valued of medieval wines, the sweet wines of Cyprus'.

derivative but constituted 'outposts of social sophistication' in their own right, developing literary genres in important ways (Duby 1997: 73). Ties with France gradually weakened, and Norman French disappeared in favour of that mix of German and Romance, our own version of Franglais, that we call English. Nevertheless the cultural bonds continued: the English who had already borrowed French terms, not only for family (kinship) relationships outside the nuclear core (aunt, uncle, cousin, etc.), also adopted terms to do with women (as in the *Roman de la Rose*) and, above all, ones relating to food and its preparation. Think for example of the list of terms for cutting up meat, game and fish which was one of the first documents printed in English by Winkyn de Worde, in his *Boke of Keruynge* (1508). It runs:

> Tranche that sturgyon
> tayme that crabbe
> ... barbe that lobster

The use of these indicative verbs, all variants of the French, took place well before the development of an *haute cuisine* in France at a time when the two countries probably did not differ all that much in their approach to food, except of course in their access to different raw products, to the grape and hence wine, to olive oil and to many of the ingredients of Mediterranean food. However, access to Mediteranean products did not differ greatly between northern France and England (except that the latter imported much more sugar, which they used in some half of recorded dishes). Most of those foods were only made popular much later in demotic England by post-war travel, as well as by Elizabeth David and other writers who have helped completely transform our tastes; and, yes, the restaurants had an effect too, at least in the eyes of anyone who remembers the situation only twenty or so years ago. London is now described as a centre of culinary culture, almost entirely through foreign imports, through the globalisation of food rather than through native invention.

The French influence on food continued during the Renaissance. In his *The English Hus-Wife* (1615) Gervase Markham writes of 'fricassée', by which he means a fry-up. 'And now to proceed to your fricassees, or quelque chose...' (1615: 42). 'Quelque-chose' becomes 'kickshaw' in English. While the French borrow English words with their spelling but do not know how to pronounce them, the English borrow orally and transform the orthography in comic fashion.[4]

But the major impact of French cooking (and of high culture generally) came at the end of the seventeenth century and was far-reaching. England had experienced its Puritan revolution in which plain behaviour and plain cooking went hand in hand, as for example in the cookbook of Cromwell's wife, Elizabeth. When the Restoration of the Monarchy came in 1660, nine years after the appearance of *Le Cuisinier français*, the royal family had lived long in France and had acquired many French tastes. In the arts Restoration comedy prevailed, as did poetic forms in the work of Augustan writers like Alexander Pope. A comment of his on court cuisine runs:

> Our Courtier walks from dish to dish,
> Tastes for his Friend of Fowl and Fish;
> Tells all their names, lays down the law,
> 'Que ça est bon! Ah goutez ça'.

The shift to French is in the spirit of the times; luxury had been banished with the advent of the Commonwealth, but it returned with a French accent which we have never lost, especially in matters to do with women and cuisine. The Restoration poet, Rochester, expressed the indigenous resistance to this influence and drew a contrast between French food and the hearty meal served at a well-known London inn:

> Our own plain fare, and the best terse [claret] the Bull
> Affords, I'll give you and your bellies full.
> As for French kickshaws, sillery, and champagne,
> Ragouts and fricasses, in troth w'have none.
> Here's a good dinner towards, thought I, when
> Straight up comes a piece of beef, full horseman's weight.[5]

These were of course the days when the roast beef of Old England could be enjoyed without further thought about infectious cows, but it still had to be accompanied by claret.

Nor was this influence now felt only at courts and among the nobility. In 1702 there appeared an English translation, *The Court and Country*

---

[4] I owe this observation to J.-L. Flandrin, who drew my attention to 'payn perdew' in Harleian ms. 279, no. 43, published by Thomas Austin in *Two Fifteenth Century Cookerie Books*, p. 42.
[5] Sillery is a type of sparkling wine from the Champagne region, one of the best vintages, well known in the seventeenth century as it belonged to a great family of ministers to the king, the Brulart (J.-L.F.).

Cook, of François Massialot's *Cuisinier roial et bourgeois*. The middle classes had definitely joined the readership. The preface runs 'It is also to be hop'd, that here, in an English Dress, as in [Massialot's] native country, where three Editions of his work have been printed and sold, in a short space of time . . .' As we see, the continental influences did not come unmodified by local tastes which offered some resistance to their total domination, especially among the more careful bourgeoisie.

From the Restoration to the death of Queen Anne, writes Mennell, there were signs in England of the emerging French courtly style coexisting with 'the lastingly different native tradition' (1985: 89). For while many aspects of French cuisine were adopted, they were also adapted to English tastes and especially to a more economical clientele. In England during the eighteenth century a number of women authors emerged who were clearly concerned about the extravagance of the courtly mode. Hannah Glasse, writing in 1769, says: 'if Gentlemen will have French Cooks, they must pay for *French* tricks . . . I have heard of a Cook that used six Pounds of Butter to fry twelve eggs.' To use less 'would not be *French*' in the eyes of someone who was not herself of the aristocratic class.

The French influence of course extended to much more than cuisine. It was equally strong in clothing, male as well as female. Both the extent and the denial of this influence can be seen in the Prologue to George Etheridge's play, *The Man of Mode* (1676), where the mode is definitely male though affected by female tastes and company:

> With modest fears a Muse does first begin,
> Like a young woman nearly enticed to sin;
> But tickled once with praise by her good will,
> The wanton fool would never more lie still.

The shift of tone from the Interregnum is obvious, but the product is also one modified by native wit:

> But I'm afraid that while to France we go,
> To bring you home fine dresses, dance and show,
> The stage, like you, will but more foppish grow.
> Of foreign wares why should we fetch the scum,
> When we can be so richly served at home?

The subtitle of the play is Sir Fopling Flutter, the name of one of the characters who thinks himself 'the pattern of modern gallantry', having

'lately arrived piping hot from France'. He wears gloves up to his elbow
and an exactly curled periwig, talks with 'a pretty lisp' and affects an imita-
tion of 'the people of quality in France'. A complete gentleman, he maintained, 'ought to dress well, dance well, fence well, have a genius for love
letters, an agreeable voice for a chamber, be very amorous, something dis-
creet, but not over constant'. A central theme of Restoration drama was
adultery; the libertine was constantly portrayed on stage. The London theatre reopened with the production of *Love in a Tub* in 1664, with an elitist
audience and an orientation towards relations between the sexes that differed radically from Shakespeare's time, although the private diaries of
Pepys display somewhat different attitudes to those that appear on the earlier stage or in Puritan discourse. In fact theatre had started again in London
before the end of the Commonwealth; Davenport's *The Cruelty of the
Spanish in Peru* was played at Drury Lane in 1658. This later sexual permis-
siveness contrasted particularly strongly with the passage of laws against
adultery and fornication by the Puritan parliament, embodying a sentiment
that was certainly not altogether dead. For there was a strong reaction
against the themes of what Thackeray, not altogether correctly, saw as this
foreign import, namely Restoration drama; in 1698 the Reverend Jeremy
Collier, an Anglican, blasted off about the immorality of the stage, which
then reverted to a diet of bland drama during the eighteenth century.

But while both males and females took France as a model for behaviour it was in fact the female one that stuck, while the adoption of the attire
of male foreigners was considered foppish, even effeminate. By the middle
of the eighteenth century the more enterprising milliners, women entrepreneurs, kept a female agent at Paris who had 'nothing else to do but to
match the Motions of the Fashions, and procure Intelligence of their
Changes; which she signifies to her Principles' (Campbell, *The London
Tradesman*, 1747: 207–8, quoted Pinchbeck 1930: 287–8). The Japanese
photographing the windows of the boutiques in the Boulevard St-Germain
had his British predecessors. Other milliners made visits to Paris and
informed their clients on return of what had been brought back. Paris fashions were all the vogue for women. That included hairdressing. 'Rising
standards of luxury and new French fashions demanded a male hairdresser
and a French one at that. "Now the ladies cannot be obsessed with elegance", claims Collyer in the *Parent's Directory* of 1761, "except a French
Barber, or one who passes for such, by speaking broken English"' (quoted
Pinchbeck 1930: 292).

Nor did the influence extend only to England. French fashions, claimed Mercier in 1780, were an art form which had entered all the palaces of kings and the house of the nobility: 'tout ce qui concerne la parure a été adopté avec une espèce de fureur par toutes les femmes de l'Europe' (Mercier 1780, *Parallèle de Paris et de Londres*, quoted Ribeiro 1995: 76). It is not by accident that the words for women's dresses, above all for their underwear, their lingerie, so often derive directly from the French. With more democratic trends, French men, however, became affected by anglomania; many of the deputies to the First National Assembly, members of the old Third Estate, wore English-influenced styles which were equated with progress and democracy, abandoning for example the wig (Ribeiro 1995: 84).

Nevertheless attitudes to the French were highly ambivalent. On the one hand there was the borrowing. Before the French Revolution,

> the British man or women of letters relied heavily on literature and criticism in French. This feature was often suppressed or denied, but the frequent attempts to assert Britain's cultural independence from France demonstrate how powerful was the bond that some wished to be broken.
>
> (Brewer 1997: 92)

Thus the villains in sentimental literature have usually adopted the vices of the court, 'which are those of the aristocracy and the French' (Brewer 1997: 135). Here the British saw themselves as superior because of their free constitution and commercial economy. Much of the local criticism dwelt on the aristocracy's love of all things French, and its adoption of florid measures associated with the sycophantic conduct of a despotic system. 'French court society, for example, was characterised by indiscriminate mingling of the sexes, excessive male solicitousness to women, and constant sexual intrigue' (p. 91). In Britain too, many critics, presumably male, saw the role of women in the arts as leading to 'the feminisation of a culture they believed should embody masculine virtues', associated with war and commercial success (p. 88).

In the eighteenth century there were numerous female writers, painters, actors and musicians. Aphra Behn, playwright and novelist, was the first professional woman writer to be buried in Westminster Abbey. Between 1750 and 1770, six of the twenty most popular novelists were women. During that period 185 editions of novels were published by

women, whose central contribution to bourgeois culture had first manifested itself in France in the mid seventeenth century, when *haute cuisine*
really emerged. Women were also great consumers, readers of periodicals
and novels, devotees of the circulating libraries, most of the audience at the
theatre, opera and pleasure garden, enthusiastic participants in the mas-
querade, the collectors of prints and the purchasers of paintings, the organ-
isers of amateur dramatics and theatricals (Brewer 1997: 86). This was by no
means the first time women had played important roles in social life, in
England, Europe or elsewhere. With dowry systems women in upper
groups always received part of their parental wealth, appropriate to their
status. That was true in both France and Britain. In Anglo-Saxon England
high-born women possessed property, wrote wills and bequested land and
movables to kin, friends and the Church. And in societies with written cultures women had long made some contribution to literary pursuits. What
happened now was that they became central to the arts, some as creators,
many as consumers. 'Women of the same social standing as men were much
more likely to own both books and pictures' (Brewer 1997: 103).

That centrality brought about a reaction. In discussing Coleridge's
condemnation of sensibility, Brewer points out that the usual object of
criticism was

> a woman who indulged in or was controlled by feelings provoked
> by literature and romance . . . the ill-disciplined reader of novels,
> the giddy girl who loses all practical sense of the world because she
> is misled by the romantic tales of sensibility was repeatedly
> satirised and attacked, not least because it was feared such women
> were easily seduced and likely to lose their virtue.
>
> (Brewer 1997: 135)

This feminisation of culture (that is, high artistic culture) was certainly
stimulated by increasing levels of literacy in England as well as by the
importation of French novels after the Restoration; and all three of these
elements – feminisation, literacy and France – also contributed to the adoption of a cuisine from across the Channel.

That process of the transmission of the feminine was only partially and
temporarily interrupted by the French Revolution. It brought about (for
example) a drastic simplification of dress, partly for fear of standing out,
partly for democratic reasons, because styles were now adopted from the
dress of lower groups. England too was influenced by this change, though

not to the same extent. Fashions drifted apart during the wars; French women were regarded by the British as too 'undressed'; the French criticised Englishwomen in their corsets pushing up the bosom to make, in the words of a fashion compendium, 'a sort of fleshy shelf, disgusting to the beholders, and certainly incommodious to the bearers'. Another French observer remarked of Englishwomen in 1810 that their appearance, in immense hoops, 'does not ill resemble a foetus of a hippopotamous in its brandy bottle' (Louis Simond, quoted Ribeiro 1995: 123). Soon after the restoration of the monarchy, Paris became once again the focus of attraction for 'le beau monde' in England and elsewhere; aristocratic women like Lady Bessingborough in the 1830s rejoiced in the milliners' boutiques. The city became the source of etiquette, for example, in developing, even inventing, the language of flowers, which was hastily copied throughout Europe and the United States (Goody 1993a).

Returning more specifically to food, it is sometimes said that the dominance of French cuisine in restaurants, as distinct from the tables of the court and nobility, came at the end of the French Revolution when the cooks of the aristocracy (like their seamstresses) were forced to find other work. That is only partly true. In fact restaurants had existed two decades before the Revolution, and earlier than that one could eat in taverns, inns, in hostelries and at bakers and caterers. English taverns had made their appearance during the course of that century and served meals to their clientele. Indeed, Beauvillier's great restaurant in Paris (he had been cook to the future Louis XVIII), opened in 1782 or 1786, was called La Grande Taverne de Londres. Nevertheless the Revolution greatly accelerated the establishment of restaurants and the expansion of the *haute cuisine* because of the migration of the best cuisine from aristocratic homes to the great public eating places. That cuisine then dominated the eating of much of the upper bourgeoisie in England, as in France.

Why and how did this take place? There are several layers to this domination of French cooking in England. Firstly, 'civilisation', the culture of cities, whether in the form of the Romans, the Church or the Normans, reached England through France. Most of the accounts of French social dominance, whether in England or elsewhere, take their starting point as the Renaissance, or the seventeenth and eighteenth centuries when French culture spread throughout Europe. But England had been influenced by France long before. When they invaded from the East, the Normans established a French-speaking aristocracy who supplied a model for class behaviour. France provided a major route to the Mediterranean, the Ancient World, the Middle East and Asia generally. But in fact, Mediterranean products and influences did reach England direct; her ships went to trade for sugar in Sicily and later brought port from Portugal. In Flandrin's opinion, medieval English cooking was more influenced by Arab cuisine than was the French.

Later on, while the creation of an *haute cuisine* in Europe may have begun in Italy, the original home of the Renaissance, it was subsequently developed in France, which in turn influenced England. In the late seventeenth century, French culture was dominated by the court. Mona Ozouf draws a contrast with eighteenth-century England, which she sees as basically republican since the mid seventeenth century, a monarchy ruled by parliament, to which the French Revolution subsequently turned for democratic models of dress. France had a court culture which in certain respects incorporated, swallowed up, the intelligentsia. Elias remarks (1994: 29) that 'In France the bourgeois intelligentsia and the leading groups of the middle class were drawn relatively early into court society.' By the eighteenth century there was 'no longer any considerable difference in manners'. With the dominance of the bourgeoisie after the Revolution their patterns became national because 'members of the rising middle class intelligentsia in France stand partly within the court circle, and so within the courtly-aristocratic tradition . . . Their behavior and affects are, with certain modifications, modeled on the pattern of this tradition' (Elias 1994: 40). They are 'civilised' in this sense, even if they are reformist and even revolutionary at the same time. To say that the French aristocracy were dominated and sidelined by the royal court in the later seventeenth century (and therefore, as Ozouf argues, more attuned to leisure pursuits in the company of women) does not mean that this situation was universally accepted. In the eighteenth century the aristocratic and high bourgeois culture of Paris certainly criticised the royal court at Versailles in fundamental ways. But in the cultural contexts which we are treating here there was a certain hierarchical solidarity of manners irradiating from high to low.

Elias draws the contrast with the separation of the German nobility around their small courts from the bourgeoisie, the first espousing French culture, the second rejecting its artificiality. The German courts were greatly influenced by France already at the end of the sixteenth century (that is, well before Louis XIV, well before the *haute cuisine*). By then the Duke of Brunswick had acquired a French dancing master, Antoine Emraud, who transmitted some of his knowledge to the Protestant German composer, Michael Praetorius (1571–1621), who in turn incorporated into his collection *Terpsichore Musarum* (1612) dances such as Les Gavrottes, La Gilotte, Les Passepiedz de Bretaigne, Gaillarde and La Bourée. The French notion of civilisation, writes Elias (1994: 41), 'the consciousness of the superiority of their own behavior and its embodiments in science, technology, or art began to spread over whole nations of the West' as they became colonial conquerors and constituted 'a kind of upper class to large sections of the non-European world'. But that again was much later.

The importance of an *haute cuisine* in France, which became part of this cultural dominance, also seems to be related to the position of women in urban life. It will be recalled that in the eighteenth century the Scottish philosopher, David Hume, considered France was 'the land of women'. He had of course been welcomed in the salons organised by women, which he described as the 'Etats Généraux of the human spirit'. Nor was he the only British commentator to make the point. Horace Walpole did so too; and the pioneer feminist, Mary Wollstonecraft, author of *A Vindication of the Rights of Women* (1792) and mother of Mary Shelley, saw French women as being less insipid than their English counterparts. At the same time she noted that 'an air of fashion is but a badge of slavery', indicating a Rousseau-esque counter-criticism to the worship of *la mode* (quoted Ribeiro 1995: 3).

The notion of the high status of women in France applies of course largely to Paris but not only to the court. Elias notes that the French court set a style of life which was often copied, not only by courtiers but also by the bourgeoisie, radical elements of which were at the same time providing a critique. There was a substantial diffusion of culture from high to low. And not only to the bourgeoisie. Think of those copies of Louis XIV beds that one finds today in French farmhouses in the Lot. Styles seeped down from the court to create a fashion of what Pitt-Rivers has called 'phoney folk'. This dominance of the court culture, and the tendency for seepage from high to low, was reflected in representations. Hufton points out that compared with England, the *livres bleus* of France in the seventeenth and eighteenth centuries, a popular genre taken round the countryside by colporteurs, 'draw more conspicuously upon stories of the great and famous, of high society' (Hufton 1995: 50). In fact they often drew upon works that had circulated among the elite two or three centuries before. In this way the people themselves became more orientated towards the culture of the court, even in revolting against it.

For the idea that French culture as a whole (rather than Paris and the upper bourgeoisie) differs in the behaviour between the sexes requires some modification when we look at rural France. Today the Aveyron could be earlier England as far as sexual restraint is concerned. Beteille's (1987) account of Rouergue in the nineteenth century is entitled *La Chemise fendue*, referring to the modest night-dress worn by the wife which provided an opening for sex. As elsewhere in the lower strata, nudity was avoided. However, in other respects much of France was affected, even in some minor degree, by the gallantry of the court and by such things as the cuisine that was developed in a society much of whose social life was dominated by women. Women were not necessarily the cooks, indeed rarely so in high society where men predominated, but they organised cooking, meals and social life generally. Aspects of cuisine passed down the social scale in the manner that Hume and other observers have implied. It is true that throughout Europe some aspects of culture also rose from low to high, including elements of regional cooking and leisure activities such as games (cricket and football) and folk-songs, embodied in aristocratic dances or providing themes for orchestral music. Clothing was certainly one of these items in the period of the French Revolution when democracy was the slogan of the day. Perhaps the descending influences prepare a route for the ascending ones, but in any case it is the former that are my focus here.

The notion that civilisation and manners began with the court of Louis XIV at Versailles and seeped down from there has been questioned by others. Indeed, it is as ethnocentric as many English claims about democracy and the 'mother of parliaments'. Cultured, mannered courts could also be seen in many Italian Renaissance states, and at that very time the Dutch bourgeoisie developed a strong sense of proper behaviour. As Hufton (1995: 26) remarks, 'there is nothing "uncivilized" about the tranquil settings of a Vermeer. The court was not then the only possible agency for change.' To speak of the genesis of civilisation at the French court is to overlook not only contemporary Europe but also the earlier and more extensive developments that took place in Rome, China, Japan and other parts of the world.

But what is inadequate comment for 'civilized' manners as a whole, may not be so if we look at the developments in post-Renaissance Europe with regard to the culture of women. In certain respects France is still supreme among the international bourgeoisie, that is, in *la mode*, in perfumes, in the language of flowers, perhaps in the discourse of love, even if that supremacy is now being challenged.

Mona Ozouf argues that, firstly, as compared with England, the privileged position of women in France from the eighteenth century was related to the nature of its monarchical regime and its court. England too had a monarch, but parliament was all-important; the imported German kings had neither the power nor the prestige of the French court. The whole ambience was more republican. The highly differentiated nature of the French court meant that sexual distinctions were only one among many. Secondly, under the centralised monarchy, court life deprived men of their traditional masculine activities and effectively sidelined them politically; so they were constrained to take up leisure pursuits in the same way as aristocratic women, and often in their company. Thirdly, as a consequence women were very much part of the social scene, especially in the organisation of salons. 'L'art féminin', Ozouf (1995: 326) remarks, 'civilise les hommes . . . Car la société des femmes est une école d'intelligence et de moeurs.' Women present the acceptable face of culture.

The other side of the coin was that the resultant gallantry could engender frivolity and irresponsibility. Intellectual freedom meant sexual licence. In mixed society, as Montesquieu observed in *Lettres persanes*, adultery was an inevitable accident, one which a man should learn to live with, for a jealous husband disrupts society. In such a milieu, women are not simply equal; they rule. Their dress, their behaviour, partakes of luxury and is directed towards the seduction of men. Infidelity is an intrinsic characteristic of the gallant society. In Paulucci di Calboli's tract on the trade in Italian girls for prostitution at the beginning of the twentieth century, he remarks that it is in Paris and in France that women receive their sweetest rewards: 'la donna francese ha una fama mondana superiore a qualsiasi altra per spirito e per grazia' (Paulucci di Calboli 1996 [1909]: 133), and that itself made the country a pole of attraction for all strangers.

Indeed, there are aspects of the position of women of which many, especially in middle-class Victorian England, would have strongly disapproved. For this vision of women of the upper classes in Paris is not unconnected with that town being regarded as the home of sexual freedom. Of course the English were once again ambivalent. For the young Englishman it was the home of 'les maisons de tolerance', and the French language gave its name to refinements of practice the British had hardly dreamed of. Not only gallantry, but at another level coquetterie and the very transaction of sexual intimacy was looked upon as essentially French. The pleasures of the bed as of the table were more interesting across the Channel.

I come to the third of my inter-related topics, which I must treat very briefly. The notion of the high status of women in France, at least in the towns, together with the close and equal relationships between the sexes, runs somewhat contrary to the ideas of many Anglo-Saxon historians of the family who base their analysis of the emergence of the small enclosed domestic (so-called 'affective') family in England, which they see either as a consequence or as a cause of the events leading to the establishment of what they proudly claim was the First Industrial Nation. That family is seen by Stone, Laslett, Shorter, Macfarlane and others as encouraging close relations of 'love' between the couple (who can now make their own choice of mate instead of being constrained by parents or even by the economy) as well as between parents and children. This affection, the works of these historians might suggest, characterised the position of women within the bourgeois family, whereas in France it was the gallantry of court life. But as we have seen, the high status of women was not confined to the French court, and such attitudes towards them, as Ariès points out regarding the love of children, were more widely based in Europe. I do not see any adequate evidence of the greater love of children in England; indeed, France was the first to start to shift from quantity to quality (if contraception can be taken as a measure). The notion that love between the sexes, as between parents and children, is basically an English phenomenon should be greeted with great scepticism, even in the specific form of conjugal love. That is especially true when it is linked with the idea that the position of women generally was better in England than elsewhere.

Seventeenth-century France saw the appearance of a number of women novelists. England followed, and the Restoration produced a significant number of women dramatists (Aphra Behn, Pix and others), who had plays put on in London (some at a theatre managed by a woman, Lady Delaney). Such achievements would have been unthinkable in the Elizabethan and Jacobean periods; a sea change had occurred as far as gender was concerned, and by the end of the seventeenth century there was not simply the occasional woman's voice in literature but the constant appearance not only of amateurs but of professionals like Behn. Not only the authors but the culture too had changed.

What had happened during that period? The role of women in the court culture of France, 'la singularité française', was of some importance even in England, giving greater freedom perhaps to women than during the Puritan Commonwealth, for whom, despite the contribution made by some to the running of sects and in other ways, women very much had their place. But other factors were at work. Nothing much is to be gained by talking of a change in *mentalité* without being more specific. The development of women's education was undoubtedly a major factor, facilitated by the growth of schooling after the Reformation and Counter-Reformation (since we are dealing with literate pursuits), as well as by the increasing freedom for the publication and selling of books and their greater circulation (Brewer 1997). Supply and demand grew together, especially in the form of plays and novels.

These changes have to be seen in the wider context of Western Europe. Many Anglo-Saxon historians, even feminists, take too ethnocentric a view of the development of the rights of women, seeing as the key figures Mary Wollstonecraft (and earlier pioneers such as Anstey) in England and Sylvia Anthony in the States, whose efforts were accompanied by changes in the family and outside, especially regarding divorce and property. But let us recall that the French Revolution had already introduced a divorce act in 1792 (later annulled, it is true), modified the dominant position of the father and husband, despite some qualifications about the latter,[6] and equalised the treatment of sons and daughters regarding the transmission of property in ways that became part of the more conservative Napoleonic Code.[7] Those events cannot be seen as simply created by sudden revolutionary transformations of the existing order. Queries and questioning about these practices had to have existed beforehand under the *Ancien Régime*.

Ozouf sees open commerce between the sexes as originating in the aristocracy but as having been supplemented by 'extreme democracy' during the Revolution (in which women played a notable political role), and subsequently too in the Republic later in the nineteenth century, especially in the sphere of equal education for the sexes, in which France has long given a lead.[8] Women schoolteachers were encouraged to stay on after marriage (indeed, to enter into *mariages pédagogiques*) some seventy-five years

---

[6] See M. Ozouf's comments on C. Pateman's attempt to distinguish between paternal rights (of the father) and patriarchal rights (of the husband). That distinction does not seem quite right, even given the vagueness of the term 'patriarchal'.

[7] The Revolution was ambiguous about women's rights, since widows throughout France and elder inheriting daughters in Basque country lost the right to vote, while the Napoleonic Code forbade the search for the paternity of illegitimate children (J.-L.F.).

[8] The political role of women lay not only with the *tricoteuses* but with the formation of women's groups, the expression of their complaints in 'les doleances des femmes' and the adjustment of their legal status.

before civil servants could do this in England. In 1963 43 per cent of French students in higher education were women compared to 32 per cent in the United Kingdom and 24 per cent in West Germany (Ozouf 1995: 375). Nineteenth-century republicanism may have kept French women from the vote because of male fears of the conservative influence priests might have, but it gave them an equal if separate education. These facts Ozouf sees as making French feminism very different from the 'gender feminism' of America, stressing always the continuing interaction between male and female rather than setting up conflicting spheres of activity. That inter-action has to do with what she calls 'la singularité française', defined in the first instance by the court culture of the seventeenth and eighteenth centuries.

Whether or not we accept Ozouf's thesis in its entirety, especially con-cerning contemporary feminism, it does attempt to offer some explanation for a number of features of the earlier situation that should puzzle those English historians who manage to raise their eyes to look across the Chan-nel.[9] In seventeenth-century France women in upper circles played a more significant cultural role than their equivalents in England, including the organising of salons for members of both sexes. Male gallantry, the culture of women, everything that goes with *la mode*, these were and remained one of the great attractions of France not only for English aristocrats who went to Paris to discover the latest fashions, but for much of the rest of the world besides. Is not the prestige and attainment of French cuisine since the mid seventeenth century also associated with the culture of the court and with 'la singularité française', namely the privileged position of women, at first of the upper classes, later more generally? The preparation of food was a prestigious activity, especially in the competitive context of entertaining others, where it was supervised, if not always carried out, by women (as elsewhere, the prestigious extra-domestic cooks were men). And the style and elegance of those occasions had some influence upon ordinary life and upon more ordinary households, both in cooking and in table manners (the proper subject for a work of France's most distinguished anthropologist), for the preparation of food was not simply a chore but an intrinsic part – the woman's part as nurturer – of family life. As my fanciful title suggests, there was indeed a connection between food, feminism and family in France

---

[9] For an extended account of French feminism between the two wars, see Chaperon (1996); the spectrum is more varied than Ozouf's account might suggest.

which offers a partial contrast with England, but not perhaps in the way discussed by the more nationalist of our historians.

As for the influence of France on England in the domain of food, before the opening up of the Atlantic seaways virtually all external inputs to high culture in Britain came from across the Channel, usually although not invariably from France. For political and geographical reasons France remained the dominant source and model for luxury products. That process of transfer was accelerated with the Renaissance. The same was also true for Germany and elsewhere north of the Alps, even before the flowering of the French court and the development of an *haute cuisine* in the mid seventeenth century. But those events contributed to the whole process which so strongly influenced England with the restoration of the monarchy. In the subsequent centuries it affected the middle classes as well as the court, and not only in cooking but in a whole range of women's activities, especially *la mode* and the relationships of women to men, and of men to women. In much of the culture of women, France for a long time dominated not only Britain but also the rest of the world.

Chapter 7

STRUCTURALISM, MATERIALISM AND THE HORSE

The starting point for this chapter lay in a special number of *Food and Foodways* that was directed to my *Cooking, Cuisine and Class* (1982), in which various scholars were asked to comment on my thesis. I was asked to reply, which I did in the first part of this contribution. In that reply I gave the following outline of my study.

The origin of my initial enterprise lay in an attempt to provide an answer to a particular problem that had not, so far as I was aware, been raised by others and that related to a series of revisionist analyses I had offered concerning some widespread features of precolonial society in Africa. Why was it that there was no differentiated cuisine south of the Sahara? I also discussed the ways in which certain general approaches had helped or hindered understanding of this topic.

Grande cuisine in France was partly the result of Renaissance influences from Italy on the court, whereas higher and lower cooking had existed beforehand. There is little evidence of major differences in attitude or in practice among the French and English upper classes in the medieval period, though there were some minor ones. Indeed, at one time those classes belonged to one and the same culture, one that differed substantially from that of their subjects, especially Saxons. That observation raises the question of hierarchy as well as of temporality. The problem behind my question was not primarily concerned with the meaning of food to the actors in one particular village at one particular time, nor even with the meaning to the actors in a larger society. Indeed, my point was that in eleventh-century England, perhaps an extreme case of raw conquest and exploitation, the meaning of foods, as well as what one ate and how it was prepared, depended on whether one was Norman or Saxon. The extent of cultural homogeneity obviously varies in different cultures and over time, but in the major Eurasian societies the changing balance between unity and diversity of meanings and practices must remain a matter for sociological and historical exploration, much more so than in Africa. The reasons behind this difference are what *Cooking, Cuisine and Class* is about.

It is generally agreed that I avoid the extremes of cultural materialism, but in other ways I am seen as approaching the materialist pole. In the first place this radical dichotomy between materialist and cultural approaches, as I have overly insisted, is as outdated as the mind–body one, especially when 'social organisation' is seen to fall on the materialist side of the 'opposition' (not at all the way I see social life as 'organised'). Secondly, I have always tried to draw attention to a variety of factors in any given situation and to suggest that what are deemed most significant in any specific context or for any particular problem must be considered empirically, not in an a priori fashion. Of course, I may start with a working hypothesis about the way a technology influences social life, but that does not commit me to a monocausal view, nor does it prevent me on another occasion asking the same question about the influence of a religious or political ideology.

The tendencies to polarise social theory are among the profound dangers of any analysis. Hypotheses need to be elaborated in ways that are sensitive to research and that are not dominated, though they may be suggested, by the a priori demands of general theories elaborated in other contexts of social action.

Any such approach as this runs the risk of being stigmatised as an unhappy academic compromise (Sahlins 1976) or as eclectic (Harris 1983; Sangren 1989). I find neither characterisation uncomfortable; the point is to make more sense of the universe in which we live. In any case I do not believe that in the end either utilitarians/materialists or culturists/symbolists can exclude factors that are exogenous to their initial precepts. Rather, they differ in adopting different strategies of approach, the appropriateness of which can be judged only by their contribution to explanation.

Prohibitions on and preferences for food are clearly so widespread and central a form of human behaviour that it would be truly remarkable if one type of explanation were able to cover them all. Let us therefore set aside binary 'theoretical' statements, and adopt a more particularistic form of analysis which not only deals with the existence of 'foodways' within a social system but looks at changes over time in relation to specific historical situations. We may find Harris (1975) unacceptable on the subject of the sacred cow of India, and we may be satisfied with Mary Douglas' (1971) analysis of the meal. But such conclusions do not allow us to dismiss once and for all any explanation of food preferences that has to do with survival, either in an immediate or in an attenuated form. Nor can we refuse to see any connection between these preferences and the transmission over time of a specific repertoire of food crops, which evolves not only by the cultural selection of what 'nature' has to offer but as the result of a historical process of invention and diffusion. Such a repertoire cannot be divorced from the particular conditions for growing certain crops, though these will change over time; there are specific reasons why wine has been a high-status item of consumption in England, and why beer ('real' or *fabriqué*) has formed the country's language of ordinary imbibing. In these specific instances, productive activities influence the structure of the categories and preferences rather than the other way round. Once in existence, of course, the categories in turn structure perception. But the contribution of one explanatory component does not annihilate the relevance of the other.

Some writers, including Sahlins, seem to adopt a contrary position when dealing with that culinary-categorical problem of *sheep* and *mouton* which de Saussure had earlier discussed with respect to their different meanings. *Mouton*, of course, refers to the slaughtered animal as well as to the living one. De Saussure (1966 [1916]: 115) remarks, 'The difference in value between *sheep* and *mouton* is due to the fact that *sheep* has beside it a second term while the French word does not.' The implication about the relational component of meaning ('difference') is correct enough from one point of view and could have been further exemplified by the Chinese failure, at least at the morphemic level, to separate the sheep from the goats. A similar situation occurs with the categorisation of alcoholic drinks: Hsu (Hsu and Hsu 1977) tells the story of how he declared a bottle of brandy to the British customs as 'wine' (a Chinese category covering all alcoholic drinks) only to arouse the officer's suspicions as to his honesty.

With regard to sheep, however, Sahlins (1976: 63) adds a further comment: 'So far as the concept or meaning is concerned, a word is referable not simply to the external world but first of all to its place in the language – that is, to other related words.' De Saussure's statement has been glossed so that the meaning of a world is referable '*first of all*' to other related words. The demonstration of course derived from the examination not of one language but of two, English and French; categories were compared in relation to the outside world as well as to themselves. Moreover, while the assignment of such a priority may be correct in the cases of certain words and in certain contexts, it is patently not so in others, except in a circular sense. That is, in saying 'It's going to rain', I imply it is not going to snow. But to maintain that the primary reference is *first of all* to other words requires some radical qualification.

It would not be necessary to make the point did the assertion not lead to the rejection of explanations that many, starting from a different premise, have found eminently reasonable. In a further note on the sheep/mutton problem, Sahlins recognises the Norman derivation of the series of English words denoting the butchered flesh. In *Culture and Practical Reason* (1976: 64 n. 8) he writes:

> In the same sense of a cultural construction, one may note of de Saussure's sheep/mutton that this animal takes its place in the Anglo-Saxon world as fit for butchery alongside pigs and cattle, which share a parallel declension of terms for the prepared state (pork, beef), while all differ in this respect from horses and dogs. History without structure would not seem to explain the classification, since we have no Norman-inspired word for 'cheval' by analogy to mutton, beef and pork.

Why are history and structure opposed in this way? The opposition is surely relevant only in the context of the restricted debate among functionalists and structuralists. The reference to the Norman conquest is a reference to structure, and it is difficult to see how history can ever be without it. On the other hand, can structure be without history? Since structures of whatever kind persist over time, they are in a real sense the past in the present; that is to say, they represent the past and thus reproduce it. Of no aspect of culture is this truer than of language, especially written language, because the interpretation of sounds and of words, of phonemes and morphemes, depends upon a very precise, a very tight structure, transmitted between as well as within generations. A forty-year-old father and his ten-year-old son have to speak to each other, however much their sociocultural interests may diverge. Other aspects of culture are more loosely structured.

Let us consider this particular case of parallel linguistic forms for animals in the kitchen and on the farm, the former based on the Romance root, the latter on the Germanic. The association of this division with the stratification between Norman and Saxon seems to offer a reasonable explanation, a reduplication of language initially resulting from conquest, becoming structured in a specific linguistic and class situation, and persisting over the generations by becoming part of the continuing structure of the verbal system. The division is no longer maintained by the specific 'causal' relations by which it was first established, the distinction between the production and consumption of meat now having the same hierarchical, ethnic reference but the verbal pattern remaining relevant to the distinction between farmer and butcher, field and table, living and dead. That pattern is of course important in *influencing* perception, though not in determining it, since perception and understanding are clearly not functions of language alone. In English we still recognise sheep and mutton as the same animal, if only because they have both tended to become 'lamb' for practical reasons connected with the industrialisation of food, with advertising its products, and with the butchery trade – just as 'duck' has become 'duckling', and 'hen' has become 'chicken'. The structure of language is part of a specified socio-cultural situation, endowed with a measure of autonomy but not autonomous.

The duality of this semantic patterning would seem to derive from the past; it was established at a particular point in time as the result of a set of historical circumstances. Its embeddedness in the English language provides one of the many instances of discriminations that were made possible by the way the conjunction of English and French after the Conquest offered a dual set of possibilities, which in many cases acquired early on a certain class significance. In other words, the past can reasonably be introduced to account, even partially, for the distinction. But on the theoretical level Sahlins rejected such an approach as 'history' (presumably *histoire événementielle*) without structure. And he follows up this point at the empirical level by rejecting the historical explanation because horse is not treated in the same way as other animals, being excluded from the list of English–French (Anglo-Saxon–Norman) dichotomies. But was it to be expected that Norman aristocrats would sit down at table to consume their companions in war and the chase, their instruments of destruction, the tools of booty production, the conditions of their domination? And how often, even in France today, is the produce of the *boucherie chevaline* served at a bourgeois dinner party or at a restaurant of *grande cuisine*? I do not find any recipes for its preparation in Brillat-Savarin, let alone in Tante Marie.

At an earlier period the Anglo-Saxons too may possibly have consumed horseflesh. Some fragmentary evidence comes from a report of the papal legates in 786 to Pope Hadrian, who replied:

> Also you wear your garments according to the fashion of the Gentiles . . . It is a marvellous and dumbfounding thing, that you imitate the example of those whose life you have always detested. You also by an evil custom mutilate your horses, slit their nostrils, fasten their ears together and make them deaf, dock their tails; though you can have them unblemished, you do not desire this but make them hateful to everybody.
>
> We have heard also that when a lawsuit arises among you, you cast lots in the manner of the Gentiles, which in these times is reckoned altogether as sacrilege. Also many among you eat horses, which no Christian does in the East. Give this up also.
>
> (Whitelock 1979: 838)

However, this act, characterised as 'unchristian', did not long continue, except in times of famine when even human flesh was no longer sacrosanct. The sentimental attachment to the horse was well established by the time of the earliest surviving English wills (1387–1439), in some of which horses are left by name (no dogs are named) to specific individuals. The best horse was known as the *Principal* (also Mortuary, Corsepresent, or Foredrove) and followed the corpse at the funeral, eventually becoming the property of the priest; a survival of this custom persisted at state funerals, and it is to this transaction that the proverb refers about not looking a gift horse in the mouth (Furnivall 1882: 19).

France was no different, and the general acceptance of horsemeat began quite late, with the siege of Paris in 1870. There had been previous attempts to popularise this source of protein. It was eaten during the Revolution, in 1793 and 1794, when food was in short supply, and again during the Napoleonic Wars. In the latter case it had the benefit of medical opinion. Based on his experience in the Russian campaign of 1812, the military surgeon Larrey pronounced horsemeat, which had been consumed in the retreat, to have a curative value for the wounded, and the belief in its health-giving properties persists to this day. Nevertheless it was a famine food until recently and shifted its position in culinary terms only as the result of these external pressures, combined with internal propaganda and a general rationalising, questioning tendency. From 1847 various steps were taken by

Geoffrey-Saint-Hilaire to popularise the meat. A horse banquet was arranged by the director of the veterinary school of Alfort at the Grand Hotel in Paris in 1855, the first time the meat had been served openly in a restaurant (Knab 1885–1902: 1136). The menu, given by Christian Guy (1961), was as follows:

Consommé:	Vermicelle au bouillon de cheval
Hors d'oeuvre:	Saucisson et charcuterie de cheval
Plats de Viande:	Cheval bouilli
	Cheval à la mode
	Ragoût de cheval
	Filet de cheval aux champignons
Légumes:	Pommes sautées à la graisse de cheval
	Salade à l'huile de cheval
Dessert:	Gâteau au rhum et à la moelle de cheval
Vin:	du Cheval Blanc

Eleven years later, in 1866, the first horsebutcher established himself in Paris, but only after the siege of 1870 did the meat become widely eaten. During that same siege dogmeat appeared in Parisian restaurants, sometimes described as mutton, which led one client to remark, 'Next time, they'll serve us the shepherd' (Catelot 1972: 178). The taint of 'cannibalism', of breaking a taboo, remained.

The French campaign in favour of horseflesh had direct repercussions in England, as was the case with most culinary matters (Mennell 1985). In 1868 a Mr Bicknell addressed the Royal Society of Arts on the merits of chevaline, and in the same year an imposing dinner was held at the Langham Hotel under the auspices of the Society for the Propagation of Horse Flesh as an Article of Food. But horseflesh never achieved the recognition it did in France, no doubt partly because in England alternative supplies of plentiful meat from the Americas were expanding very rapidly at this time.

The horse returns to centerstage again in Sahlins' analysis of 'food preferences and tabu in American domestic animals' which he presents in a chapter entitled 'La Pensée Bourgeoise: Western Society as Culture'. He has no difficulty in showing the 'irrationality' of a productive system that does not consume the meat of horses and dogs. The point will be disputed only by the most extreme rationaliser, those who rely upon a medical 'explanation' for the Near Eastern taboo on pork; except for those too numerous exceptions, the contention is surely as axiomatic as the alternative proposition that biology imposes limits of viability.

In discussing the centrality of meat in American culture and its association with the notion of strength, Sahlins (1976: 171) notes that it 'evokes the masculine pole of a sexual code of food which must go back to the Indo-European identification of cattle or increasable wealth with virility'. The reference to Benveniste's work on the reconstruction of Indo-European concepts is surely a matter of historical derivation rather than of cultural logic, unless logic is unchanging over time. If that is so, we might ask why the vegetarian Hindus are not equally relevant as the cattle-consuming cultures. And unless we are referring only to language, why should Indo-Europeans be more relevant as a cultural model or ancestral figures than the ancient Hebrews, contemporary West Africans, or nineteenth-century Comanche for large parts of the American population?

The analysis of this ancient cultural logic is based upon 'the domesticated series – cattle-pigs-horses-dogs' (Sahlins 1976: 174). Taboo is associated with inedibility to give the formula 'edibility is inversely related to humanity' (p. 175, following Leach 1964) so that 'the food system' can be seen as a 'sustained metaphor on cannibalism' (p. 174). It follows that dog is most consistently rejected as food because it is closer to man than horse; pig follows, being 'contiguous to human society, more so than cattle'. The cow is the most distant and the most prestigious; in the same vein, the inside of the cow is closer to man and hence less edible.[1]

Parts of this analysis are very plausible and the ideas are widely current among the actors themselves, especially the notion of the 'traditional' closeness of the horse and dog to man. But 'cultural logic' is subject to the influences of changing social circumstances, so that the domesticated series is less an independent than a dependent variable. For most of the inhabitants of Europe and America, the horse is no longer an instrument of booty production, a means of production, or a means of transport. It is surely as distant as the sheep, suggesting a potential change in dietary custom, one that in some quarters took place many years ago: among French officers during the Franco-Prussian War, in the Harvard Faculty Club during the

---

[1] The closer proximity of the inside is not easy to follow, nor is the inedibility of the stomach to tripe eaters in France, Italy and northern England, for whom it is a delicacy.

Second World War and continued as 'traditional' in its aftermath (see the menu below), and more generally among the working class and petty bourgeoisie in France.

Monday, December 10, 1979

Soup – Cream of Tomato   75 c

TODAY'S SPECIALS

21.	Chicken Chow Mein with Steamed Rice	3.00
22.	Baked Vienna Loaf – Brown Gravy	3.00
23.	Creamed Seafood Mornay en Casserole	3.00
24.	Pan Fried Horse Steak – Mushroom Sauce	3.25
25.	Egg Salad, Bacon Bits, Lettuce and Tomato on a Roll	1.50

Lunch menu of the Harvard Faculty Club. (On a more recent visit in November 1987, the 'traditional' dish appeared to have been abandoned.)

When we think of sheep, however, we wonder further about the nature of that particular series. Why not include the sheep, the chicken, and even undomesticated animals? Would distance still equal edibility? Or proximity, inedibility? The wild deer is not noticeably preferred to the cow. Nor is the chicken rejected in favour of the sheep, and the pig is not made more edible to a large part of New York's population, despite the fact that it is further from the house than the hen.

Not only is the series partly arbitrary, but the notion of closeness is used by everyone in different ways, even to explain the logic of the limited series under review. Hence the system of preference lacks the overall logic proposed. Though some elements of the explanation are certainly relevant, it is difficult to accept unequivocally that 'it is this symbolic logic which organizes demand' (Sahlins 1976: 176). We can readily agree that a variety of sociocultural factors influence both the supply and the demand for food, but 'organize' is another matter because the word implies the rejection of the role of other elements. Indeed, the author himself seems to draw back from the extreme position when he claims that 'the symbolic scheme of edibility joins with that organizing the relations of production to precipitate … an entire totemic order uniting, in a parallel series of differences, the status of persons and what they eat' (p. 176). The notion of parallelism seems redundant, but there is some recognition of the interaction between forced choices.

One further problem arises with this attempt to specify cultural logic in such general terms (for example, humanity = inedibility). The interpretation of specific cultural forms in terms of a wider logic means abandoning the cultural particularity on which the argument rests: an important body of French eaters has a different set of preferences from Americans, and yet there is no evidence that the horse is any more distant in France than it is in America. Sahlins implicitly recognises this point when he notes that Leach claims his schema of animal categories has wide validity but not universality.[2] Certainly there are plenty of instances of peoples who keep dogs and eat them too (in West Africa, for example), just as they keep tame rabbits, doves and chickens in many a contemporary French farmhouse. All animal husbandry involves a tension between cherishing the young and slaughtering the old. There may well be some general tendency to protect 'close' animals (Goody 1962a: 115), but if this is the case, it has a significance that lies outside the realm of specific cultural codes though inside that of learned behaviour; it may arise from the cognitive contradiction involved in humans having at the same time to conserve and destroy. One of the problems anthropologists face is the failure to distinguish consistently between the two general meanings of 'culture' – that is, 'culture' and 'a culture': both represent factors that need to be taken into account though in different ways. While one is linked to a language, the other may be related to linguistic activity in general, to the problems of language-using animals facing the world in which they live.

In the foregoing pages I have attempted to support the theoretical eclecticism to which my work has been linked. Monofactoral, single-track theories or approaches seem less likely to generate profitable hypotheses, certainly at this point in the development of the social sciences, than a more comprehensive search that is directed toward the problem in hand. The edibility of the horse is a case in point.

HISTORY AND THE DRY AND THE RAW

Much has been made recently of the dichotomy between the Cooked and Raw. In most societies this pair of words comprises part of a more complicated set that cannot easily be represented by a simple matrix, since the

---

[2] On animal categories, see Leach (1964) and Halverson (1976).

concepts are overlapping. Drying can obviously be regarded as one form of cooking; we place plums in an oven to turn them into prunes. Equally, 'fresh' and 'raw' are linked at various points. Again, dry is often opposed to 'wet', not only for the weather but also, in the domain of food, for fish (at least in English, though the phrase 'wet fish' seems less common nowadays, especially in the South).

I have argued that at one level the sheep–*mouton* problem discussed by de Saussure must be related to a historical situation where difference emerged in a specific socio-cultural context. The structure of categories in French and English was the result of a series of events setting up a system of social stratification which has a productive, culinary and linguistic dimension. When that specific situation in England effectively disappeared, the parallel classification of living animal and dead meat continued as an established feature of the language.

A similar situation exists with regard to the English and French terms for the fresh and dried versions of certain fruits. Just as English segments the living and dead animals, by using one word with a Germanic root and one with a Romance one, so in a slightly different way it segments the living and the dead produce of the vine and the plum tree, adapting a word in the one case and using a Germanic root in the other. Consider the following series in the two languages:

English	*French*
(bunch of grapes)	grappe
grape	raisin
raisin (dried grape)	raisin sec
plum	prune
prune	pruneau

An Anglo-Saxon word, *wynberry* (Goth. *weina-basi*; Fr. *vigne*), belonged to the long series of berry words in English (straw, rasp, goose, black, blue, wortle, logan) and specified very clearly the use made of grapes, namely to allow the fruit of the vines to ferment into an alcoholic drink. But the term was supplanted by the French, who were the major suppliers of the fruit. In fact, what had happened in the case both of the grape and of the plum is that the French word for the fresh fruit became the English term for the dried product. The reason is not hard to discern. As with most vegetable products before the age of mass transportation and refrigeration, the objects of export were the dry rather than the fresh (or wet or raw) goods; to create these the raw had been subjected to the desiccating heat of the sun. Hence they were goods that also tended to travel from South to North, from hot to cold, since climatic factors were important. But of course similar effects could be obtained, as with much of the Atlantic food trade, by means of fire, possibly the oven, to dry the perishable fresh product or to do so by means of the desiccating qualities of salt. Hence the whole cult of the dried fish in north-west Europe: the kipper, dried cod, smoked salmon. It was the dried, the salted, the pickled – in other words, the preserved – that were not only the objects of trade but also made distant sea voyages a real possibility.

Dried vegetable products too became the object of early long-distance trade. From the standpoint of Europe, the phases of this trade included:

1 The early spice trade, dating at least from Roman times.
2 The Mediterranean trade in dried fruits, many of which were initially of Near Eastern origin and include dried grapes (raisins), dried dates, dried figs, etc., which are still associated with festive occasions.
3 The American trade, principally in tobacco.
4 The eighteenth-century trade in tea from China (and later from India), plus of course coffee and sugar.

It was these dried products, especially the spices, the dried fruit, the tea, that formed the basis of the grocer's shop, known as the *épicerie* in France and *kolonialhandlung* in Germany.

Among the dried fruit one found not only raisins but currants and sultanas; central constituents, together with spices, of rich (ceremonial) cakes, of gingerbread, of hot cross buns, of plum puddings, and so forth. 'Sultana' is another distinct lexeme by which the English refer to a form of dried grape from the eastern Mediterranean, known to the French as *le raisin de Smyrne*, that is, from Smyrna or Izmir in Turkey. 'Currant' is yet another form of dried grape or raisin, with a more complex semantic field. In French the currant is *le raisin de Corinthe*, indicating more precisely its origin in trade with the Mediterranean. In England the word also acquired quite another meaning, referring to the black and red fruit of the *ribes* which were introduced into England from Scandinavian countries some time before 1578. Their similarity in shape and colour led to the assumption that here was a fresh version of the 'black currant' from Corinth but whose original identity was concealed in its shortened nomenclature.

In French the *ribes* were allotted different lexemes, *cassis* for the black and *groseille* for the red. Like 'currant' in English, *groseille* refers to not one but two fruits of distinct species, that is, also to the gooseberry (sometimes with the addition of the epithet *maqueraux*), which, leaving aside the ubiquitous 'berry', appears to be a transformation of the same root as *groseille* in French: indeed, as dialect forms in English one finds gozell, groser, goosegog. The double usage seems to have a similar origin to that for 'currant', which at first was also referred to as the overseas gooseberry in English; the gooseberry too is a *ribes* and has common features with the currant from the North.

These complexities of the category systems for fruit in English and French can be paralleled in the world of the vegetables – *pomme de terre/ciel*, endive and chicory, artichokes, and other items. Their elucidation serves to make one obvious point: there are many ways in which classificatory systems relate to the outside world, to the interaction of persons, and to other aspects of the conceptual system. In the case of the grape and raisin we see ecology and interaction (in the form of trade) as significant determinants of the relationships between lexemes. The damson likewise reflects the Syrian (Damascene) origin of a small plum that was introduced in early times into Greece and Italy. But once established, the different lexemes and identities take on a life of their own, since language, being arbitrary, must be inherently conservative in order to communicate not only within but between generations. The original rationale, the earlier associations (currant/Corinth) become lost, and one can unravel (and in that sense explain) the relationships only by historical inquiry. Etymology lives because it incorporates the concepts and social relations of past time.

Chapter 8

THE GLOBALISATION OF
CHINESE FOOD

Asian food has long had a great appeal to the West, less often for gourmets than for the general populace. When I first went to Cambridge University in the year before the outbreak of war there were already a number of Indian restaurants in the town, and one Chinese-American establishment. The Indian restaurants were generally run by Bengalis and served a standard menu of curries and pilaus of the kind that had been directed to British servicemen abroad; the Chinese restaurant, the Blue Barn, served chop suey and chow mein (possibly sweet and sour pork) of the type beloved by Americans wanting a taste of the exotic. Both types of restaurant served inexpensive food, partly because Asian foods have a smaller percentage of those costly ingredients, meat and fish. Consequently they had great appeal, not only for their stranger value but also for their cheapness. Undergraduates could afford to sign out from a meal in college and use the savings to buy a restaurant meal.

After the war the number of Indian restaurants in Cambridge increased rapidly, patronised by many who had had experience of Indian cuisine in the sub-continent itself. They remained inexpensive, though their menus gradually widened to include tandoori, balti and other varieties. The fact that they were open at all hours, even after the pubs closed, was an additional attraction. Before the war there had been few Chinese restaurants in Britain except in the dock districts of London and Liverpool. With the end of the war, the final stages of rationing and the attraction of new tastes, the number increased, many offering meals of moderate quality, others later concentrating upon take-away, a service that was becoming more and more popular with changing patterns of work, especially women's work. Chinese restaurant workers, especially from Hong Kong, increased rapidly.[1] The numbers of restaurants expanded so that even remote Scottish townships were hardly complete without their Chinese take-away, while the Chinese community provided cooks and assistants for many other 'ethnic' restaurants in larger towns throughout the country. Not only did they benefit from the shift of emphasis towards a restaurant culture that was taking place in the country but they were also taking over the running of some indigenous institutions, in particular that deeply British form of take-away, the fish and chip shop. The Chinese chip shop became a commonplace of the urban environment.

For the establishment of the restaurant is only one stage in the spread of Chinese or other foods. Most traditional English public houses in Cambridgeshire now serve food (an index of the spread of the restaurant culture), some offering Thai or other exotic foods. I know one at least that changes its foreign choice every night: Monday night is Indian night, Tuesday Chinese. Of course, unlike the ethnic restaurants this food is not cooked by native cooks and suffers as a consequence. But exotic dishes are not confined to the restaurant since a vigorous trade has grown up in take-away and delivered meals – you phone your local restaurant when you want a special meal and they bring it round in a short space of time. Frozen foods in supermarkets play much the same role, and in my local Sainsbury's I can buy a range of ready prepared ethnic dishes. But I do not need to rely on the cooking of other individuals, since ethnic cooking can now be prepared in my own home, thanks not only to foreign food shops (for example the Chinese emporium in Florence catering for the restaurants) but even the supermarket now has a whole variety of different rices and other ingredients, while one of the most vibrant sections of the publishing trade lies in producing cookbooks of a range of foreign cuisines. Cultural differentiation in foods enters the kitchen.

One reason for the popularity and success of Indian and Chinese restaurants lay in the good value they gave. Partly this was due to inexpensive 'ethnic' labour, partly to the relatively low cost of food that did not include large portions of expensive meat. And while not exactly vegetarian, they were less heavily orientated towards meat than were Northern or Western 'barbarians'. That made them increasingly attractive to generations concerned to protect the environment from large-scale cattle ranching and the consequences for the world's forests, as well as touching upon a

---

[1] By 1970 there were 1406 Chinese restaurants in the UK (Watson 1975: 104).

certain feeling that the Americans (with their hamburgers and fast foods) were commanding too much of the earth's resources. The advent of mad cow disease (BSE) can only reinforce this trend.

The establishment of Indian and Chinese restaurants in Britain was a very different process from Australia, where they mainly resulted from migration on a considerable scale, leading to the formation of ethnic communities with their own eating places which also catered for the wider public. In Britain these restaurants were established by immigrant workers and deliberately aimed at providing food for the host nation. They filled a niche, in this case the culinary vacuum in post-war Britain, and the nature of their migration as 'restaurant workers' was linked to their relations with the host community (largely self-enclosed) and their intention to return home. They were, in intention, long-term labour migrants rather than refugees or settlers, and were involved in a food-led movement.

Of course even in Chinese restaurants the food served is somewhat modified to local tastes. The main male character in Timothy Mo's novel, *Sour Sweet*, knew what he liked and that 'the food served from the "tourist" menu was rubbish, total *lupsup*, fit only for foreign devils' (Mo 1982: 17). Watson (1975) describes two types of restaurant in London. The authentic variety, first established in the dock areas to cater for Chinese sailors (for example, The Good Friends), now in central London in *Tohng Yahn Gaai* ('Chinese People Street', that is, Gerrard Street), caters mainly for Chinese customers (and some expensive restaurants where the non-Chinese are welcome); the general type of 'chop suey' restaurant offers food adapted to local tastes and prepared by non-specialist cooks.

The Indian restaurants were often based on labour that had been recruited from kith and kin, in the home country. These individuals were working off the debt they had accumulated through the costs of the voyage and so were prepared to work long hours for low wages. Watson's study of Chinese restaurant workers in Britain showed them to be even more organised, mainly based on a single lineage village from which kinsfolk were recruited for work. The extension of Chinese restaurants from Britain into western Europe, including Scandinavia, was carried out largely by members of that one lineage, called Man, inhabiting a walled village, San Tin, in the New Territories of Hong Kong, and who even ran their own travel agency. The fact that all the workers are members of the same lineage facilitated not only recruitment but entrepreneurship, since many restaurants are organised as partnerships, often with every employee as a partner, holding shares, until they themselves become managers. Few partnerships are formalised by written agreements, since if problems occur these have to be solved within the lineage framework. In other words, the presence of kinship ties provides advantages not only in recruiting labour but in raising capital based on trust and social control, in contrast to the 'bureaucratic' participation claimed to have been essential in the development of Western capitalism.[2]

The inhabitants of San Tin were originally agriculturalists growing rice. This was not a lineage of cooks, but they had learnt the trade because of a downturn in farming and passed it on to other members. While the results were not always spectacular from the culinary point of view, they provided inexpensive and adequate meals for the masses. For while the best of Chinese cooking is a genuine *haute cuisine*, prepared for elite customers with a gourmet appreciation of food, a range of restaurants also provided for the wider public. The scroll depicting the southern Sung capital in the fourteenth century (the Spring Scroll) already shows a wide variety of tea and eating places, while in the markets, as Marco Polo recounts, tofu provided a ready-made cooked food for the poorer classes, an early case of take-away. Certainly these aspects of culture were developed to a much greater extent than in the West at an equivalent period. China was the restaurant culture *par excellence*, where cooked food was prepared for the many in an extra-domestic environment; for a large number of people for a long time, cooking has not been confined to the home, a feature that is associated with the great development of urban society where raw food has to be brought in from outside the towns and prepared to provide for the part of the population not working in a domestic environment.

But restaurants and tea houses were not limited to the large towns. Even in small ones people go out to eat to celebrate private and public events. Moreover, this is not only a restaurant but a banqueting culture (as is India) in which life-cycle rituals and religious ceremonies are marked by large-scale feasting. Of course in simpler societies sacrifices also provide for the public consumption of food and drink for the participants, rather differently from the largely 'family' eating associated with the Seder or with Christmas. But in the Chinese case the preparations are often very extensive, especially of roasted pork, which is served at lineage festivals to all bona fide members, the supplies being provided out of corporate funds.

---

[2] On the supposed opposition between individual and 'collective' capitalism, see Goody (1996a).

For the villagers of San Tin the most exciting prospect is the round of New Year banquets thrown by returning restaurant workers. 'The banquets are almost literally the only thing many elders have to look forward to during the entire year.' They are held in ancestral halls which have kitchen facilities, and professional cooks are hired from nearby towns to provide nine-course feasts. Such banquets may celebrate a migrant's return to the village or a son's first birthday.

Restaurants come in all shapes and sizes. In 1989 I visited the island of Chueng Chow in the Hong Kong group. We had lunch at a noodle shop, where the food came to the table directly out of an iron pot boiling on an open fire. The restaurant itself consisted of a few trestle tables under a canvas awning at the side of the road. After the noodles we ordered *chai* (tea). What we were brought was hot water in cups, which the poor of the area referred to as 'tea'.

The usage emphasises firstly the widespread practice of 'eating out', even among the poor. It also suggests (tea = hot water) that nevertheless the reference of even the poorest restaurants was some higher point in the culinary hierarchy, as when modest English restaurants call the bill of fare a menu, or give French names to local dishes.

The advent of Chinese restaurants to Europe came at a time when the canteen culture of the wartime period was disappearing. In a sense this had been a highly socialised form of feeding, carried out collectively whether in the army, in the factory or in communal restaurants (called British restaurants) which showed the restrictions of the limited restaurant culture, with its supplies being rationed and its prices being controlled. That system was highly egalitarian and began to disappear, under pressure of economic growth, expanded supplies, consumer choice and – it has to be said – boredom with uniformity, with egalitarianism.

That wartime, post-war system broke down to the advantage of the Chinese and other foreign (or exotic) restaurants, and it broke down at the time when such an egalitarian cooking was making its mark in China itself for specifically ideological reasons,[3] although that factor was also present in wartime Britain, as witness the election of a Labour government in 1946 and the continuation of rationing as a way not only of sharing scarcity but of avoiding inequalities. The same happened with clothing, furniture, schooling and other consumer items.

---

[3] On this point I am indebted to Prof. Yu Chang-jiang on Beijing (1998).

The globalisation of Chinese food is part of the globalisation of world cultures, the culture of the global village. In capitals of impoverished African countries such as Ghana the smarter restaurants are often Chinese (more often in anglophone than francophone countries, although in these the south-east Asian eating places are of equal importance). But there are two aspects of this process of globalisation that proceed concurrently. The first is homogenisation, whereby bread for example comes to play a dominant role in cultures throughout the world; or McDonaldisation whereby one product (previously Coca-Cola) comes to dominate world markets in fast foods or non-alcoholic drinks. Frequently these items are American because of the very significant contribution of that country to the industrialisation of food in the later nineteenth century, for example in the processes of canning food, invented by the French at the time of the Napoleonic Wars but later developed in England and the US, giving to the world Heinz cans, orange drinks and breakfast cereals. In this context the world is following the trend of industrialisation into monocultural paths where it has no real need to tread.

The parallel process is one of global differentiation rather than global homogenisation, which consists of the adoption (or the spread) of local products, in this case forms of cooking, around the world, leading to multiculturalism. It is not simply Chinese food but Indian, Italian and not least French which have become international, first in the restaurant, later in the supermarket and home. French cuisine became the basis of a homogenised international bourgeois mode of consumption, employed in major hotels throughout the world. The Asian cuisines were part of the later process of multicultural globalisation, though their advent had a marginal effect compared to the homogenisation of cultures related to mass production and the mass media. However, that is the story of Chinese cooking and Chinese restaurants, enriching industrial cultures by giving them a global dimension. This enrichment has happened with cooking, especially restaurant food, since the end of the Second World War. London is now reported to be one of the best centres for restaurants in the world, but the food very rarely has anything to do with local tradition; it is world food. In suburbs of the capital one can eat Pekin cuisine, vegetarian Gujerati cooking, Russian, Persian, Balkan, Turkish and many other dishes within a very limited area.

The process of globalisation has been a gradual one. It is a Western conceit or prejudice to view that process, like the establishment of a world system or modernisation or even capitalism in the broad sense (that is, not confined to industrial capitalism) as an adjunct of Western domination. These processes began long before and they were given a boost by European activity from the sixteenth century. But at that time Indian and Chinese consumer goods (printed cottons in the first case, coloured silks and porcelain in the second) overwhelmed Western markets, changed the nature of domestic tastes in radical ways, and opened the path to the industrial production of these self-same manufactured items that had been imported from the East and now became among the major exports of the West (at least cottons), resurrecting an earlier pattern of Roman exports of pottery and glass in India and East Asia.

All those movements of goods, and with them their ideas and identities, gave rise to a measure of globalisation. But that was not always a homogenising process, like the universalisation of Coca-Cola and the hamburger, of the sandwich and the whisky, of pizza and campari, but one that also added to difference, to what it is fashionable to call cultural diversity, of cultural enrichment.

While food in general has become globalised, that process has happened selectively. There has been no effective globalisation of African food, even in the form, culturally prestigious in some circles, of 'soul food'. The reasons are not hard to seek. There was little hierarchically differentiated cuisine in Africa for reasons I have elsewhere tried to explain (Goody 1982) and that are connected with the nature of land tenure and the lack of extensive socio-economic stratification. Consequently there was no *haute cuisine*, no differentiated food, no higher cooking as distinct from a lower one. And for other cultures it is mostly the higher rather than the lower elements of cooking that got translated into restaurant, or at least into hotel cooking. One does find some lower elements, in America the hamburger and other fast foods, in England fish and chips, in China tofu as a take-away, in other areas services to market traders. But not for 'dining-out' foods. In any case, African food plays little part in either – restaurants serving such food being rare exotica – with of course the exception of Ethiopia, which has provided restaurants worldwide. But from this standpoint Ethiopia is not an African country but a Near Eastern, a Eurasian one, with plough agriculture, similar forms of stratification and a hierarchical cuisine that with its spicy foods, its bread and stew (*injera* and *wat*), attracts not only an internal but an international clientele.

Was Italian spaghetti or pasta an earlier example of the globalisation of food? The Romans did not know this dish, and it has been fancifully proposed that it was introduced from China by Marco Polo, much as silk worms were brought back from the East by monks into Byzantium to inaugurate the Western silk industry. But that seems to have been a myth of the same order as the claim that French cuisine owed its origin to the marriage of the Florentine Catherine de' Medici to the future King of France. More acceptable perhaps is the suggestion that both cultures derived such products from the countries of central Asia.

Of course, this kind of cultural differentiation occurs only minimally with the more technological facets of culture; nuclear power stations, automobiles, electronic equipment vary relatively little wherever they are manufactured, and their production follows major industrial trends. On the other hand, the popular music of the world's youth no longer consists only of Western originals or imitations, though there is plenty of this. In addition there is the cult of 'world music', which incorporates wider traditions from other cultures. But food represents the major cultural dimension involved in this process of multicultural globalisation by means of differentiation. Like music it is not affected by language which inhibits communication outside the group. And while it has its particular technological requirements, in the shape of the instruments of cooking (the frying pan and the wok), these differences are relatively small and easily overcome.

The spread of Chinese food affected a wider field than culinary practice alone; it also involved a migration of personnel. The life of these immigrants required a minimal adjustment to the host culture. The hero of Mo's novel, Chen, worked long hours in a Chinese restaurant, spent his leisure in a Chinese cinema, played Chinese games, mixed with his fellow countrymen. His wife patronised emporiums in Chinese Street in Central London, ate frugally and saved to establish their own business, if only she could persuade her husband to break away. She remained attached to Cantonese customs throughout.

> Sweet after salty was dangerous for her system, so she had been taught; it could upset the whole balance of the dualistic or female and male principles, *yin* and *yang* . . . For four years, therefore, Chen had been going to bed tortured with the last extremities of thirst but with his dualistic male and female principles in harmony.
>
> (Mo 1982: 2)

As Watson pointed out in his survey, many immigrants never learn

English, except for the waiters who have to communicate with the customers: 'Most of the Mans seldom venture beyond the security of either the restaurants or the recreation centers where Cantonese is spoken' (Watson 1975: 125). Indeed, most hope to return to Hong Kong when they have accumulated enough money. Until the 1970s that was the case: they remained abroad for some twenty years. During that time they supplied the village from which they came, San Tin, with remittances; this was essential, since 85 to 90 per cent of the able-bodied men were employed in Chinese restaurants in Britain and other parts of western Europe, leaving behind only women, children and old men (Watson 1975: 2). Even when families went abroad, the children were sent back to receive part of their education in their 'native place' which, rather than finding itself in the forefront of modernisation, was turned into a highly traditional settlement, a kind of thatched cottage village to which the traveller, the sojourner, could return in his later years.

Only Chinese prepared Chinese food professionally; only they ran the restaurants, only they were employed. Such restaurants needed immigrants, but they also encouraged the importation of Chinese furniture and ornaments, as well as of Chinese ingredients, for the restaurants. They greatly expanded the spread of Chinese artefacts, personnel and culture generally. In some larger towns both restaurants and the auxiliary services tended to cluster into segregated areas, into China towns which were socio-cultural foci for the Chinese community. As such they encouraged other, more notorious, aspects of Chinese life, brought out by Timothy Mo in *Sour Sweet* (we have to rely on fiction as it is not a topic into which the social sciences can delve with ease). The Chinese are inveterate gamblers, in ways that are likely to be controlled or condemned by the host society and its 'official bandits'. In London Chinese gambling dens were unofficial but flourished as they only catered for the Chinese community and were largely overlooked. Some Chinese have also long been users and distributors of drugs, which in the eighteenth and nineteenth centuries were encouraged by the British and other merchants (especially by Jardine-Matheson and the Sassoons) in the form of opium imported from India, against the wishes of the Chinese government. Now the situation is reversed. Such illegal activities encourage the presence of parasitic elements, of protection rackets operated by gangs such as Triads that have their own tight organisation, their internal loyalties, their use of the threat and actuality of violence. In New York one sees branch offices of such groups openly indicated, some of whom are involved in illegal migration and illegal imports as well as illegal 'protection'. At the same time they perform less dubious services for the Chinese community, loaning money (at interest) and maintaining relations with kin back home, who, as we have seen, are often in receipt of assistance from funds repatriated by the workers abroad. They may also help to maintain a specific Chinese identity overseas, since that is what their livelihood depends upon. The dependence of Chinese workers on Chinese employers (and vice versa), on Chinese food, on a ghetto environment, on Chinese protectors, on Chinese films, videos and newspapers, makes for a relatively closed community without many integrationist ambitions or prospects.

The underworld associated with Chinese restaurant culture abroad is not peculiar to the overseas Chinese. In his account of Suzhou in the lower Yangtze delta in the sixteenth and seventeenth centuries, McDermott sees the underworld as an intrinsic part of commercial culture. Its members organised the Duanwu festival and its myriad activities, using their toughs to maintain order in what even in ordinary times was not only a centre of high gentry culture but also a violent city. The gangsters (*wu-lai*) mainly belonged to China's 'bachelor subculture' and were organised in relatively tight-knit groups under the leadership of one man. They were dependent as ever on running protection rackets as well as controlling transactions in a variety of spheres, giving rise to full-time secret societies in the eighteenth century. Their role in the Duanwu constituted a public affirmation of their power and influence.

The export of Chinese cooking has added a multicultural element to the process of globalisation which does something to offset the homogenisation of world cultures brought about by the mass production of industrialised foods. Since it has to be carried out by Chinese personnel, that has led to the emigration (largely of males) as well as to the export of Chinese material culture and the gambling, drugs and protection rackets that accompany the establishment of an overseas community of this kind. That community remains very insulated from the host cultures (thinking their own much superior), with the immigrants aiming to return to their 'native place' rather than settle abroad. They have little contact with the host cultures but maintain close ties with the home communities, sending remittances for personal and public purposes, making frequent visits and in many cases eventually returning home to villages which have been rebuilt with repatriated funds in a very traditional manner. Nevertheless the effects on the host communities have been considerable, especially in the culinary sphere, where Chinese dishes play a significant part in consumption, not only in restaurants but in take-aways, in prepared dishes from supermarkets and increasingly in the repertoire of the foreigners themselves, stimulated by the countless cookbooks that have now made their appearance.

Chapter 9

WHY NO WINE ON THE TABLE?

Why is the very area that first cultivated the grape the one that rejects or inhibits the drinking of wine? While there was a concern with health in these societies, that was not in this case the primary motivation behind the prohibition. It was, rather, other social reasons.

The first visual evidence of the cultivation of the grape comes from Hittite sculpture dating from the third millennium BCE. That is part of the very area where the drinking of wine has been forbidden since the conquest by and conversion to Islam. There is an important distinction to be made between the prohibition on consumption, which is rare, and the condemnation of excessive consumption (drunkenness), which is very widespread. But the two are related, as are the reasons for refusal or restraint. Jews and to some extent early Christians were also somewhat apprehensive about wine, although it was of course a central part of the major rites of the Eucharist and the Seder. Today Jews use a thick sweet wine in their Passover service (the Pesach) but they do not drink or produce much wine; in Israel production is rather in the hands of Christian Arabs, while consumption is abroad. That was not the case in earlier times. There are many references to wine in the Bible, for example in the incident of Christ turning water into wine for the wedding at Cana. It was the same in ancient Israel. The text of the Old Testament contains over 140 references to *Yáyin*, the fermented juice of the grape. It was drunk at meals (for daily use and for feasts) as well as in rituals. There seems to have been no objection to drinking wine, only to drinking to excess. The psalmist praises God for making crops to grow so man can 'produce wine to make him happy' (Psalm 104). It was regarded as health-giving by Saint Paul, who in the first letter to Timothy advised him, 'Do not drink water only, but take a little wine to help your digestion, since you are ill so often' (I Timothy 5: 23). However, there are also warnings about excess, condemnations of drunken rulers who cannot do their duty (Isaiah 5: 22; 28) as well as of the ordinary man whom drink leads away from the worship of God:

> The Lord says, 'Wine, both old and new, is robbing my people of their senses! They ask for revelations from a piece of wood.' They give themselves to idols and their daughters become prostitutes. 'After drinking much wine, they delighted in their prostitution, preferring disgrace to honour.'
>
> (Hosea 4: 11–15)

In other words, wine not only distracts from the worship of God, it also leads humankind to address idols and into sexual excess. Indeed, explicit prohibitions occur in the Old Testament. The Nazarite who had wholly devoted himself to Yahweh had to abstain from wine and spirits (Numbers 6: 3 ff.), just as did the priests before administering the sacred rites (Leviticus 10: 9). According to Diodorus Siculus, the Nabateans also abstained from wine; one of their gods was called in their inscriptions, 'the good god who drinks no wine' (Weinsinck 1953). But such prohibitions were not general. How therefore did today's reluctance among orthodox Jews to drink come about? Did there develop an element of 'puritanism' or 'moral restraint' in the situation of the diaspora which set them aside from their Christian neighbours, a sacrifice that brought them closer to their God?[1] Clearly their social position was much more delicate as migrants, and excessive drinking would have been badly looked upon. What seems to have happened is that wine became so identified with ritual that its secular use was discouraged or deemed inappropriate. Such a dichotomy between sacred wine and secular abstinence also marked many non-conformist sects of Protestants, who reserved the drinking of wine (symbolising – rather than identified with – the blood of Christ) for ritual occasions. I want to take some of the emphasis away from the religious context and direct it towards the inherent contradictions that are found in the use of what are (or were) luxury, inessential, even threatening products. Such contradictions at the level of society give rise to ambivalences at the personal level.

---

[1] I recognise the problems in using 'puritanism' as a term in cross-cultural analysis, but this is a general question in the development of knowledge and should not lead to avoidance or to the adoption of uncomfortable neologisms (see Berlivet 1996).

Similar ambivalences occurred in Islam. There seems to have been at first no general prohibition on the drinking of wine (_Khamr_) in Arabia. Muhammed's companions engaged in drinking parties, and Sūrah xxi: 67 praises it as one of Allah's gifts to mankind. 'And of the fruit of palmtrees, and of grapes, ye obtain an inebriating liquor, and also good nourishment.' But the consequences of drunkenness, and specifically the interference with prayer ('come not to prayers when ye are drunk', Sūrah iv: 43) led the Prophet to be critical and banish wine altogether. In a sense this rejection of excess consumption before prayer is paralleled by the rejection of excess drinking before driving a car. Both may lead to a wider rejection because excess consumption of a pleasurable substance tends to loss of control. 'O true believers! surely wine and _maisir_ and stone pillars and divining arrows are an abomination, of the works of Satan; therefore avoid them, that ye may prosper' (Sūrah v: 90). Once again wine is associated with false gods and hence forbidden. That prohibition was then taken over by the doctors of the law and elaborated in the Ḥadīth.

Later restrictions on wine also indicate a certain ambivalence about its use. These restrictions on (and outright rejection of) wine on the table were made partly on religious grounds, partly on ecological ones, partly because of class and partly because of individual tastes or prohibitions. For some, wine was seen as a luxury rather than a necessity and therefore not something to be encouraged in the ordinary man. Partly, too, the drinking of wine could lead to behaviour of a rough and rowdy kind, when participants might forget their relationship with God and with their fellow men and women. The fear of excess may lead to total rejection, as in Islam. Or it may result in an emphasis on moderation. These religious prohibitions have to do not so much with wine as with any alcohol, although wine plays a special part in Judaism and Christianity because of its ritual role, while in northern countries, the difficulties of producing wine gave it a special, luxury, status.

In early Europe there was of course a fundamental divide between the beer-drinking Germans in the North and the wine drinkers of the Mediterranean. But it was mainly the latter, adherents of orthodox Christianity, who were 'primarily responsible for the spread of the Romance-Christian dietary models in northern Europe'. In accounts of their consolidation of the power of the 'true faith' over the Arian heresy, 'wine occupies a strategically central role of political and cultural legitimation' (Montanari 1994: 17). The lives of saints are filled with individuals who to promote the

Christian faith planted vines and cultivated wheat (because bread played an analogous role). Remigius, Bishop of Reims, gave Clovis, King of the Franks, a flask of wine 'as a blessing' before his decisive battle with the Arian Alaric, King of the Visigoths.

But the culture of wine was not established without resistance. Beer continued to be used in pagan sacrifices, leading Columban to refer to 'the sacrilegious liquid'. As late as the twelfth century, the son of Henry Plantagenet refused to drink wine, which he considered a 'foreign drink' (Montanari 1994: 20). Beer was gradually adopted by monasteries in the North as the everyday drink. But within the Christian world wine always had a higher prestige; it represented after all (indeed, presented) the blood of Christ.

There are certainly different perceptions of the kinds of alcohol, partly for ecological reasons. Beer drinkers may look down on wine drinkers, more usually the opposite because of the Christian tradition. But in doing so they are often expressing a preference for their local beverage and downgrading that of their neighbours. By and large such preferences follow the ecological patterns of cultivation: wine is preferred in temperate southern areas where there is sufficient sunshine to cultivate it. But nevertheless wine has long been a drink for upper groups (the aristocracy, the clerics, the grand bourgeoisie) in northern climes. When the Greeks established themselves at Marseilles, they cultivated the grape, made wine and exported it northwards to the Germanic chiefdoms along with the material goods used in its consumption (Dietler 1990). It was a prestige good, and so it remained for the British yet further north who imported large quantities of wine from Bordeaux from the thirteenth century, and had already under the Romans tried to adapt the grape itself to more northern climates. In the early Middle Ages vineyards were found in many parts of Europe including England and the Low Countries. By degrees the wines of three or four major regions came to predominate – Poitou, Gascony, Burgundy and the Moselle – all of them with flourishing vineyards dating from Roman days. England concentrated on the wines from Gascony and imported over four million gallons in 1415, supplying Gascony with grain in return (Postan 1952: 123–4). It is partly relevant to the question of puritanism or moral restraint in the consumption of wine (or alcohol more generally) that the great wine-producing areas are attached to the Catholic religion while the areas dominated earlier by beer drinking are Protestant. Nevertheless, the regions are not homogeneous and strong contradictory tendencies exist, as we see from the history of the Reform in the south-west of France and earlier from that of the Cathars and other 'heretical' sects.

It is from Britain that I draw my ethnography, a country that had to import its wines but produced mead (hydromel) locally in Anglo-Saxon days, as well as beer, gin and (in Scotland) whisky. Until recently wine remained a luxury drink for the middle classes, one for special occasions but rarely for everyday imbibing. In my Cambridge college, fellows were entitled as their 'commons' (rations) to a loaf of bread and a pint of beer a day; at feasts one had wine; whisky never appeared. In the late 1960s a francophile Steward argued that a glass of wine cost the same as a pint of beer – the substitution was made, which was indicative of a much wider change in *moeurs*. Wine was hitherto a luxury and viewed as such by the beer drinker in the public bar. That has changed very much in the last thirty years. Even before the Common Market and the consequent reduction of taxes on imported wine, greater prosperity and holidays abroad had led to a spread of wine drinking to other groups, more especially to women. Throughout the country in the 1960s, special containers made their appearances in the bar, containing an inferior quality of white and red *vin ordinaire*. More recently that array has largely disappeared in favour of wine poured from ordinary bottles, a testimony at once to increased consumption and often to better wines. For many pubs now offer a choice, with monthly 'specials', of wines from France, Italy, Australia and elsewhere. One is no longer slightly ashamed of ordering a glass of wine; it is much more a matter of daily life and not a focus of general resentment, as in the case of true luxuries. The expansion of wine drinking in pubs happened at a time when there was increasing competition from wine bars and cafés, and when the whole character of food, first in restaurants and then in supermarkets, was changing to take on a more continental (indeed, international) air.

Those earlier restrictions were stronger for women than for men. It was partly that drinking in a public bar was virtually forbidden to respectable women, who before the Second World War were allowed entry to the saloon bar but not to the public equivalent. That separation continued much later in Scotland, Australia, Canada and Northern Ireland. Beer drinking was not for them. They went for sweeter fortified wines like the cheaper qualities of port ('port and lemon'), Madeira or sherry. Men's drink was beer and whisky. Among the upper bourgeoisie, wine was widely drunk at dinner, with port afterwards for the men, the women having withdrawn. Before-dinner drinks were not gendered; it was sherry, and occasionally American cocktails, a sign of post-First World War freedoms, the age of jazz.

In Britain alcohol as a category, all alcohol, was also the subject of some hostility in sections of the respectable working class because everyone knew of histories of individuals whose lives and families had been 'ruined by drink'. This picture is painted of a certain section of urban life by the artist William Hogarth in the eighteenth century. The lower classes drank gin, 'mother's ruin', and their drinking was regarded as dangerous to the social order, since a drunken mob was a threat to the upper classes, whose drinking was considered safe and civilised. But it was not only the demands of social control from the top that led to a reaction: from below there was also an aspect of self-improvement. In the nineteenth century drink continued to be viewed as a cause of poverty and as disrupting social life. It was men rather than women that tended to deplete the family finances through drink and thus inhibit a rise in the social hierarchy, either for the couple or for the children. Such expenditure went against the injunction to save and postpone immediate gratification, sentiments that resulted in the importance of the Temperance Movement in Britain with many from the petty bourgeoisie and working class agreeing 'to sign the pledge' and renounce all drink, beer and wine as well as spirits. While the religious and health aspects of this movement were important, expenditure on alcohol also prevented the poor from becoming better-off. In the years before the First World War my father himself was one of those who signed, no doubt because of the unfortunate break-up of his natal family. My mother had similar tendencies, but hers were more directly sectarian. She came from a bourgeois milieu in the north-east of Scotland that consisted of ministers, teachers and small merchants. Calvinism had long been the established religion in the form of the Free Church, and I do not recall seeing any alcohol in their houses in the vicinity of Turriff. Though not far from the whisky-producing area of the Spey and around Banff, drink was regarded by that family as the very devil, and taverns as places of ill-repute. That background did not stop my mother, when she migrated South, from having occasional recourse to some alcoholic drink 'for medicinal purposes', in the shape of Stone's Ginger Wine or Wincarnis (a 'health' drink), neither of which would fall into the category of *vin de table* but rather *vin de penderie*. Later on, when my father had long since abandoned the pledge for the occasional beer or whisky (always in the house, restaurant or hotel, never in the pub), she accepted a bottle of brandy now and again from which she used to fortify herself after dinner, on either gay or harassing occasions, as when her sons went off to college or to war.

There is one other condition in which wine is not placed on the table, and that is because of the physiological reactions of the drinker. That reaction happens to some people under some conditions in Western societies. But it occurs very much more frequently in China and Japan, where many inhabitants cannot drink any alcohol without adverse consequences. That difficulty did not prevent China from importing the grape or from making rice wine, but for many it does place severe limits on their consumption.

We have noted that at the ecological level wine is not always on the table simply because the grape is not grown. But cultural pressures may take up and expand upon this raw fact. In northern Ghana where I worked among the LoDagaa, the better-off citizens now drink beer of a European variety, although made in the country with imported ingredients. European beer corresponds to the local beverage, which is a true beer made from fermented guinea-corn in a manner that completely parallels that of Europe (see for example Goody 1972a). Immediately over the Black Volta river that formed the (colonial) boundary between Ghana and Burkina Faso lived other members of the same ethnic group whose elite had adapted to wine rather than beer because they had already lived in a francophone country for some forty years when I first knew them. What is as remarkable to me now as it was then, is how profoundly these tastes for different alcohols, following the preferences of their colonial conquerors, have become part of the cultural repertoire of these divided peoples, serving not only as markers of new identities (that is too facile an account) but as particular sources of pleasure.

However, just as there are cultural factors that distinguished between wine and beer-drinking areas (as earlier in Ghana the forest palm wine drinkers were distinguished from the millet beer drinkers of the savannah, again primarily for ecological reasons), so too there are areas which deny themselves the pleasures of alcohol altogether. In Africa these are basically the places that have been influenced by Islam, for its believers are told to abjure alcohol in the holy scriptures. This injunction is widespread (but not universally obeyed by Muslims), as we see from the cases of Europeans being prosecuted in Saudi Arabia. In parts of India it was the same. Gujarat is a dry state (except for the liquors made by untouchables), and to purchase alcohol you have to have a special addict's licence. The prohibition derives not from Islamic influences, of which there were many, but rather from

Gandhian objections to luxury and indulgence. But traditionally the production of alcohol was in the hands of the lower classes, and so by and large
was its consumption. The drinking of alcohol was never a characteristic of
the priestly caste of Brahmins who set the model for much social behaviour.
I do not know of anything in the Hindu scriptures that prevents the consumption of alcohol. It was rather a luxury phenomenon to which objection was made by a puritanical trend in that society. In Buddhism it is a
restriction rather than a rejection of wine, although the highest forms of the
path do include abstinence.[2]

The religious uses of wine are of fundamental significance in considering these rejections. Islam and the Indic religions do not use wine for any
religious purpose. Judaism does enjoin four glasses of wine with the ritual
meal, the Seder. That practice was taken up and developed in Christianity,
where the wine represented the blood of the sacrificed God and the bread
his body. This association had two possible consequences. Firstly, the
sacramental use of wine might legitimise its use for secular purposes. That
was not the case with many Protestants, for whom the communion wine
(unlike the communion bread) remained something totally apart. In a sense
wine was the blood of Christ, not to be consumed on other occasions. On
the other hand, in the Catholic Church quite the opposite effect seems to
have been produced. We have here the grounds for the emergence of a religious ambivalence. The deep-purple wine from Cahors, made from the
Malbec grape, was exported down the Lot through the Mediterranean to
the Black Sea to be used in Orthodox communion services because of its
blood-like properties, giving rise to the word Cahorski for such sacramental wines. The identification of a particular wine with the blood of Christ
could well have led to it being considered appropriate for the church but
not for the table.

Puritanical trends were widespread in Europe, especially among
Protestants who considered alcohol not only a luxury but a temptation to
the poor that would prevent them raising their families and worshipping
God. Hence the presence of these beliefs in north-eastern Scotland during
my mother's time (and today too among a small minority), as well as the
strong prohibition among the inhabitants of New England, for whom
cider was 'sweet cider' (that is, non-alcoholic), and the later outbursts of

---

[2] See Sigalavada Sutta in the Digha Nikays (ch. 31), T. W. Rhys Davids (transl.), *Sacred Books
of the East*, vol. 4, published for the Pali Text Society by Luzac and Co., London.

Prohibition that swept through America in the years between the World Wars (and still persist in some communities). That was what gave rise to the bootleggers, to speakeasys and to Dillinger and his gang, because there was an attempt at rigorous government enforcement of the protest about drink rather than leaving it to religious and welfare movements.

What is interesting about this puritanical position is that it tends to go along with objections to other activities that one might regard as luxury, or at least as inessential. New England Puritans were also against iconic representations, against the theatre and against the reading of novels. The same trends were to be found in early Christianity as well as in Judaism and Islam. That went along in early Christianity with objections to perfumes and fine (coloured) clothing.

Nor was this limited to the Near Eastern religions. We find similar but not identical trends in Hinduism as well as in Buddhism, although everywhere features such as aniconic attitudes changed over time. In other words, there seems to be a cluster of objections to the luxurious and the aesthetic that are found in different times and places through the major Eurasian societies. I have argued that this is partly due to internal reflections on the heavily stratified societies of the Bronze Age which produce an abundance for some and a dearth for others. That disparity opens the way to philosophical, political and social critiques of the distribution of goods and of the existence of luxury. Rebellion or revolutionary thoughts take the shape of rejecting the activities of the rich; in other words they arise from cognitive contradictions implicit in the organisation of society.

But there is more to the situation than that, at least as regards some of these features. Let us take the example of icons. I have argued (1991 and 1997) that aniconic tendencies are found even in African societies with a very different socio-economic system. The evidence for this lies in the demonstrable reluctance to figure the High God, and often indeed other gods as well. Indeed, in societies such as the Tallensi of northern Ghana, which resolutely reject all Muslim influence, one finds no iconic art of any kind; shrines are 'abstract' rather than iconic. This uneven distribution also holds true of the theatre and the cult of relics. I do not suggest this pertains for all the other items in the puritanical complex, drink for example. In most traditional societies in Africa the inhabitants drink millet beer or palm wine. I do not know any (except Islamic ones) who reject beer, especially as it is seen as a 'food', in the case of millet beer another way of transforming grain. Nevertheless there are some individuals who reject these drinks, and this seems to point once again to a certain ambivalence about its consumption. For example, my first neighbour among the LoDagaa was the caretaker of the resthouse, who was also an important diviner. To perform this part meant he was constantly in touch with the beings of the wild. He was a thin, tight, unsociable man who kept himself very much to himself and his shrines, except when people approached him for consultation. His isolation was reinforced by the fact that the beings of the wild had forbidden him to drink beer, a fact that made it difficult for him to participate fully in social or ceremonial gatherings.

Some individuals, even in a society of drinkers, reject alcohol. That was often true of priests and monks. Of course, many have similar taboos of other kinds. But these individual rejections do seem to feed into the social or sectarian ones we have noted before. These as we have seen relate to anti-Epicurean, puritanical, views about the consumption of 'the good things of life', to forms of puritanical renunciation that are particularly prevalent in the 'luxury cultures' that developed in the Bronze Age. Today this kind of renunciation and abstinence tends to disappear in contemporary consumer cultures, where those 'good things' become more widely distributed and lose the luxury tag. Partly too it is secularisation; the notion that man can control affairs of the world by abstinence, which was also present in China, receives much less credence than before.[3] Of course, such prohibitions continue to exist among fundamentalists of an Islamic or Christian kind, as well as in revolutionary situations which attempt to put an end to luxury and to concentrate upon the more equitable production, distribution and consumption of essentials. In this rejection reasons of health, except perhaps spiritual health, play a relatively small part, except among a minority in the contemporary West. There is always the special problem with alcohol that encourages opposition, namely, that drunk in excess it leads to loss of self-restraint and possibly to social disorder. But such conditions are more often associated with 'strong drink' (spirits) rather than with wine or beer. By and large, just as Fridays and Lent have lost their taboos, so wine appears more frequently on the world's tables, partly because of developments in transport and the expansion of markets, but also because much of the ambivalence arising out of its luxury status has disappeared. Certainly

---

[3] A Chinese decree of 1678 declares that because of the drought 'We have on this account directed our efforts towards reflecting upon the reformation of our character, practising abstinence, and devoutly praying for sweet and prolonged rain...' (Elvin forthcoming: 8).

in the case of those countries that are consumers rather than producers, some of the cognitive contradictions have been resolved.

Part III

DOUBTS

In the last section I am dealing with a set of problems that have most recently attracted my attention and which mainly have to do with those that centre upon ambivalence and doubts that representations create, especially in the culturally differentiated countries of Europe and Asia. There the differentiation is based on the existence of class sub-cultures, including luxury cultures, but also on the important division into literate and illiterate which obviously does not affect oral cultures. Chapter 10 discusses the Great and Little Traditions in the Mediterranean, concepts based essentially upon the presence of a writers' (great) tradition and the parallel existence of a (little) popular culture. The cultural divide means that while there is a measure of homogeneity of local cultures, literate groups have often been closer in significant ways to the literates of neighbouring peoples who shared the same written traditions (in Islam, for example). Popular culture tended to differentiate localities, high culture to bring them together. But there is also some opposition between high and low, for these are also class distinctions related to access to resources, or to poverty against riches. Joint ceremonies, such as the Feast of Cockayne in Naples, do not simply imply solidarity, as Durkheim's approach suggests, but also bring out the fact of cleavage and hence the doubts about sub-cultural values and goods.

The problem of doubt and its particular relationship to complex stratified cultures, including the literate–nonliterate dimension, is brought out more clearly in chapter 11, where I am specifically dealing with agnosticism primarily in religions but also in the secular sphere. Agnosticism has been seen by some as a development of the Enlightenment, by others as already present in Greece. I argue that it is more generally a feature of all written cultures, Eastern as well as Western; while a developed agnostic tradition, a tradition of unbelief, is probably confined to such societies, doubts about gods are certainly not. Scepticism is widespread in oral cultures; not everyone automatically believes everything. And one of the reasons, as I discuss in chapters 11 and 13, has to do with the cognitive contradictions that may emerge in the context of particular ideas and practices, for example the ideas about the origin of the world and man's culture, and whether this was by slow evolution or by sudden creation. Each of these notions embraces contradictions which may lead to the adoption, perhaps contextually, of the other, leading as I suggest to quite different emphases in the Bagre myth of the LoDagaa. The cognitive aspect of myth is of primary significance, despite much stress on symbolic interpretations, and difficulties about one approach may lead to the adoption of another. Or it may lead to the contradiction being 'resolved' in ritual, as when some killing is condemned (in the case of homicide) and some praised (in warfare), but both involve the dangerous act of shedding the blood of fellow human beings. Those contradictions are built into the interaction of language-using animals with the world, outside and inside; they are an intrinsic feature of the use of words as representations.

Some contradictions are evident in people's attitudes to nature, since animals clearly have to be protected as well as killed for meat. Among the LoDagaa a number of rituals centre on this contradiction, which produces an ambivalence that may find expression in hunting rituals and in satanic beliefs. In societies with writing, once again these implicit contradictions often become explicit, hence a number of religions, especially the Indian ones, and many individual vegetarians today, avoid killing and eating animals, indeed, shedding the blood of living things.

The final chapter returns to the problem discussed in the first section, expressing doubts about the way Westerners, scholars and others (especially historians and social scientists) have represented the East in their search to account for the recent dominance of the West. In doing so they have tended to look for long-term differences (many either imaginary or irrelevant) to account for short-term advantage. One such feature has been civil society. I end with a discussion of its global distribution, suggesting that treatments of politics by Western scholars have been too concerned with European categories and events. Ignorance or the disregard of the politics of others has endowed the regimes of that continent alone with special characteristics, such as the presence of 'civil society' or commercial law, that have been considered critical in its modernisation. I argue that this is wrong not only for the so-called despotic states of Asia but also for the 'tribal' polities of Africa.

Chapter 10

THE GREAT AND LITTLE TRADITIONS IN THE MEDITERRANEAN

As is well known, the notions of the Great and Little Traditions were developed in an Indian context by the Chicago anthropologist Robert Redfield. The idea was then extended to his version of 'peasant studies'. I want to ask what we have lost as well as gained by the application of the idea to the Mediterranean world, especially in relation to other axes of differentiation, such as class.

The notion draws attention not simply to the plurality of Mediterranean cultures but also to the divisions that cross-cut 'cultures', 'societies', nations. It stresses the fact that not only are there limitations to seeing individual 'cultures' as wholes (a tendency of fieldworking anthropologists engaged in community studies), but also that within those cultures both persons and traits may have closer associations outside their boundaries than within. For the Great Tradition is a written one which extends outside the boundaries of a specific social or cultural group, as usually conceived. It may also divide internally as well as unifying externally. We have to pay attention not only to local knowledge but to what comes from outside in a relatively decontextualised form; there are not only 'the religions' (each group its own) but 'a religion' with its relatively fixed texts as points of reference, leading to systems of layered knowledge.

Many scholars of the Mediterranean (particularly anthropologists) have tended to deal in unities, talking of Greek or Italian cultures as if, from time immemorial, they had been wholes in a significant sense. Their usage is the commonplace one that refers to cultural units as defined by the boundaries of modern nation-states, which are with few exceptions monolinguistic (at least administratively) and strongly centralised groups that encourage a certain cultural uniformity; writing makes such pressures stronger than in purely oral situations. The fact that modern democratic nations are unified politically, constitutionally (by definition, as for example with written laws), ritually (with orders of service or with books of rites, as in China) and linguistically (by origin, choice and convenience) naturally means that there is some common ground among its members; under modern conditions similar (written) laws apply in theory (though not always in practice) to all citizens, and all members can communicate through the national tongue.

Although scholars are only too ready to talk about (for example) the Italian family, the implied notion of a unified culture, perhaps justified for some aspects as we have seen, conceals important internal differences in others. Few 'cultures' are even wholly linguistically unified; and from the standpoint of citizenship few do not distinguish between the rights of males and females, as well as between those of native-born citizens and immigrants, especially the recently arrived. There is considerable internal difference in family structures, and hence in the position of women, not only hierarchically but of a regional kind, say, between north and south Italy. Or in France in inheritance practices between the regions of the *langue d'oc* and of the *langue d'oïl*. However, the differences in culture that I want to examine here are hierarchical ones that characterise even the groups that are central to the culture, not just the marginals or the regionals. We have to make room not only for the caste system but also for the dalits (or untouchables) and their opposition to that system, for they are part of its very existence. Opposition and resistance to culture, including that of gender, are intrinsic parts of that culture. For despite holistic notions and approaches, we are all aware that Western culture is and has long been culturally stratified in a number of ways, so that how people acted in upper groups differed substantially from the ways that they acted in lower ones.

In India, where the distinction between the Great and the Little Traditions was first developed, the notion referred primarily to adherence to or deviation from the Hindu tradition, which was of course a written one. To a significant degree the distinction referred to that between literate (or attachment to the literate tradition) and illiterate. But by no means entirely; there was also differentiation in other cultural spheres, in cooking for example, in drink, in the arts such as music, and in the nature of male–female relationships.

This differentiation between high and low works in a complex manner so that it is easy to oversimplify the situation. For example, only in limited contexts is it possible to speak of a Great and Little Tradition as if they were quite distinct. One reason is that in any locality, whether in Europe or India, all elements normally speak a language that is largely mutually intelligible. It is within this framework that dialects and usage differ, for example between what in England in the 1950s was called U and non-U, so that it is possible in most situations to divine by his speech and actions into what group an individual has been born or what education he has received.

Let me insist that there was always communication between the culture of the literate and that of the illiterate. Hinduism, Islam and Christianity were all written religions. However, they were adopted by or forced upon those who could not read themselves but followed the lead of those who could. The illiterate only followed in certain broad respects, though, for they also made adaptations or even continued and created other religious practices associated with mother goddesses, with djinns, with nature spirits or with various forms of 'magic', elements that have been described as belonging to 'popular religion' or to 'popular culture', suggesting that we can analyse such religions in terms of higher (written) and popular (unwritten) components. But the distinction can never be so neat. As we have seen, both 'traditions' rely on intercommunication for organising social relations, even those of superordination and subordination. The fact that one element, the upper, is also literate divides people but not necessarily culture, since the illiterate can learn about the written religion from spoken sermons and from graphic representations, from 'the Bible of the Poor'. Such adherents may, in their way, be even more convinced of the truths of that religion than its literate representatives.

There is communication over the hierarchy in other ways too. Styles of life of the upper groups gradually seep down and are adopted by the lower ones, leading to a new synthesis. Nor is such communication only downwards. Even a Marie Antoinette at her French court mimicked the supposed ways of a shepherdess. Clothing such as jeans and headscarves certainly came up. More substantially, composers of upper music incorporate the songs and dances of the peasantry in their more formal compositions, for which writing is a sine qua non. So too with cooking. Elements of *haute cuisine* descend from above by way of cooks employed by the rich. In Renaissance Florence for example, before a grand banquet the dishes were displayed to the public, who also learnt from the scraps given afterwards to the poor from the rich man's table. In the contrary direction regional cooking gets taken 'up' into the written recipes of the bourgeoisie and on to aristocratic as well as restaurant tables. Medicine is another case, in which the learned, literate remedies developed in the Egyptian, Greek and later traditions, initially built up from oral practice, are continually replenished by the alternative folk traditions, with the higher being more identified with the former, the lower with the latter, but both elements cross-fertilising one another.

This process of transmission between upper and lower clearly depends upon the degree to which the traditions and the people concerned are separated physically and socially, and that degree is a matter of variation between different places.[1] The cultural collaboration and at the same time opposition of personnel and performance was a particular feature of the social life of Naples. In that town there was little segregation of social groups in specific neighbourhoods. In the quarter of Santa Lucia for example, palazzi and popular housing stand cheek by jowl, so that the inhabitants are always conscious of the life of the other. That does not of course eliminate differences in styles of life between social classes or groups, but it does lead to the development of two features: firstly, joint participation in common rituals and, secondly, the reflection of the activities of one group in the life of the other.

Joint participation is of course a widespread feature of many hierarchically divided societies; Srinivas well analysed the situation for the Coorgs of southern India, where each caste played its part in the joint annual celebrations. Indeed, nearly all public festivals have this communitarian character, which both brings together and holds apart. In Naples part of the Carneval consisted in the construction of the 'alberi di Cuccagna' (as in the spring festivals of much of Europe), but these were incorporated into the *gioco-rito*, as Scafolgio (1977) calls them. That happened above all in the sixteenth century, when floats loaded with food were first placed on display and then pulled to pieces by the poor, in counterpoint to the Florentine banquets of the rich. In the following century, the festival took place in front of the royal palace, where at a signal from the king the indigent were

---

[1] In his comments Peter Burke provided excellent examples of this changing process from Ariosto and the composition of *Orlando Furioso*, from the carnevals in Brazil (with fluctuation between elite and popular control), and with the Spanish bullfight, so different in its aristocratic version in the south from more popular forms in the north.

free to pillage the cheeses, hams and other foods that had been built up into the shapes of buildings. Royal control over the Carneval was strong and aristocratic participation necessary to mark and preserve status, as well as to provide a safety valve for popular feelings of resentment, albeit implicit, against the hierarchy. Indeed, some felt that the festivities gave too much rope to the poor, and there was opposition on these as on other grounds. The Secretary of State, Tanucci, saw the Cuccagna as 'useless and serious for the government as well as dangerous', leading to aggressivity and violence. In 1778 he succeeded in having it suppressed. Turning the world upside down is not simply a symbolic safety-valve; ritual can turn into riot. And riot can be a factor in changing the culture. In other words, the seeds of change lie embedded within the culture itself, in the shape of cognitive and social contradictions.

Opposition came from other quarters too. The 'culture' was in no way agreed upon the value of these performances; it would be a simplification to see in these actions the core of culture, as 'performance theorists' like Turner have claimed, for not only elements in the government but also in the Church strongly disapproved. 'Culture' includes opposition. After the Council of Trent the Church attempted to suppress from its services all folkloristic elements, just as it had tried much earlier; the Carneval was 'uno spazio tollerato ma mai del tutto accettato' (Scafolgio 1997: 51). The religious authorities in Naples insisted upon the town's prostitutes being shut up, which ran against the liberty traditionally accorded them to wander about freely during the Carneval period. In 1590 the Church tried to forbid religious parables and blaspheming practices in the Carneval, refusing to allow the laity to don ecclesiastical habits. Masks were forbidden to be worn near churches, especially on holy days, as was the use of obscene acts and words. Sacred drama within the church was seen as a direct contrast and higher alternative to street theatre, combating the licentious spirit of the Carneval.

To indicate that this ambivalence is not confined to Christianity, that a general rather than a specific problem is raised, I turn to an account of the Duanwu Festival of Suzhou in the lower Yangtze valley, held on the fifth day of the fifth lunar month, which runs:

> During every transition from spring to summer [the men of Suzhou] deceitfully say that the god is descending. Thus groups of vagrants, pursuers of inessential occupations, gangsters, and

desperados magnify this need . . . Row after row of plays and the overlapping of solemn ceremonies open the minds [of the people] to thoughts of deceit, they increase misbehaviour, and they lengthen the practice of contention.

(Quoted McDermott n.d.: 8)

The festival was designed to please the gods so that they would bring prosperity and ward off illness. Even the literati withheld their 'conventional . . . disdain for such licentious waste' (McDermott n.d.: 21).

In Naples it was a question not only of joint participation in Carneval by aristocrats and populace, in which the power differential always played a prominent part. There were parallel performances; those pieces that were put on at the royal court theatre of San Carlo were re-enacted soon afterwards on the popular stage, often in the form of parody expressing a critique of that very differential in power. In terms of content there was also a lot of borrowing one from the other; the opera buffo fed into comic opera, popular masks were recontextualised in the masked dances of the elite. One fed into the other, sometimes in support, often in opposition. The 'culture' was strongly divided not simply into popular and elite, into the Little and the Great, into the illiterate and the literate, but above all by class and by the interests and views of the component estates, in particular of the Church. It is plainly unsatisfactory to speak of any such culture having a single, unitary ideology in any monolithic sense, while the 'ideology' of the Church clearly cross-cut national boundaries, as did the interests and passions of royalty and the aristocracy, even if it was rarer for the peasants or workers to unite across political frontiers.

There is two-way communication but there is also two-way rejection, with the upper throwing out what they consider as lower and the peasantry objecting to some of the foppery of the court – at the same time as in southern France in the twentieth century the rural population for example universally adopts the bourgeois evening dress for a wedding costume. Especially for festivities and rituals, there is emulation as well as resentment or rejection; that lies at the root of the process of inter-group communication in hierarchical societies. It even encourages a measure of self-criticism among the privileged, as upper groups attempt to get closer to the supposed simplicity of pastoral life, or as luxury is widely eschewed by certain trends in world religion.

Let me explain in more detail what is involved in the Carneval and in the cognitive and social contradictions that are embedded in it. The social contradictions (or here, conflicts) are obvious, since they appear in the opposition between the classes, in this case in relation to food. The cognitive contradictions should be equally evident, since they relate to the perception of humanity as one (demanding redistributive justice) and the actuality of class stratification that gives more to some than to others. This contradiction strikes even some member of the upper groups, intellectuals and especially philosophers and priests, who are more sensitive to such matters than the bulk of the population and whose explicit written comments may lead to social changes.

The differentiation in styles of life was long a feature of the Mediterranean as of elsewhere in Eurasia, and this was related to social class as well as to the Great and Little, to the written and the oral. Why is it then that this programme has no reference to class?[2] That omission cannot be altogether explained by current antipathies to Marxism (which has of course no monopoly of the concept of class), nor contemporary sympathies with 'post-modernism', which phrases its objections in very different terms. It has long been an aspect of the anthropological version of the Mediterranean more generally. Is that because there has been a tendency for 'Mediterranean studies' to treat such differences under the heading of the Great and Little Traditions, as if they could be best understood within the framework of hierarchical variations in tradition within a particular culture, rather than as a social system that was often split in fundamental ways that the holistic notion of 'culture' tended to gloss over? As a description, that is a bland and even evasive notion even for 'peasant' societies.

Of course the situation varied over time and place in Europe. Initially the conquests of the Romans and later the Goths and other invaders established hierarchical regimes that differentiated upper and lower in terms of culture as of social position. The archetypal case is perhaps the Norman conquest of England, which threw out local landlords and churchmen on ethnic grounds and installed the Duke's men from Normandy. As a result the supremacy of the invading elite based originally on booty production had to be maintained, as did that of the English in Ireland, by harsh laws and practices which in turn sustained the romanticised rebellions of Hereward the Wake in the marshes of the fens and later of Robin Hood and his

---

[2] I refer here to the conference in Aix-en-Provence of May 1997 to celebrate the twentieth anniversary of establishing the field of Mediterranean anthropology.

company in the forest of Sherwood. In many cases time saw a softening of the lines of division, the establishment of greater cultural communication and the adoption of a single language (sometimes by the suppression of one, as with Celtic in Scotland, or the contrasting disappearance of French in England). But that process of softening cultural differences, which was true of many areas, did not of course eliminate class, nor did it always remove the kind of cultural differentiation referred to by the concepts of the Great and the Little Traditions.

I want to suggest that the extent of these cultural differences, which in fact represent polarities (with shifting orientations between them) rather than hard and fast dichotomies, has to do with the emergence of the radical stratification that came into being as a result of the transformations of the Bronze Age and produced profound class divisions based upon the ownership of and access to the means of production. To some extent reinforcing this hierarchy was that distinction between the literate and the illiterate which until the last hundred years was a fundamental feature of societies with writing, that is, of post Bronze Age life.

Unlike contemporary cultures of mass media and mass consumption, dependent in the long run on mass means of industrial production, earlier pre-industrial societies, based on the intensive agricultural systems of the Bronze Age, were luxury societies in a significant sense. That is, luxuries (created locally or imported from abroad) end up in the hands of the upper groups although they often become objects of emulation by lower ones. At the same time they may be rejected by some members of the community, and such rejection is especially associated with the writings of philosophers, churchmen and moralists. Think for example of the way that Roman moralists, and later on Christian ones, condemned the use of spices, perfumes or silks from the East by either men or women but especially by the latter, whose use of these luxuries was seen as sapping the strength of (male) Roman society. A similar kind of condemnation comes from the pen of those Chinese philosophers who criticise the use of luxuries by the rich and support the cause of the poor. Such dichotomised, ambivalent, attitudes are found even among members of the elite in stratified regimes of this kind. That is, elements of the Great Traditions may criticise luxurious behaviour, constituting a form of self-critique by philosophers and others whose very position, however, is based on the accumulation of a surplus which gives rise to and supports literacy (and hence the Great Tradition itself), as well as luxuries and class. With the development of mercantile cultures, luxuries expand to the middle class, including a range of artistic developments, as in the great towns of southern China or those of western and southern Europe. Consumer cultures in Europe began to take shape with the imports of Indian cotton and Chinese silks and ceramics at the time of the Renaissance, which was paralleled by an expansion of literacy in its artistic as well as its practical form. But they took off with the radical shift in productive systems towards industrialisation and the mechanisation of farming. Then luxury cultures move towards consumer ones, in which material goods and cultural products generally are shared more widely among the mass of the population.

Mass production leads inevitably to mass culture, not everywhere (there are always pockets of resistance, pockets of marginality) but in every region, including the Mediterranean. Of course, some elements of this culture were present whenever earlier proto-industrialisation occurred, for example with the red, stamped sigilatta ware, the production of which migrated from Arezzo in the first century CE to Gaul at Graufesenque (Millau), and from there to North Africa in the second century, thus spanning the Mediterranean in a commercial operation whose range extended from north Britain to south India (Whittaker and Goody forthcoming). Such production was largely for elite consumption in luxury cultures.

In some ways the shift to consumer cultures was gradual, depending upon the general rise in the standard of living and the increasing imports of formerly luxury products that sea voyages and overseas conquest made possible. That was the case with Indian cotton cloths in Europe, as the sea trade took over from the land-based caravans, inevitably associated with luxuries, to provide for the burgeoning bourgeoisie of the seventeenth century, whose desires were mainly fulfilled through the quantities of bullion acquired from overseas.

That process was fuelled by the mass production of consumer goods in Europe beginning in the eighteenth century and leading to the Industrial Revolution at its end. Even so, their consumption was still limited, but it advanced radically with what has been called the Second Industrial Revolution of the 1870s. That period saw the industrialisation of food, leading to considerable standardisation at least of national diets. It also saw the mass production of information in the shape of popular newspapers and, above all, of universal education, which evened up the disparities between male and female rates of literacy. This was not the same thing as the use of literacy, however, since women were probably greater readers than men, especially of novels, which they increasingly created.

Mass newspapers (and consumption of newsprint, the extension of the reading public) was followed by the development of the cinema, the phonograph, the radio, the television, the various components of the mass media, which again resulted in the further democratisation of culture. Earlier forms were not replaced; the cinema may well have encouraged the theatre, as the television may have stimulated the reading of plays. Instead they added another dimension, extending enormously the audience for certain types of cultural performance.

It is the mass media that have led to the globalisation of many 'cultural' forms, so that the cinemas in Sète show the same films as those in Birmingham, the discos in Bouzigues play the same music as those in Clacton. Local production of spectacle and song is not entirely swamped but it is marginalised and folklorised. It is no longer central to local culture, so that the young can move where they wish and still be à la mode. Of course there are certain places that resist more than others, partly to proclaim their opposition to the Coca-Cola culture which has descended upon the Mediterranean like most other parts of the world.

It is the same with vacations, with the growth of a holiday culture that now influences not only the Mediterranean but the greater part of warmer climes. Earlier in the Middle Ages 'leisure' travel abroad had taken place largely in a religious context, for local pilgrimages (as in the *Canterbury Tales*), for visits to distant monasteries or for educational purposes (the wandering scholar). In the eighteenth century we get the growth of the Grand Tour and similar visits made by the aristocracy and upper bourgeoisie to other countries, the kind of visiting epitomised in Byron's *Childe Harold*, or in the tours of the novelist, Smollett, or of Boswell, Samuel Johnson's biographer. These were essentially elitist products of minority culture; the lower classes travelled only as soldiers in foreign wars or in colonial occupations from Britain, to South Africa, the Sudan or India. Leisure tourism expanded with the coming of the railway and the steamboat (in its various disguises), which also permitted cheaper travel for migration and for commercial purposes. But at first the Riviera was reserved for the aristocracy and upper bourgeoisie, while intellectuals made the shorter journey to the Dordogne. It was only after the Second World War that mass air travel developed to Eastern Europe (through entrepreneurs such as John Bloom[3] in England) and new tourist resorts such as Benidorm in Spain, patronised by trades unions and enabling the retired to live materially better abroad than they could at home. Of course, the democratisation of travel and holidays in Europe, promoted earlier by measures such as the compulsory four-week holidays brought in by Leon Blum's Socialist government of 1936 as well as by shorter and more traditional holidays in northern England, meant a relative saturation of many tourist areas such as the south of France, which had now to cater for a mass rather than an elite market. That changed the whole tone of the resorts, so that the high bourgeoisie were obliged to go further afield or to use select locations that exclude the mass traveller by a variety of means. The result was a radical change in the social structure of the recipient societies, whether Stratford-upon-Avon or Miami, meaning that a considerable number of the inhabitants of such places were engaged in catering for tourists, by means that varied from the straightforwardly commercial to the outright criminal. Strangers and temporary visitors could be treated in ways that one's neighbours could not, but in ways that could often lead to an increase in prosperity and, indeed, in local facilities, since tourists required museums, good restaurants, luxury shops, which the natives had done without. Tourism means disruption but it also means survival and much more.

This general process of development had its cognitive side in the shape of the revival of learning in the Renaissance and the scientific revolution of the seventeenth century. That scientific revolution had a double effect, of promoting a changing technology and of encouraging secularisation. The push towards secularisation greatly influenced not only conceptions of the world in a general sense but also the conduct of personal life which had been so much under ecclesiastical control. This process saw the advent of divorce, of closer marriages, of birth control and many other of the features that mark contemporary domestic life.

At the same time there was a shift from minority to mass literacy. Universal literacy was attempted only in recent times, beginning with the Second Industrial Revolution. Nevertheless its advent has not altogether abolished the distinctions between upper and lower traditions, between for example the preferences for *haute* and *basse cuisine*, or between lieder and pop songs, or even between 'upper' and 'lower' women. While it has increased the communication, decreased the barriers, between the two

---

[3] He was also the manufacturer of cheap electrical goods on a mass scale, providing new benefits for the working classes.

poles, it has not produced completely homogeneous cultures; there are still important differences related to cultural activities, some of which are linked to formal education and therefore to the Great Tradition, as Leavis and Snow reminded us in their acerbic discussion of 'minority culture' and 'the two cultures'; one of Leavis' major works was entitled *The Great Tradition*, which he saw as constituted by a line of English-speaking authors in some sense nourished by popular culture (the Little Tradition). Other differences still arise from class background, which is always ready to introduce or elaborate new criteria of what is elite behaviour, even when in the age of universal media communication these may be rapidly dissolved and need renewing in a different form within a relatively short space of time. These developments gave rise to the more aggressive popular cultures, the growth of mass tourism (the Benidorm phenomenon), of mass 'culture' (especially pop, the shift from chamber concert to rock, from theatre to cinema) that includes many of the elements, including violence, that are so inimical to the grand bourgeoisie. Grand bourgeoisie, Great Tradition, these are partners in luxury cultures.

I want to emphasise the following points. Firstly, while the opposition between the Great and the Little Tradition has some merit, it has to be seen from a wider perspective that does not use this dichotomy to conceal the influence of socio-economic class, nor yet the division between written and oral traditions, or rather between literate and illiterate persons, which is not the same thing. Secondly, any opposition must always take into account the interaction between these traditions and the actors involved, in which there is movement predominantly down but also up.

For the interplay generally involved a hierarchical dimension, between dominant and sub-dominant; but the latter was certainly not entirely suppressed, because it would be wrong to see bourgeois or peasant culture as always being under the thumb of the aristocracy. The former had more than a measure of independence, in China as in the Mediterranean, and played a part in contributing to what there was of common concern as well as to their own distinctive sub-cultures. That was especially true in relation to the written tradition, since the ruling class was often at pains to differentiate itself from the scribes, the clerks and other specialists in the written word, who belonged to lower, employed groups and yet were the ones most likely to make substantial contributions to the ongoing literate culture. The middle classes were most frequently the playwrights, novelists, chroniclers and poets.

Even in overall political terms the hierarchy does not always remain the same – quite apart from the differences in the internal system of cultural values – but it changes over time. Within European and other cultures the bourgeois gradually became dominant over the aristocratic, which correspondingly took on a less significant role. Upheaval in the society meant upheaval in the culture. The French Revolution, like the earlier English one, radically changed dominant beliefs and practices about the world, as is shown by the story of the tree of liberty cut down from the lord's forest and its subsequent outgrowth, the statue of liberty; the *mai*, formerly the pole of May Day, is still erected for electoral victories and marriages in the Lot in rural France. At the same time the new politically dominant classes adopted the dress of lower groups (or of English parliamentarians, dropping the wig), either for their own ideological reasons or to merge inconspicuously with the masses. Paintings were at first destroyed in an iconoclastic fervour, the theatre abolished, established religion swept away. Many of these changes did not endure, but a residue did. For the gradual introduction of democratic procedures placed the majority in a position of power against traditional elites so that politicians had now to pay greater attention to what they said and how they acted, thus modifying the overall class relations as well as the position between the bearers of the Great and Little Traditions. Similar transformations have occurred wherever democracy and majority voting have been introduced, doing away with the minority white governments of Zimbabwe and South Africa, breaking the power monopoly of the Tutsi in Central Africa and threatening the rule of established elites throughout Africa. That was one of the time-bombs left by the retreat of colonial powers, and it accounts for much of the turmoil in Africa today, a turmoil that destroys the existing relationship between elite and popular cultures. That is not to say that their representatives, the new holders of power, will not try to adopt the dress and behaviours of the earlier elites. There is inevitably much cultural continuity; that was also true even in Soviet Russia or Nazi Germany, but the newcomers modify these practices in adapting to them, and in any case there are powerful checks and balances in the inertia of national traditions and in democratic regimes, in the shape of the voters at recurrent elections.

Let me turn to the topic of specific hierarchical differences in the three spheres I have discussed, namely wine, women and song. I will discuss the last first as it is the most straightforward. Like all others, Mediterranean cultures gave birth to examples of that particular rhythmic combination of voice and melody that we call song. In simple societies song is usually a common cultural possession. In the hierarchical cultures of the Mediterranean, we tend to get an early division between the written songs of the elite and the orally created and transmitted songs of the people at large, including folk-songs and other popular music. The elite music was at first largely created for courts and produced by specialist musicians for specialised instruments. With the increasing power of the middle class, the advent of widespread education and the ensuing spread of literacy, that exclusivity ceased; while classical and popular traditions continued to lead separate lives, individuals were no longer themselves exclusively identified, certainly over their whole life-course, with one or the other. Of course there had always been interaction. Classical composers took up the themes of popular music; some like Liszt and Bartók made a career of that. At the end of the sixteenth century the Protestant German composer, Michael Praetorius, incorporated into his work dances such as Les Gavrottes. The French peasants had made it to the German court, at least in terms of their music. At the same time aspects of written culture made themselves felt at the popular level, as in many of the famous recordings made by Parry and Lord in their effort to show that Homer was an oral poet.

While song is differentiated hierarchically and influenced by the written tradition, wine occupies a somewhat different position in Mediterranean cultures. The culture of wine was probably first introduced into France by Greek traders; the vine was a cultigen of Anatolian origin that spread from East to West. But it was not adopted in an unambiguous way, since there were always doubts about its effects on the human condition; there were some ambivalences about the use of substances that altered states of consciousness, rendering mankind less in control, especially of their communications with God, although in other cases disassociation in trance was seen as a mark of successful intercourse. As such it was more closely identified with warrior elements in society, as in the Bulgarian and Macedonian epics discussed by Jean Cuisinier, rather than with women or with the more saintly representatives in the community. For warriors, drinking stood for prowess and virility. The Church of course also made ample use of wine for secular and sacred purposes, but for puritans there was often a contradiction between the use of wine in the communion service to represent the blood of Christ and its use to induce riotous or uncontrolled behaviour, resulting in the kind of domestic impoverishment and violence that led to the Temperance Movement and to the total rejection discussed earlier in chapter 9.

Moreover it was a luxury product, a vanity not a necessity. As a result of these various features wine was in fact little used in the areas of its origins, either by the Jews or less so by the Arabs. The objections arose mainly on religious grounds. Mediterranean culture was split in two regarding the imbibing of alcohol (and the nature of consumption more generally) largely because of religious affiliation: Christians and pagans drank, Muslims and Jews did not. But drinking (like other consumption) was also stratified in relation to class as well as in relation to religion (and hence literacy). Cooking is perhaps more obviously so. Both on the African and on the European shore elite cuisine was not only preserved but developed in writing, in the cookbooks analysed by Rodinson for North Africa and by Flandrin for Europe. Those developments applied to more than one culture. Indeed, there were influences that cut across the two shores of the Mediterranean. Europe adopted a number of luxury traits from the Arabs during the medieval period: the sugared flavours (sugar came from India through the Near East), the golden colours, and many spices; some special dishes such as blackbirds baked in a pie which formed the theme of a current English nursery rhyme were found in both areas, for luxury was often expressed in a foreign garb, adopted from abroad.

That was also at first the case with wine. Coming from the East, wine was imported to Marseilles in amphorae and sold to local dignitaries. Eventually it was produced in the south of France and exported northwards where it became a favourite luxury of the chiefs of the Germanic tribes, whose followers were confined to locally brewed beer. Not only did the chiefs adopt wine, as later African chiefs adopted gin (there was no distilled liquor south of the Sahara), but they also imported the utensils associated with drinking, as described by Dietler (1990) in his article, 'Driven by drink'. In the North there remained a distinction between the local plebeian culture that adhered to beer, and the luxury culture that drank imported wines.

But wine too was a stratified drink. There were the local wines, the *vins ordinaires* or even the almost undrinkable *piquet* produced on peasant holdings, and there were the *grands crus* of the chateaux-bottled wine. In Bordeaux that aristocratic production fed into the export trade principally to England (and later to the whole world) that began as early as the thirteenth century, changed the agricultural landscape of Gascony and led to the importation of cereals from Britain and a certain measure of English culture (including rugby football) in exchange.

Finally I want to deal with the most complex problem of the three, namely the stratification of women, which paralleled that of men. One of the most significant features of kinship in the Mediterranean, discussed in the earlier chapters as well as in the volumes on Mediterranean anthropology, was the fact that many women took into marriage a dowry. This has been visualised in terms of honour and shame as well as of gender, and such considerations were certainly present. But looked at from a wider point of view, we find that dowry is a feature of all the major Eurasian societies, as distinct for example from Africa, where marriage transactions are characterised by bridewealth. One does not find the equivalent of bridewealth in the major Eurasian societies; what is often there referred to as brideprice is almost invariably either a counter-transfer or a feature of lower-status marriages in which the wife is endowed indirectly by the groom's family rather than by her own. Or in Arab and Jewish societies (where divorce, in contrast to post-Christian Europe, was common) it may represent a necessary financial protection for the wife if she were to be set aside.

Unlike bridewealth, which is usually made up of a standard sum, dowry is essentially variable since it consists of an endowment of a daughter out of parental wealth. It expresses and creates difference of status, and in the post-Bronze Age societies we are discussing, it reflected the substantial stratification of an economic and cultural kind. In African societies where there is little such economic stratification (though in states there is a political one), men and women usually marry out; sometimes, if the system is exogamous, obligatorily so. In the Mediterranean, as in the other major states of Eurasia, it is important to maintain and even advance the position of daughters as well as of sons as a matter of family status and prestige as well as sustaining the earlier way of life (now culturally differentiated). So we find what I have called diverging devolution, with the property of both parents going to the children of both sexes, not necessarily in equal proportions or at the same time. Daughters tend to receive it earlier at marriage rather than as an inheritance at the death of the parents. Usually they receive less, but sometimes they get it not only earlier (which is itself a gain) but in greater quantity, as has been reported for areas on the European coast of the Mediterranean (for example Cyprus).

Daughters are not only differentiated in the amount they receive, leading them by and large to marry men of similar wealth within their own group, endogamously, isogamously. But they also differ in the type of endowment they receive. Women of lower groups may have to accumulate their own dowry by working, by a process of self-accumulation. Others were provided for by charitable institutions, as at the Neapolitan Carneval, when twenty poor girls were endowed (Scafolgio 1997: 42). And yet others are endowed by their husband's family rather than by their own, with an indirect dowry that usually goes to the girl rather than her natal kin, as it would in African bridewealth. That was an important class difference distinguishing one sort of woman from another. It was a hierarchical difference that was only distantly related to the existence of the Great and Little Traditions but very directly to socio-economic stratification.

The danger in taking any region for social analysis is of concentrating on the search for common qualities. It is that commonality which justifies the original decision to designate a 'culture area'. There are certainly important similarities within the Mediterranean zone, but concentration on this search tends to neglect important distinctions, such as those that developed after the seventh century between the two coasts of the Mediterranean, north and south, deriving from the influence of Christianity and Islam respectively on the institutions of kinship and marriage (Goody 1983). These are not marginal considerations; they profoundly affect systems of transmitting property at both the familial and societal levels. There is no particular virtue in stressing the cultural as distinct from the physical unity of the Mediterranean if it means neglecting those ties of the northern littoral with Christian Europe as a whole and of the southern with the Near East and with Islam more generally.

The distinction between Great and Little Traditions was relevant to both coasts, although Christianity and Islam (and the educational traditions that developed from these) certainly affected each in their own way the nature of the cultural hierarchy. But we must not let an analysis of elite and popular cultures, of the Great and Little Traditions, lead us to neglect the important socio-economic or class differences to which they are related, directly or indirectly. The change to mass consumer cultures has profoundly influenced the nature of class relations and of national 'cultures' generally. In terms of class, there is more communication, including marriage, and less distance; the constant themes of post-Renaissance literature concerning the misalliance and the servant–master relationships are no longer central concerns of creative work; class differentiation takes more shaded forms, especially in America. But such modifications should not lead us to neglect the cultural importance of class in earlier luxury cultures, nor yet its persistent character. American writers, of whom Redfield was one, have been particularly prone to neglect its importance, partly because its exponents tended to be associated (rather narrowly) with Marxist or socialist interpretations of the world, partly because the notion of equality has played such an important part in American thinking about themselves. Rather, they have tended, abroad as at home, to mask its significance in emphasising differences in styles of life or in Great and Little Traditions. That tendency has been strengthened by those writers on India who see caste as excluding class, or interpret hierarchy mainly in religious terms. I would myself have emphasised the role of the written tradition (and with it of education) as well as of religious factors, and have attempted to give these some independent weight in the examination of culture and of kinship (see Goody 1983 and 1990). At the same time it would be quite misleading to see these factors, as many commentators do, as denying or replacing the hierarchy of class, even in its modified contemporary form but certainly in Europe before the Second Industrial Revolution.

Chapter 11

A KERNEL OF DOUBT

This chapter was written in response to an invitation to celebrate the name of T. H. Huxley, son of an unsuccessful schoolmaster who was progenitor of a line of intellectuals. We remember him partly because of his support of Charles Darwin on the occasion of the debate about evolution with Bishop Wilberforce at Oxford in 1860 (a year after the appearance of *The Origin of Species*). The occasion represented a major public assertion of the independence of science from theology, a breach that had been in the making since Galileo and long before. Indeed, I want to argue that doubts, ambivalences, about the role of God and divinity in human affairs (as well as doubts about secular matters too) has a much longer history, one that relates not so much to science or even naturalism in the restricted sense as to a transversal scepticism about the role of deity arising from the human situation itself.[1] A similar phenomenon arises with other notions about this world, such as those of creation and evolution, which I discuss in the following chapter.

Huxley had himself played an important part in scientific biology, working as an assistant surgeon on HMS *Rattlesnake* which had been fitted out for exploration in the Southern Seas. As for Darwin, and as for anthropology in general, Imperial rule provided the opportunity to expand Europeans' knowledge of the world, as commercial imperialism does for contemporary powers. But Huxley was much more than a natural scientist, becoming president of the Ethnological Society, as well as honorary principal of the South London Working Men's College and a dominant member of the first London School Board, and serving in many other capacities beside.

---

[1] Transversal, not universal but widespread in a variety of cultures.

His commitment to a scientific, empirical approach to problems led him into conflict with established religion but not to a complete rejection of the supernatural. His own attitude was expressed by the term 'agnosticism', which he first used in 1869 at a meeting of the Metaphysical Society in antithesis to gnosticism or to the gnostic, 'who professed to know so much about the very things of which I was ignorant' (quoted Flew 1974: 312). While Huxley may have invented the English word, the Greeks already had a concept of *agnôstos*. For Hermetic philosophers, God himself fell into this category. He could not be known except by looking inwards to our soul, which was itself a part of God (Besançon 1994: 80). Although first employed in a religious context, the word was later applied by Lenin (1908) to David Hume and Immanuel Kant referring to the Enlightenment idea of the unknowability of the nature, or even the existence, of things in themselves (that is, of the realities beyond appearances).

That topic was taken up by many writers in the second half of the nineteenth century, McCosh (1884) comparing the agnosticism of Hume and Huxley, Ward (1899) devoting the Gifford Lectures of 1896–98 to the subject, and Baron F. von Huegel, founder of the Cambridge Museum of Archaeology and Ethnology, leaving behind some literary remains devoted to the notion (1931). Others too produced vigorous defences (see Cockshut 1964 and Lightman 1987). The theme was also taken up by philosophers like Strawson and by historians of thought, but all these discussions involve an almost purely Western view of the topic, as if others had no similar doubts.

Agnosticism stands apart from atheism, which asserts there is no God and which is not a manifestation of doubt or ignorance but an outright denial. Agnosticism is closer to scepticism, though it is more concerned with recognising the limits of human knowledge and with the necessity of empirical investigation; as such, it connected not only with scientific enquiry but with the positivism of Auguste Comte and with the logical positivism (or logical empiricism) of the Vienna School. Both the latter are heirs to the Enlightenment since they imply the questioning of other forms of knowledge as well as religion; that is, they imply a scepticism about traditional beliefs and a measure of doubt about their validity.

So agnosticism did not suddenly emerge in the nineteenth century, though its scope was certainly widened at that time. It had existed before, especially in the form of doubt or scepticism. I want to pursue that notion of scepticism, since its existence in human societies is important as a paradigm for the development of other features of human cognition. When did it first emerge? Some commentators, including many philosophers, have perceived a great divide between 'traditional' and 'modern' modes of thought, with only the latter manifesting scepticism, rationality or logic. Modern historians like Keith Thomas have seen the decline of magic as taking place in the sixteenth century. Historical sociologists like Max Weber saw in this same period the disenchantment of the world and the concomitant development of the Western rationality of world mastery. Philosophical anthropologists like Ernest Gellner and Jürgen Habermas have seen this change as linked to the Enlightenment. That movement looked back to Descartes and gave birth to David Hume and eventually to Kant; some have seen scepticism, especially atheism, as its product. Important developments clearly took place at both these periods, but others look further back. Armstrong argues that the return to the book, the literal rather than the symbolic or allegorical approach to religion, in the Age of Reform (for example, the rejection of Copernicus and Galileo because their heliocentric theories contradicted the Bible) in effect prepared the way for the advance of science and the attack on the existence of God (Armstrong 1993: 334 ff.). Before these times, Laslett has claimed, all our ancestors had believed; attendance at church was compulsory and faith universal.[2]

That notion has again been challenged by other historians. Wootton (1985: 98) has pointed out that in the period 1540–1680, 'there existed a coherent culture, both oral and literate, both popular and, above all, intellectual of irreligion' which he sees as fostered by absolutism. A typical figure of pre-Enlightenment scepticism, indeed atheism, was the playwright Christopher Marlowe, one of the 'University Wits', who represented a group of alienated young men. Under pressure of torture, his friend Thomas Kyd told how Marlowe used to 'jest at the divine scriptures'. Richard Baines, a government agent, spoke of his 'scorn of God's word', of his claim that '"Christ was a bastard and his mother dishonest", that the twelve disciples were "base fellowes neyther of wit nor worth", and that "the first beginning of Religioun was only to keep men in awe"' (Watt 1996: 30, quoting Kocher 1946). In other words we need to look further back for the origins of this divide. Indeed, many classical humanists have

---

[2] Of the middle of the sixteenth century Laslett writes that it is 'the time when every living person in England was both a believing, fearing Christian and also by compulsion a member of the national church' (Laslett 1965: 176–7).

seen the beginnings of Western rationality as emerging right back in the classical period. Sceptics such as Sextus Empiricus (second and third centuries CE) challenged all knowledge that went beyond the immediate experience. That is to say, the sceptical traditions of the Enlightenment looked back not only to the revival of classical knowledge in the Renaissance but further back to the development of those thoughts in Greece and Rome.[3] Right at the so-called beginnings of (written) philosophy, we find criticisms of earlier concepts of divinity by Xenophanes, Heraclitus and others. In addition there emerged among the early Ionian philosophers a distinct strain of naturalism (see Lloyd 1979). The culture of the greatest of these city-states, Miletus, has been described as 'humanistic and materialistic' (Guthrie 1962: 30). Its 'physical philosophers', who were interested above all in nature, tried to get behind the multiplicity of the observable world and seek the underlying One. Their work led directly to the Atomism of the following century; in this scheme of things there was no problem of the world suddenly coming into being, of a creation story, since it consisted of small particles that could be combined in a variety of ways. The notions of Democritus and others excluded that of divinity in the ordinary sense. According to these authors men pray to the gods for their health, but that was in fact in their own power.

The Sophists too excluded religion as man made, adopting 'a humanistic agnosticism' (Armstrong 1957: 23). According to Protagoras (c. 485– c. 410 BCE), 'man is the measure of all things', and in *Concerning the Gods* he found there was not enough evidence on this subject to make up one's own mind; as a result he was, like others in the alternative tradition, accused of impiety. The dramatists of the fifth century BCE, especially Euripides and Sophocles, also displayed considerable ambivalence about their gods. Meanwhile medical writers quietly pursued a parallel tradition of naturalistic explanation, mostly disregarding the final causes beloved by Plato. Although Galen was committed to the notion of final causes, their work continued like Plato's to dominate much European thinking until the seventeenth century. In history, too, Thucydides tried to explain past events without seeking supernatural causes. Subsequently the Hellenistic age saw the rise of competing philosophies that included Epicureanism and Scepticism itself. For the former, gods played no part in the creation of the

---

[3] On the revival of Pyrronhism (scepticism) in the Renaissance by Montaigne, see Popkin (1964).

world (Epicurus accepted the materialistic stance of Democritus) nor did they in human affairs; there was no 'providence', the soul was not immortal and nature was non-teleological. The Sceptics continued the earlier Greek trend of speculative thought that considered the understanding of the world too difficult a task. These doctrines had a great effect on the Middle Academy, especially under Arcesilaus (c. 316/315–241 BCE), who called for a 'suspension of judgement', and Carneades (c. 213–129 BCE), both of whom levelled their criticism at theistic beliefs. However, what Academic Sceptics always questioned was not so much belief in the gods, whose validity was deemed sanctioned by custom, but rather efforts to prove or show reasons why they had to exist. These philosophers strongly influenced the Roman writers, Cicero (who gives a classic statement of this position in *De Natura Deorum* III, 6–9), Lucretius and Pliny the Elder.[4] The dominant philosophy of the early Roman empire was Stoicism tinged with Platonism, in other words a theistic system. But much ancient classical religion centred upon practice as much as belief, and scepticism could arise from hopes unfulfilled by recourse to rites. Cicero did not, comments Schofield, become a sceptic in the modern sense of an unbeliever.

> Rather, he had come to think with the Academy that whatever philosophical views a person holds had better be entertained not as firm convictions but simply as the best views that appear to be available after he has run through and compared the arguments on either side.
>
> (Schofield 1986: 47–8)

It was this kernel of doubt that led to the need for a suspension of judgement; Cicero saw much force in the arguments both for and against divination. He asked 'questions on all points, often with hesitation and without confidence' (Cicero, *Div.* Bk II, 11.8; Schofield 1986: 59).

These ideas contributed to a mood of cynicism towards religion that achieved its most significant political expression in the work of the Emperor Marcus Aurelius (121–180 CE), who has been called 'the saint and exemplar of Agnosticism'. That may be an exaggerated view. For he was a Stoic, touched by Platonic ideas; though there were 'obscurities and

---

[4] On Cicero and the question of divination, which is particularly relevant to a consideration of scepticism as it concerns prediction, see Schofield (1986). Bottéro sees its study as a forerunner of scientific enquiry.

ambiguities' in his religious attitudes, he nevertheless declared 'And so too with the gods; from my repeated experiences of their power, from these I apprehend that they exist and I do them reverence' (M. Aurelius, *Med.* XII, 28; Rutherford 1989: 209). He was a man who neither believed nor disbelieved, unable to make up his mind between gods and atoms.[5]

I have tried to link part of these processes of rationalisation (as I would prefer to call them, seeing a continuing series of changes rather than the abrupt invention of rationality) with changes in the means of communication. Watt and I have suggested that the introduction of writing, and specifically the development of a fully alphabetic script among the Greeks, provided humankind with an easy method of 'transcription' (though much more was involved) that led to the development of sceptical thinking and a sceptical tradition (Goody and Watt 1963). The development of sceptical thinking was encouraged by the fact that writing provided a measure of decontextualisation of speech and thought. The example we used was the writing down of Greek mythology. Since this was initially linked closely to the society in which it appeared, the written versions took on a different 'truth' status when that society changed with the passage of time. With the emergence of new social values, they became out of kilter. Myths were then discounted as the 'fables of men of old', in Xenophanes' words, or had to be reinterpreted in allegorical fashion, as happened centuries later during the Renaissance. Similar consequences must have arisen from the writing down of the results of divination which recorded the negative as well as the positive results, whereas in memory the former tend to get forgotten in favour of the latter. The sceptical attitudes encouraged by these written procedures were not of course the only ones to prevail; writing itself gave rise to new forms of divination such as horoscopes, and new forms of religion, the religions of the Book. But it did help to establish a continuing sceptical tradition alongside the 'religious' one, leading to a tension between the two that reached its apogee in Huxley's time. It provided a new measuring stick with which to establish 'truth' of a secular kind.

Such notions are clearly not confined to the post-Enlightenment period, for they were prevalent much earlier. Some classical humanists assume this explicit expression of doubt in the form of agnosticism or atheism to have been a feature of the Greek tradition, related to their sceptical

---

[5] For the earlier references in this paragraph see Thrower (1980: 222–3), quoting F. W. Myers and T. R. Glover.

mode of enquiry, their search for proof (Lloyd 1990), which Watt and I considered to emerge from their use of alphabetic writing (1963).

What was wrong about our earlier statement was that we confined such sceptical traditions to alphabetic writing and so to the Greek (and hence to the Aryan, the European) heritage. That was an unduly ethnocentric, Eurocentric view. For developed notions of this kind are found in other literate cultures, as a counterpart to ideas of rationality. I have argued that the use of syllogistic reasoning, to take the most prominent of the Aristotelian procedures, was found in embryonic form in Mesopotamia and in more developed ones in India, China and Japan, while Islam had incorporated Aristotelian logic at an early period, long before Western Europe (Goody 1993b, 1996a).

A similar distribution is found with organised forms of scepticism. A century ago Dillon presented an account of *The Sceptics of the Old Testament* (1895). That is to say, in the very heart of the major religious work of Judaism and (to a lesser extent) of Christianity and Islam, lay a tradition of doubt, even of disbelief.

The book of Genesis had elaborated a special view of world processes, since the monotheism of Judaism implied a radical separation between divinity and nature. Nature was the creation of the one God but could not directly claim any religious awe or worship. This totally transcendent God also forbade the creation of 'graven images' and hence the worship of anything humans had themselves constructed; he 'denigrates and relativises all human values and their representations' (Thrower 1980: 235, quoting H. Cox). Such transcendency may also lead to the desacralisation of the universe, leaving humankind freer to explore it without any reference to divine interference.

But agnosticism and atheism were also present in more explicit ways, in the Wisdom Literature of Proverbs, Job and Ecclesiastes, which manifests strong links with similar traditions in Egypt, Babylon and Greece. The Bible records the views of one Agur who declared 'I have no God'. While he is quoted only to be refuted, that nevertheless provides evidence of the presence of such thoughts. Ecclesiastes is more specifically agnostic, so much so that some theologians have queried the inclusion of such a pessimistic and fatalistic text in the Jewish or Christian canon. But there is also a more positive component, the encouragement of humankind to enjoy life. 'So then eat your bread with cheerfulness and drink your wine with a glad heart ... Enjoy life with the woman you love all the fleeting days that God grants you under the sun, for it is your rightful portion . . .' (Ecclesiastes 9: 7–9).

Such attitudes appear in some Babylonian texts, including the *Epic of Gilgamesh*. They can also be found in Egyptian Wisdom Literature, which again is paralleled by a more deliberately naturalistic approach to the world that lies at the basis of medical texts such as the *Edwin Smith Papyrus*.

So the roots both of the criticisms of the religious view of the world and of the establishment of a naturalistic understanding were already present in the classical period of European civilisation, as well as in the Near East more generally. However, the 'pagan' philosophical schools that propounded those views were gradually closed down under the Christian emperor Justinian. Up to the 560s, the pagan professors of Athens 'dominated the intellectual life of the cultivated classes'. But during the Middle Ages Western thought was subject to the theistic *Weltanschauung* of the Church (Brown 1971: 177). That supremacy was formally challenged with the revival of classical learning beginning in the twelfth century and culminating in the eighteenth after the Italian Renaissance, fed partly by Byzantium where a classical elite had survived and which did not therefore have to go through the same experience of a rebirth.

What I am insisting upon is that scepticism, agnosticism, like rationality, did not have their origin in the European Enlightenment, whatever further achievements were made at that time. Part of the appearance of the growth of secularisation and the disenchantment of the world at that period has to be seen against the earlier hegemony of Christian ideas which had done something to suppress most formal expressions of agnosticism and scepticism over some thousand years. In the classical period, which saw such major advances in the growth of knowledge, things had been different.

Also I now want to argue that these developments were not only earlier but non-European as well, appearing in other literate civilisations in Asia. We find a note of scepticism in certain sects of Islam, notably the derviches, but the scepticism is about the ways of approaching God rather than about God *per se*. In particular the poetry sung by the Bektachi brotherhoods was sometimes very severe about Islamic ritual, even about the book and the mosque:

Approche dévot, sors le Coran de ton giron,
Ce livre ne te conduira pas vers le salut,
Allah est un mystère qui n'est pas contenu dans une maison,

Celui qui se prosterne devant les quatre murs est un sot,
Le but est de se réjouir sans faire le pelerinage.

(Zarcone 1993: 453)

It was this scepticism that led writers like Riza Tevfik to try to reconcile enlightened sufism with modern Western philosophy by way of free-masonry, a movement that became widely adopted by modernists such as the Young Turks in eastern and central Asia.

The Indian situation is particularly instructive, as we are dealing with a tradition largely distinct from that of Greece, Europe and even the Near East. That sub-continent has been seen by many, Asians as well as Europeans, as being dominated by the religious world view. In Radhakrishnan's words (1953: i, 21, quoted by Chattopadhyaya 1959: 3), 'The characteristic of Indian thought is that it has paid greater attention to the inner world of man than to the outer world.' That has been the view of many anthropologists. But there was also an 'alternative' tradition as Thrower calls it, attributed to the mass of the people, which was 'instinctively materialist' and was known by the name of Lokāyāta, a word that appears to be derived from that for 'the natural world' (*loka*) and possibly from *ayatana*, 'the basis'. The extent to which this tradition formed a relatively consistent philosophy is unknown, since we are only aware of its existence through the commentaries of opponents, such as the fourteenth-century *Sarra Darsana Samgraha* by Madhavacarya. According to this author,

the Lokayatikas denied the validity of any source of knowledge other than immediate sense-perception. And therefore denied all realities except the gross objects of the senses. There was no God, no soul and no survival after death. It followed naturally that the Lokayatikas denied all religious and moral values and cared only for the pleasures of the senses.

(Chattopadhyaya 1959: 9)

In other words he viewed these doctrines as 'the cult of those crude people who little understood the higher values of human existence'.

The extensive account by Thrower of the history of disbelief starts with a dichotomy between the magico-religious world view and a naturalistic one which eventually comes to dominate. He rightly queries the idea that the latter came into being only at the Enlightenment, or indeed even with the Greeks, seeing it as much more widely distributed in human cultures. In India he sees 'sceptical, agnostic and naturalistic strains' as embedded in the Vedas themselves. Doubt as well as faith is present in passages such as the following:

> I ask, unknowing, those who know, the sages, as one
>   all ignorant for sake of knowledge,
> What was that ONE who in the Unborn's image hath
>   stablished and fixed firm these worlds' six regions.
>   (*Rig Veda*, Book I, hymn 164 v. 6, translated Griffith 1889)

This, 'the earliest recorded speculation of ancient man', was connected, Thrower suggests, with the growing practice of asceticism which was inspired by a desire for knowledge, leading to a breakdown of earlier Vedic beliefs as exposed in the Upanishads (Thrower 1980: 38). Agnosticism is thus an intrinsic part of the Vedic hymns, as is clear from the 'Hymn of Creation' (the *Nāsadīya*) which Basham (1954: 247) has described as 'one of the oldest surviving records of philosophical doubt in the history of the world':

> Non-being then existed not nor being:
> There was no air, nor sky that is beyond it,
> What was concealed? Wherein? In whose protection?
> And was there deep unfathomable water?
> ...
> None knoweth whence creation has arisen;
> And whether he has or has not produced it:
> He who surveys it in the highest heaven,
> He only knows, or haply may know not.
>   (*Rig Veda*, Book X, hymn 129, translated Macdonell 1922: 18)

Max Müller called this doctrine 'adevism', the doubting of the devas, which constituted a sub-theme throughout the history of Indian religion. While the orthodox associated such thoughts with the Asuras, regarded in the Upanishads as devils, they represented the unspoken doubts of many about the role of deity in the world. In the words of the *Sarva-siddhānta-sagraha* of Śakara:

> Who paints the peacocks, or who makes the cuckoos sing?
> There exists here no cause excepting nature.[6]

---

[6] Radhakrishnan and Moore (1957: 235), from the translation by Cowell and Gough (1904).

Naturalism represents one outcome of doubt, of disbelief in those representations we speak of as gods which cannot be directly perceived and whose existence is therefore liable to be questioned. Even ancestor worship came under the critical eye of the doubters, and one of the tenets of the Lokāyāta was that 'there is no immortal soul and nothing exists after the death of the body', so that *karma* itself is an illusion (Tucci 1926; Thrower 1980: 86). They looked upon 'priests' not merely as wrong but as fraudulent, as leading people astray by advocating offerings to non-existing agencies and encouraging them to believe in an imaginary life-after-death. They dwell upon the virtues of asceticism but, as the Materialist comments in the ancient drama, *The Rise of the Moon of Intellect*, this too has its limitations:

> These fools are deceived by the lying śāstras, and are fed with the allurements of hope. But can begging, fasting, penance, exposure to the burning heat of the sun, which emaciate the body, be compared with the ravishing embraces of women with large eyes, whose prominent breasts are compressed with one's arms?
>
> (translated Taylor 1911: 20,
> in Radhakrishnan and Moore 1957: 248)

Such hedonism, which paralleled that of Epicurus in the Greek tradition, was linked by Chattopadhyaya with the Tantric cults which had followed *deha-vada* beliefs (where the self is the body) as well as magico-religious practices, and which stressed sexual enjoyment, a fact that condemned it in the eyes of many orthodox Brahmins.

In many great myths like the Mahābārata or the Bible, indeed in many epics, we find a kernel of doubt present. One character questions the ideas of the hero or the dominant party. Sometimes the devil himself plays that role. Such questioning is almost a structural necessity, both artistically and ideologically. How would Pilgrim make any Progress had he not obstacles to overcome, had he not had to negotiate the Slough of Despond? Artistically, this intervention creates a necessary tension; ideologically, the dominant trends are questioned so that doubts can be overcome. But the doubts are not so easily quelled; they continue to exist in the minds of many of the faithful who need to convince themselves of God's powers and yet are led into scepticism. Both acceptance and rejection, giving rise to ambivalence, are the essential countercurrents of faith, not necessarily in the minds of everyone but in those of some elements of the population. Agnosticism is

the counterpart of gnosticism, inherent in doubts about the conceptualisation and representation of supernatural agencies and their requirements of
gifts and asceticism.

Such doubts are certainly prominent in written religion where they
may even come to constitute their own alternative tradition, as in the case of
Confucianism in China and possibly of Lokāyāta in India. India in the sixth
century, which is when Lokāyāta emerged as a definite school of philosophy, seems to have been a place in which a considerable amount of free-
thinking took place, a fact that might be connected with the more
widespread literacy following the introduction of an alphabetic script, a
development that would have led to increased reflexivity (Thrower 1980:
62).[7]

China has a similar history of doubt. Buddhism spread from south to
east Asia. Early Buddhists in south Asia held certain practices in common,
such as the rejection of sacrifice and of caste. They denied the existence of
God (though not always of the supernatural) but they disagreed on the subject of transmigration. For the doubters, 'no one . . . has ever observed the
transference of consciousness from one body to another'. But China had its
own indigenous tradition of doubt. Well before the advent of Buddhism, in
the Spring and Autumn period (722–481 BCE) we meet in the *Tso-huan* evidence of those who have lost their belief in supernatural beings and even in
the 'Way of Heaven'. 'The Way of Heaven is distant, while that of man is
near. We cannot reach the former; what means have we of knowing it?'
(Legge 1872: 671, quoted Thrower 1980: 106). Later explanations by means
of *yin* and *yang* (*c.* fourth century BCE) implied a naturalistic as distinct
from a theological view of the universe, which was subsequently incorporated into much of Daoist thinking. Lao Tzu, the supposed founder of this
native religion of China, subsequently advocated what has been called a
'pantheistic naturalism' in which the *Dao* was the whole order of nature.
However, the Chinese generally avoided abstract speculation about
absolute values or concepts like 'nature'. Nor was there any absolute distinction between this world and the next, so that it would be a mistake to
oppose belief and unbelief in too sharp a manner; both could be present in
one speaker.

---

[7] See also Morris (1990), who sees Sankhya philosophy as being a learned expression of popular materialism. It was founded by Kapila, who rejected the notion of a supreme being; his
ideas appear to have influenced Buddhism.

While Confucius recognised the existence of an impersonal Heaven, spirits and ghosts, he maintained what Joseph Needham has described as a 'worldly social-mindedness' and adopted an agnostic attitude to the supernatural as well as to his own knowledge. He was primarily interested in things of this world, which was what could best be understood. In Weber's opinion, Confucianism is more rational than any other ethical system except that of Jeremy Bentham. That notion is often espoused by recent Chinese and other intellectuals. However, this view of his rationality certainly has to be modified (as does that of Western rationality), partly because the separation of the domains of the sacred and the secular was not as clear as in the later West. Confucius was interested in the practice of rites (including ancestral ones) rather than in religious beliefs; as we have seen in ancient Greece and Rome, a measure of doubt is inevitably associated with the hopes that such practices often fail to realise.

Confucius did not stand alone and was followed by many others of a critical turn of mind, of whom the most outstanding in this context was probably Wang Ch'ung (27–97 CE), whose general scepticism discounted the whole basis of the systems of divination and divine communication. Heaven and Earth do not listen to prayers; they do not reply to questions. His line of thinking was continued by many others. As Needham (1956: 386) remarks: 'Throughout subsequent Chinese history the sceptical tradition runs on.' This continuity of the literate counter-culture is critical. It was developed by some neo-Confucians of the Sung (960–1279 CE) in opposition to the strength of Buddhism and popular religion, as well as by various scientifically inclined individuals, right down to the seventeenth century when China came into contact with the Western science brought there incongruously by Jesuit missionaries.

So while the term 'agnosticism' was an invention of nineteenth-century Europe, indeed of England but derived from the Greek, the kind of doubt it embodies is not confined to the post-Enlightenment West. It was not uniquely associated with what Weber referred to as 'Western rationality' and the disenchantment of the world, nor yet with the European heritage going back to the Greeks. As a developed tradition it is also found in the other major literate cultures as a complement to their formal rationality. That is not to say that scepticism is applied to all topics equally at all times and all places. Even in contemporary societies there are plenty of situations in which some citizens doubt (and perceive as irrational) what others passionately believe. That is the essence of a plural culture. Some consider that not enough scepticism is applied, whether to political, religious or psychological doctrines. Others acquiesce in established beliefs. But opposition has always existed, although time has certainly seen an extension of the boundaries of 'rationality', doubt, scepticism and agnosticism, to ever-widening realms of knowledge, if not always to day-to-day behaviour.

Another theme to which I earlier referred was that scepticism was not in my view confined to literate societies, though it has been significantly developed there into a persisting alternative tradition. In our original argument Watt and I did not deny a measure of scepticism to oral cultures, but we wanted to call attention to its efflorescence in literate ones. One of the central functions of writing has been to make the implicit explicit. In this case a tradition (or counter-tradition) of scepticism emerges within written cultures, whereas in oral ones such doubting thoughts tend to get swallowed up (and renewed) in each generation. But contrary to the superficial opinions of some observers, not everyone in oral cultures believes what they are told, any more than in Tudor England. It is often considered that non-literate cultures are ones in which the members inevitably believe in local gods, as automatically as they speak the local language. That it is part of the custom which, as Montaigne declared and as Fortes approvingly reminded us, was sucked in with one's mother's milk. That view was reinforced by Durkheim's notion of solidarity, especially mechanical solidarity, in the simpler, undifferentiated societies, in which deviant notions would be eliminated in a kind of homeostatic process whereby the oral memory erased what it found uncomfortable (Halbwachs 1925; Bartlett 1932; Goody and Watt 1963). However, doubts do exist about the efficacy and even the existence of gods. The presence of such doubt even among hunter-gatherers is delightfully illustrated by an aboriginal song from the Northern Territory, Australia:

> The God-men say when die go sky
> Through pearly gates where river flow
> The God-men say when die we fly
> Just like the eagle, hawk and crow –
> Might be, might be; I don't know.
>
> (quoted Flew 1974: 312)

The song is obviously influenced by Christianity but it nevertheless displays an embryonic scepticism, by which I mean that in the absence of writing such doubts were not embodied in an independent tradition of thought but tended to get overwhelmed in each generation by the dominant ideological mode.

That situation is more general, despite appearances to the contrary. Anthropologists often see themselves as specialists in systems of beliefs. They record ideas about this world and the next, whether in the shape of myths or mythologies, the latter informally expressed, the former formally recited, which are elicited in answers to their probing questions. That data constitute the basis of many books on the religious systems of such and such a people. The results are expressed in a monograph on the religion of a particular group, of a specific culture, as a system of beliefs and practices common to all.

There are two major problems with this approach. Firstly, religious beliefs are not totally circumscribed by communities and states. It is true that 'primitive' religions – that is, the beliefs of oral cultures – tend to get defined by the place, the ethnic group, whereas in written cultures they are defined by a scriptural tradition, a set of texts that are read by various peoples and travel independently. Buddhism, Islam and Christianity are not 'tribal' religions. They are ones that involve conversion, change, and hence the discarding and discontinuance of a previous set of beliefs and practices. There is some discarding of these in oral African religions too, but on a more particularistic level. Beliefs in one medicine shrine may be discarded in favour of another, and I have argued that this turn-over has been a long-standing feature of African religions, not simply an outcome of the 'contact situation', though this contact with the West undoubtedly added a further dimension (Goody 1957).

These beliefs tend to be seen and defined in ethnic terms. The Asante practise Asante religion; no one else does. Yet objectively beliefs are not always strictly limited in this way, for not only do medicine shrines travel across ethnic boundaries, indicating their acceptability on both sides, but facets of divination or sacrifice are also understood and accepted by travellers to neighbouring communities. Moreover, in West Africa the outside observer can perceive many similarities in the beliefs and practices pertaining to the Earth, to the ancestors, to the beings of the wild, the High God, the rain and the sun, not to speak of similarities in symbolic and narrative usages (see for example Parrinder 1961). We are not dealing with wholly different entities, unless we choose to define them as such. That we often do, as the observer normally works with one particular group and takes on their perception of difference, tied in with their identity.

Defining religion in ethnic terms means asserting, on the basis of normative utterance, what the LoDagaa believe in. We take these utterances, these replies to our questioning or these statements in formal ritual situations, and we construct from them an integrated system of belief and practice, a structure of positive assertions. The result is that the belief systems of the simpler societies are often contrasted with those of literate or 'modern' cultures in terms of the commitment made by individuals to those beliefs. This is clearest in the contrast made by many philosophers of such a world view with that of the Enlightenment, in which doubt and questioning were accepted as an intrinsic facet of rationality. Indeed as we have seen, for some scholars Western rationality began at that moment. I have argued elsewhere (1993b; 1996a: chapter 1) that this notion of rationality is far too ethnocentric. Formal rationality of the Aristotelian kind is intrinsically literate, but it is not confined to alphabetic scripts and is certainly not limited to the Western tradition. There is I believe a significant difference here between literate and oral cultures. That does not mean that informal rationality or logic, the ability to utilise sequential reasoning, does not exist in oral cultures. It certainly does. So too does an element of doubt and questioning. But that countercurrent does not always emerge, since the holistic approach of the ethnographer to custom, to normative situations, to *moeurs*, tends to exaggerate that other side of the coin and to neglect the absent, the failure, the doubt.

That doubt is brought about by (among other things) perceptions of the failure of supernatural agencies always to deliver what is expected of them. The God who failed is a feature of simple as of complex societies. In West Africa it leads to the obsolescence of some shrines that are rejected in favour of new ones and hence results in a turn-over of gods. Not the major agencies in the case of West Africa, but of minor ones, of what have been called medicine shrines. That is also true of systems of divination, which are necessarily procedures that are likely to go wrong. Evans-Pritchard and others have written of the ways of coping with unacceptable or mistaken results – ignoring the prediction, fiddling the oracle, trying another practitioner – but they have tended to see the belief system itself as untouched, with its credibility continuing to be maintained. That is not altogether the case, since whole systems of divination change, greater credibility being placed in the new rather than in the old (see Goody 1975). In other words, substitution is made in the techniques of determining the truth (*yel miong* in LoDagaa). Among the LoDagaa these techniques are often associated with the beings of the wild (*kontome*), but these agencies are, as the Myth of the Bagre shows, as capable of concealing as of revealing the truth. Sometimes they confuse the results of divination, and hence in the invocation to the recitation of the myth the Bagre deity is addressed as 'the lying god'. A central theme of the first Black Bagre I recorded is that these beings have led mankind away from God's path, to which the performance of the Bagre was bringing humanity back (Goody 1972a).

In discussing the Azande, Evans-Pritchard (1937) writes of faith tempered by scepticism, and Lewis (1986: 18) has perceptively discussed 'the key importance of the skeptical informant who, being partly external to, or unconcerned in, a given situation, can stand back and take a more dispassionate, and in our terms "objective", view of what is happening'. I would go further than attributing scepticism to an outsider's view; it seems to me intrinsic to the nature of religious belief itself.

While I have just suggested that in West Africa it was largely the minor deities that were rejected and replaced, doubt can spread yet further, even to the High Gods themselves. In the Near Eastern religions, God is approached by prayer and supplication to meet the needs of mankind. In Africa, that God is a *deus otiosus* who created the Universe and then effectively retired from active participation in the doings of this world. But the notion of a Creator God who takes no further interest in his creation contains the ever-present possibility of change, as does that of a God who is able to help humankind but does not always do so. Both contain contradictory elements that can lead people to doubt and then to take up an opposed belief. In the African case, humans may be led to call directly upon God to exercise the powers he had earlier displayed. In one such case I observed, a new cult, that of the Little God which was spreading to the LoDagaa and neighbouring groups, offered the possibility that God would return to sweep away the evils of the world, especially witchcraft, creating a breach in the prevailing conceptual scheme (Goody 1975). Equally the omnipotent God of the Near East does not always choose to exercise his powers, potentially creating doubts in the minds of men as to whether he really possesses them, and possibly giving rise to agnosticism and even to atheism.

Doubts about deities exist in virtually all societies. It is true in polytheistic schemas that this often leads to a search for new cults, whereas in monotheistic religions (which are religions of the Book) the alternative may be exit rather than voice, the adoption of new loyalties, although one way out may be offered by a shift of sect, a change of patron saint, or by blaming one's own faith or the priesthood rather than one's god. Nevertheless doubt breeds doubt. A 'counter-cultural' tradition emerges.

In this discussion I have indicated some broad lines of long-term development. Aristotelian logic, associated with the growth of Greek science, was one of these, though it had its parallels elsewhere. The emergence of modern science was certainly another; although it had its links with medieval enquiry, both in Europe and elsewhere, new standards of investigation, proof and scholarly communication were established, not unconnected with the use of movable type to print an alphabetic script.

Literacy had earlier made possible the development of a more continuous tradition of sceptical enquiry. It seized on elements present in oral cultures, where some measure of doubt already existed. That component has been partly concealed, though not among the best ethnographers (such as Siegfried Nadel in his analysis of Nupe religion) because of the nature of anthropological enquiry. That enquiry looks for the presence rather than the absence, and the mental sets and procedures of the anthropologists may lead them to search for committed beliefs, for norms and certainties, in contrast to the greater uncertainties of contemporary life, especially in the religious sphere. Both factors induce a certain methodological and conceptual laziness, which can be countered by fully taking into account Huxley's post-Darwinian doubts, that is, his agnosticism.

What is the relationship between doubts about the supernatural (agnosticism) and the cognitive contradictions that I perceive in other forms of representations, such as iconic ones (Goody 1996b, 1997)? Supernatural agencies are of course representations, in the mind, in speech, in writing, in icons. The fact that religious icons are sometimes prohibited is an indication of the tension that may surround the representation of the immaterial by the material. But a measure of tension also emerges when one is dealing with words about deity. Why does the omnipotent choose not to exercise his omnipotency? Why does the good create the bad? How does sacrifice and prayer communicate? How does communion transform? These problems of understanding both the world and ourselves allow of several outcomes. The deist view has its difficulties or its complexities. So too does the materialist. Doubts often arise about the validity of any particular solution because of the cognitive contradictions involved in each. Such contradictions arise out of the human situation of having to represent in language the experience of that world and one's participation in it. Gods are created by language; so too are doubts about their existence. Both gods and doubts are widespread, transversal if not universal aspects of culture, the result not of inbuilt processes but of the interaction of talking men with their social and natural environment.

Questioning was in fact built into the human situation in which language-using animals create representations of entities to help deal with their intellectual, social and psychological needs, whose status is open to doubt. There are cognitive (and other) contradictions involved in the conceptualisation of supernatural beings, whose presence can only be deduced from their possible effects. Such dilemmas involve doubts as well as doctrines; agnosticism is part of the social universe that humanity creates for itself by the very use of language, which re-presents experience in a totally transforming way, and always contains a kernel of doubt.

NOTE

I want to acknowledge my great indebtedness to the work of James Thrower on unbelief and the alternative tradition. I am also most grateful to Joe McDermott and Malcolm Schofield for their comments.

Chapter 12

MAN AND THE NATURAL WORLD: REFLECTIONS ON HISTORY AND ANTHROPOLOGY

When I first began to work in the social sciences, history was a field from which anthropology wished to set itself apart. Now every other title in a series I help to edit includes the word 'history'. It is important to understand how this change has taken place.

The earlier separation did not arise because Malinowski and the other functionalists, structuralists or structural-functionalists agreed with Henry Ford that 'history was bunk'. They were concerned with two points. The first had to do with the kind of attention to the past that many of their predecessors had given. The so-called evolutionists (not a very good description) had concentrated, to use the title of one of E. B. Tylor's books, on *The Early History of Mankind*. So too had lawyers like L. H. Morgan of Rochester, NY, whose long-range reconstructions of social life were later taken up by Marxist writers, especially in the USSR. That interest in *la très longue durée* was also a feature of the work of Herbert Spencer and other sociologists, and it was clearly influenced in a general way by archaeological and biological discoveries of the post-Darwinian era.

This approach was rejected by many anthropologists who followed, for very specific reasons. Firstly, the paucity of available evidence meant that these reconstructions of early social life were often highly speculative, based on the use of somewhat unsystematic methods of comparison and an atomistic view of human society. For these were armchair anthropologists who had little idea of how societies worked, how the pieces they were playing with fitted or didn't fit together. As a result of the Darwinian success they tended to bring in, to impose, 'evolutionary' or developmental explanations when these were not warranted. For example, there was the well-known attempt to explain the many customs displaying a resistance to marriage on the part of women, typified in the earlier British practice of carrying the bride over the threshold. These widespread customs were interpreted as survivals of an earlier form of marriage by capture. The alternative approach that the functionalists offered was to see this behaviour in terms of the changing structural position of adult women, a kind of institutionalised reluctance to move (she had to be seen to be unwilling) especially when entering a virilocal marriage where residence was determined by the man's location. The earlier explanations were referred to as pseudo-history by the fieldworking structural-functionalists who followed, and were firmly rejected. There were never the same objections to the kind of historical reconstruction of the recent past of particular non-literate peoples that Boas, the American anthropologist, went in for – what is sometimes called ethnohistory. Nevertheless the shift to professional fieldwork in other cultures meant there was now a concentration on how things work rather than how they came to be as they are (or were); you analysed what was going on under your eyes. Moreover, since this fieldwork was mainly carried out among non-literate peoples, even as far as the past was concerned there was more interest in how notions of it were manipulated or represented, in myth, legends, genealogies – that is, in the actor's view of the past – rather than in narrative history of the academic kind. For many historians, on the other hand, anthropology was either too general, like other social sciences, or else dealing with so-called 'primitives' who were outside the range of historical enquiry and, by definition, uninteresting.

I present this thumbnail sketch to explain how it was that history and anthropology came to be separated from one another. But it was not a very deep divide. For there were always some anthropologists who crossed it, especially those influenced by Marx and Weber, and those who were interested in long-term change. For historians, L. H. Morgan's schema of the development of marriage and kinship made its impact by way of Engels when he sketched out his notion of the general development of human society, especially regarding private property, including sexual property. In this way that schema influenced early developments in studies of women and the family, although family history probably owes more to Engels' own early work on *The Condition of the Working Class in England* (1845). On quite another topic Sir James Frazer's discussion of sacred kingship in *The Golden Bough* was taken up by Marc Bloch in *Les Rois thaumaturges* (1924). Using the works of social anthropologists, later historians have added a dimension in their treatment of phenomena such as religious cults, social movements, carnevals, ritual more generally. There were other topics including the family and literacy in which there has been valuable collaboration between anthropologists and historians. A few years ago I worked in Paris at the great centre of French historical research founded by Marc Bloch, now called the Ecole des Hautes Etudes en Sciences Sociales. Every other course in history advertised there included the words 'Ethnologie' or 'Anthropologie', even to excess. But then that institution had been founded with the social sciences in mind (especially anthropology) in an attempt to modify the dominant traditions of political and narrative accounts towards the socio-cultural accounts favoured by the Annales School.

For just as anthropology was changing its emphasis over the century, so too was history. Through the revival of social history, it was increasingly taking into account the affairs of those who made minor appearances in the documents of state, especially the lower classes, the illiterate, the underprivileged, the ethnic minorities, as well as other neglected groups such as women, children and alternative sexualities. In order to create a history that included all these you had to examine sources which earlier scholars had overlooked, or even to draw upon the oral tradition and field enquiries in a way that brought history closer to anthropological practices.

So too did the extension of Western historical scholarship from the local and European past to that of the world as a whole. This broadening of academic history to include other major civilisations (India and especially China) meant that some practitioners had to take more seriously the study of other cultures, of other forms of social life. One could not work on India without some understanding of caste hierarchy, nor on China without coming up against comparative aspects of lineage and marriage. But the contact with anthropology became especially strong when history was extended to the new nations of sub-Saharan Africa and the Pacific, who were more different in structure and did not have the same depth of written tradition as the major civilisations of Europe and Asia. For this reason their past had been largely disregarded in academic circles; it had to be created by other means. The development of African history was mainly due to Africa itself, where around the time of Independence new universities and established secondary schools (following the lead of politicians and people) demanded a history of their own. Its extension to the curricula of the rest of the world followed, and the process gave authority to different methods of reconstructing the past. For in Africa it was necessary for those scholars who normally paid attention only to the written word to collect and evaluate oral as well as documentary sources, to look at the spoken as well as the written, at the utterance as well as the text.

The use of oral sources was not entirely new: little is. The father of (Greek) history, Thucydides, had already made use of personal recollections in his *History of the Peloponnesian Wars*. But formally trained historians became committed to documentary sources; the oral smacked of folklore, of sociology, of reportage. When it came, the change affected Europe as well. E. P. Thompson made use of folkloristic materials; those dealing with the twentieth century turned to oral accounts, especially of popular life (for example in the work of Raphael Samuel (1981) and others such as Ellen Ross (1983) on London's East End). Naturally the focus shifted from the literate middle classes to the not so literate working classes, to subaltern history, as it has been termed in India. And it had been stimulated by the enquiry of the anthropologist, Oscar Lewis, into what he called the culture of poverty in Mexico.

The result of these endeavours was to extend academic history to those whom Eric Wolf referred to as 'the peoples without history', meaning documented history; for while past and present are often closely intertwined in oral cultures, no society is really in the position that the anthropologist Boas described for the Eskimo, who were said to regard the world as if it had always been as it is now. All societies have some sense of the past, which it is an important part of an anthropologist's task to examine.

The scope of history was certainly broadened by this experience in more than one way. Historians of regions such as Africa inevitably had to try to evaluate the results of archaeological, linguistic and ethnological reports, as well as learning something about the analysis of non-literate societies. Indeed, in francophone countries much of the detailed historical work on local kingdoms, as well as more general studies of the past (for example, on slavery and warfare), has been carried out by people who have a foot in both camps: Terray, Meillassoux, C.-H. Perrot, Tarditz, Izard and others.

Equally, the reverse process was also taking place, with contemporary anthropologists taking up historical problems for a variety of reasons. Observational studies of so-called traditional societies that have not been swamped by the expansion of 'the world system' have become increasingly difficult. The reconstruction of earlier systems, as anthropologists of North America knew well, involves 'antiquarian' as well as observational skills. Moreover, administrative documents on the recent past have now become available to investigators in Africa in a way they never were (given a sixty-year closure on files) to a previous generation of scholars, whatever their theoretical outlook. In addition those anthropologists more interested in the contemporary rather than the 'traditional' scene are often concerned with the process of development, with social change, giving rise to a different kind of investigation, but one which again stresses the time dimension because a comparison is being made of the situation at time A with that at time B (possibly the future). Moreover, the very speed of recent changes is often of profound significance (at the conscious level) to the actors, to the human agents themselves, having affected the course of their own lives. Looking at this aspect of people's existence involves an increased attention to memory, to personal recollection and to the experience of individuals, subjects which form a focus of some recent 'cultural anthropology'.

An understanding of this dimension is important for a number of reasons. We need always to be on our guard against the misrepresentation of others, whether of the Oriental other or of the other next door (or even the other in our own house). The total avoidance of misrepresentation may well be beyond our capacities. But that is no reason for shirking the task, especially since the process of representing the other will continue, whatever we think or do about it. School children will be taught history and adults will make judgements about other cultures. It is surely the job (or one of the jobs) of the universities and others to make certain those products and those judgements are the best that it is within our power to make. We should not conclude, as some have done, that the way out is to throw up one's hands in despair or to take refuge in the indulgence of frankly fictional or personalised accounts. That may be a way out; it is no way forward.

It is time I turned from considering the past of scholarship to looking at what I see as *one* way – certainly not the only way – forward. The example I draw on inevitably has to do with my recent interests that concern the comparison of attitudes to nature and their relation to developments over time.

Recent anthropological discussions about nature have taken a variety of forms. Firstly, there has been the well-known structuralist dichotomy between nature and culture, often assumed to be a feature of all or most societies. That opposition in turn has been linked in various ways to the dichotomy male–female and other binary categories. I myself do not find that this approach has added greatly to our analytic armoury; indeed, I have argued that these decontextualised oppositions, for example between black (= night, witchcraft) and white (= day, openness), have been grievously misleading in understanding symbolic usage, leaving insufficient room for different contextual usage, for deliberate reversal and for inventive word-play, for what I call the black-is-beautiful problem.

Secondly, much work has been done on the way different cultures classify natural objects and link them by homologies to other classes or perceive them as anomalies. The work stems originally from that of Durkheim and Mauss on 'Primitive Classification', and one strand is exemplified in the influential studies of Mary Douglas on *Purity and Danger*.

Thirdly, there has been the ecological interest in the cultural exploitation of and adaptation to the environment that has been especially prominent in studies of hunters and gatherers. Such studies have told us much about the livelihood of these peoples, often implicitly praised for their respect of nature compared with our own more devastating attacks upon it.

These studies have dealt rather sketchily with attitudes to nature which are not easy to determine from the total flow of oral communication; it is a much easier task (though not necessarily easier to make an adequate assessment) when one selects a limited number of written texts such as the works of Gilbert White or Wordsworth's *Lyrical Ballads* as a basis for analysis. Again, little enough has been done to integrate such enquiries with the abundant material on modern societies, except for Scott Atran's work on classification in natural history and except for the work on the rural and urban gardens of ordinary people that has been carried out by French ethnologists. If I approach the question from quite a different perspective, that of wider cultural comparison, it is because I have been stimulated by historians who are concerned with developments in Europe, especially by Keith Thomas whose study is entitled *Man and the Natural World* (1983).

Those who were brought up on the work of the Romantic poets imbibed the view that England developed a special attitude to nature at about the time of the Industrial Revolution. Indeed, they saw a close connection between the advent of 'the dark Satanic mills' and William Blake's paean to England's 'green and pleasant land'. Earlier in the eighteenth century one aspect of the appreciation of nature had been directed towards the rural displays of cottage plots and the attempts of aristocratic gardeners to modify the formal layouts of the Renaissance and the Restoration (the first under Italian, the second under French influence). This attention was directed not so much to nature itself as to its cultural transformations.

The understanding of popular conceptions has been greatly refined as a result of Thomas' book. What I want to do is to offer some thoughts on how his thesis might be extended and modified by pushing the discussion outward to other societies (including non-literate ones) and backward to earlier ones – in other words by seeking help from comparative history and comparative sociology (or anthropology). I do this partly because it raises for me the question of the Uniqueness of the West in the process of modernisation (or industrialisation or capitalism) that is of prime concern not only to transcultural studies of an academic kind but also for understanding the world as it is today. I take Thomas' work as the focus partly because of its anthropological background (he was influenced by Evans-Pritchard, especially in his earlier work on *Religion and the Decline of Magic*) and because it carries me along the way I want to go, at least in considering the broader historical problems and setting them in wider framework.

The subtitle of Thomas' book is 'Changing attitudes in England, 1500–1800', and these changes are to be seen, he explains, in the growing number of people who 'had come to find man's ascendancy over nature increasingly abhorrent to their moral and aesthetic sensibilities'. The direction taken by English society during that period meant that the inhabitants of towns developed a new longing for the countryside so that the confident anthropocentrism of Tudor England was upset by 'the growing conflict between the new sensibilities and the material foundations of human society' (Thomas 1983: 300–3). Despite his characterisation of the general attitude in earlier periods, that nature was made for humanity, Thomas recognises that different views were evident in the sporadic naturalism of English medieval art, and yet earlier in the works of Aristotle. Nevertheless, early modern naturalists he claims 'developed a novel way of looking at things, a new system of classification, leading to subsequent changes in these man-centred attitudes' (p. 5).

Even before the modern period, we find not only some elements of naturalism but also important contrary currents of another kind: 'if we look below the surface we shall find many traces of guilt, unease and defensiveness about the treatment of animals'. Europeans, even the ancients, also knew something of the respect paid by Jains, Buddhists and Hindus to the lives of animals (though these views were often treated with 'baffled contempt'). The references are of course to earlier written cultures. Even locally in Europe, contrary attitudes to the eating of meat were earlier prevalent among Pythagoreans, Manicheans, Cathars, Lollards as well as among Benedictine monks. Moreover, in the earlier Tudor period, Thomas recognises that some 'hypersensitive persons' took up different positions about, for example, animal rights.

At the same time as acknowledging these contrary attitudes, Thomas also perceives a general shift of sentiment and attitude. For him the early modern period 'generated feelings which would make it increasingly hard for people to come to terms with the uncompromising methods by which the dominance of their species had been secured' (Thomas 1983: 302). These feelings are described as 'new sensibilities'. Equally he finds a 'new attitude to', 'a new kind of taste for', wild nature developing in the theological controversies of the early seventeenth century, with the English themselves going furthest in the process of the 'divinisation of nature' (pp. 259, 261). The author takes pains to defend himself against the charge that the charting of such developments may look like 'a Whiggish search for the intellectual origins of . . . the Friends of the Earth' (pp. 15–16). In its place he seeks to 'reconstruct an earlier mental world in its own right'. Nevertheless, despite this disclaimer and the contrary evidence he cites, he is committed to a specific chronological approach which includes the vectorial notion of the development of these ideas over time and in space. And since his discussion is about England, where the divinisation of nature went furthest, that notion of development cannot be dissociated from the idea of the emergence of that country as the first 'modern', capitalist and industrial nation.

We are presented with a difficult analytical and intellectual problem. On the one hand dramatic changes in attitudes are seen as taking place; on the other there is evidence of ambivalences that relates, as Thomas notes, to 'the material foundations of human society' (Thomas 1983: 302–3). There is change and there is continuity, and it is a question of sorting out the different elements and defining their nature. I want to argue that Thomas is essentially correct to point to earlier doubts about man's mastery of nature, and that this realisation should lead him to modify the penchant of the modern historian for seeing modern thoughts on these matters as first emerging at the time of the Renaissance. That is not to deny changing attitudes, but for evidence of ecological awareness we need to go back not only to earlier literate societies (from which he draws his example) but even to oral cultures. That is to say, we doubt whether these general attitudes concerning 'the divinisation of nature' or doubts about the way man treats it are linked to England, to Europe or even to literate civilisations. The basic dilemma leading to these doubts (and the associated reversals of attitude) lies in the human situation itself and the cognitive contradictions to which it gives rise in the human mind. On that let me turn to the anthropological evidence.

Many anthropologists would be inclined to draw a contrast between the integrated relationships between humanity and nature in the simpler cultures and the antagonistic ones in industrial societies. Clearly there are differences in the degree of integration or antagonism in such relationships, but some of these differences appear to be strongly linked to the calls on the material means at man's disposal at different periods. All societies are engaged in a struggle with nature. The destruction of wild life, the denuding of forests, the problems of erosion, these are to be found in simpler as well as in complex societies for they relate to their 'material foundations'. That does not imply the existence of an exclusively anthropocentric mentality in the earlier period; nature is often personified, at least in religious terms. We moderns have not invented worries about the exploitation of the natural world. Indeed, the so-called animist or nature-worshipping religions (I am deliberately using a nineteenth-century terminology) can be seen in this light, as part of a dialogue with and about nature (E. Goody 1994). For example, the agricultural LoDagaa, like many African peoples, interpose a category of being between men and gods that are called *kontome*, 'beings of the wild' as I render the term, 'fairies' as they are often called in West African English. In their long myth known as the Bagre, which includes an extended account of the origin of man and his culture, these beings are seen as intermediaries between the two, for they occupied the hills and rivers and forests long before mankind developed the cultivated spaces. Their herds are the wild animals, their food is gathered from the forest. But they also knew of the arts of civilisation, and it was they who taught the first man, one of two brothers, how to smelt iron, how to make a hoe, how to grow grain, how to shoot animals, how to fight. None of these cultural acquisitions was wholly unambiguous for humanity. And today the beings of the wild (who resemble in some uncanny ways those European creatures we moderns have set on one side as trolls or dwarfs and enshrined in Disneyland) exact from humans penitential sacrifices if they have killed certain of their flock or damaged certain of their trees. Such sacrificial offerings, which may weigh heavily on an individual, can surely be seen as an ecological payment for man's destruction of their habitat and their herds.

Early on in my stay in that society I was surprised to find a local friend reprimanding me for swatting a harmless insect, on the grounds that it was one of God's creatures, though he was not above exterminating in a violent fashion what he thought harmful. Such attitudes are often less explicit. I have argued that among the LoDagaa even the honourable destruction of human life, the shedding of blood in war, had to be ritually condoned (Goody 1962a). And that perhaps one aspect of the taboos whereby clans forbade the eating of one wild animal but consumed many others (that is, totemism in one of its varieties) had a similar role of apologising for the killing of living things by each clan preserving one species. The blood sacrifice of domestic animals, which was virtually the only way that meat was consumed by the LoDagaa, could also be regarded as sacralising the murder of a living being that had blood in its veins.

It is not only the destruction of animal life that causes second thoughts. Think too of the sacrifices, discussed by Sir James Frazer in *The Golden Bough*, to the dying but resurrected god, that were made in the Near East at the time of the cutting of the corn, for such an act was seen as the killing of the corn spirit. Even the harvesting of domesticated crops involved a slaughter of the living plant, which called for some spiritual redress. The harvest sacrifice was thus not merely a thanksgiving but an apology as well. In this sense it resembled the ritualised slaughter of meat in Judaism and Islam, to which the modern West often takes such exception. We butcher in a more rational, secular, 'humane' manner, leaving the apologies to be made, the doubts to be expressed, by the increasing number of vegetarians among us.

Such ambivalent attitudes, though widespread, are not necessarily universal, and they differ from place to place and from time to time. They are not embedded in the cultural or racial genes but arise out of the situation of the human actors in their contact with nature. In certain times and places, as among the followers of the Indic religions, such attitudes have long been much more developed than they are even in the modern, vegetarianised West. For some Westerners that is precisely the appeal of those creeds.

In other words the kinds of attitudes towards animals that are expressed in the Greek writer Porphyry's *De Abstinentia*, a tract partly directed against Christian omnivorousness, are examples of widespread feelings of ambivalence about humanity's relationships with the natural world. At different times and different places, one or other pole of this ambivalence is emphasised in a way that takes various forms depending on the particular cultural context and upon long-term trends. The relative weighting placed on these aspects is something for scholars to work out. But to describe recent changes in Europe or England as 'new feelings', much less 'new' 'mentalities', is to run the danger of overlooking the ambivalences of others and of attributing too much to Western modernity, and in the present case especially to England's contribution to its growth.

I have spoken so far of earlier and other ambivalences about the exploitation of nature. There is the further question of the straightforward appreciation of nature, which is often seen as a post-Renaissance development. For example, attitudes to wild nature, in particular to mountains, are seen as changing with Petrarch's visit to the Rhone valley in 1336 when he climbed Mont Ventoux, rising to a height of 1,912 metres. That attribution of a completely new mentality disregards not only the earlier concerns of the Romans but also the wider perspectives of cultural history. We find a largely non-anthropocentric attitude towards the wild, especially mountains, in the Chinese landscapes of the Tang period; that was seen as a place to which to retire from the troubles of this world, especially the political ones, encouraged by Daoist notions of the sacred mountain. Indeed, some of the drugs with which Daoists experimented are said to have created a compulsive desire to walk or climb; it has even been claimed that there is a connection between drug addiction and the early development of Chinese nature poetry (Hawkes 1989: 47). The realistic rendering of landscape, thought by Dubs to be the result of Roman influence on a Han battle scene, goes back much earlier, to tiles in a tomb at Nan-kuan in Honan and to a bronze *hu* from *c.* 300 BCE, where hunting and sea battles are depicted.

Despite the perceived differences between Eastern and Western landscape painters (the former being said to display 'an abridged realism impregnated with spirit', the latter 'a palpable naturalism'), there may well have been mutual influences, both then and later (see Sterling 1931; Cart 1960). The introduction of pictorial art into the Islamic culture of Safavid Persia in the fifteenth and sixteenth centuries certainly owed a great deal to Chinese influences brought by the Mongols to western Asia. That tradition in turn may have affected the painters of paradise gardens in Western Europe (Goody 1993a). The sixteenth century in Europe also saw the development of the specialised genres of still-life and landscape painting. Still-life had emerged in the Low Countries partly from the representations introduced in border illustrations to illuminated books. They included many 'oriental' features which came to Holland through the Eastern trade and made it a major centre for curios. Landscape painting developed from the tortuous backgrounds to Gothic art into more realistic landscapes later in the sixteenth century, a process that may have been influenced *by* the East, in a reversal of the suggested Roman importation *into* the East. A number of art historians have pointed to the analogues in composition between East and West at this time, and it has been suggested that Western art of the Renaissance may owe something to the pictorial motifs on eastern ceramics, textiles and lacquerware available from the fourteenth century onwards (Lach 1970: 73–4). The famous *têtes composées* of Arcimboldo (1527–93), in which natural objects were arranged into fantastic portraits of humans, may have been inspired by Mughal paintings of fantastic animals (Lach 1970: 77). None of this is at all certain, but the opening up of the Renaissance was certainly much more than a rebirth of Rome; it embodied and developed themes from other cultures, as is especially clear in the history of woodcuts and engravings, and earlier in textile design.

The influence of Asian designs on textiles in Byzantium and Western Europe was transmitted through Sassanid weavers of Persia from the third to the seventh centuries CE (see Lach 1970: 96). In late antiquity, 'In northern Europe, every great church was hung with Byzantine silks; . . . saints were inappropriately buried in shrouds of Persian silk, showing the griffins of Zoroastrian mythology and the hunting feats of pagan shahs in the Iranian plateau' (Brown 1971: 158). Knowledge of the silkworm had come to the Emperor Justinian through Soghdian middlemen in central Asia (a sub-Iranian society), who a century previously had sold Roman glass-making techniques to the emperor of China. 'Dragons, fabulous birds, and floral motifs from Chinese textiles . . . helped enrich European iconography and to give a rhythmical quality to Romanesque ornament', though this movement came to a temporary end with the rise of Islam and later with the domination of Gothic art in the thirteenth century. However, with the establishment of the European silk industry first at Palermo in the twelfth century (though Islamic Spain copied Egyptian textiles as early as the tenth century), then by 1300 on the Italian mainland and in the thirteenth century at Lucca, weavers borrowed directly from the motifs on Chinese textiles, flying birds, the lotus flower, waterfalls, rocks, stylised cloud forms, and often entire landscapes, to produce 'Tartar cloths'. This interchange of images between West and East in both directions argues for a broad similarity of approaches and conditions, rather than the dominance of one over the other. As with the scientific fields examined by Joseph Needham in his great series, *Science and Civilisation in China*, the traditions took roughly parallel courses over the long run, except for that remarkable dip in Western knowledge systems after the classical period and the subsequent rise beginning in the fifteenth.

My own direct interest in this topic has been of a more specific kind but concerned nonetheless with the West and the East, as well as with the North and the South. It was generated by noting the relative *absence* of the use of flowers in Africa as compared to India and Bali. It was not difficult to account for the difference in the use of domesticated flowers, since the first appearance of what I may loosely call an aesthetic as distinct from a utilitarian horticulture occurred at what it would be correct to see as a subsequent stage in the evolution of the agricultural economy than Africa had reached. It is true that this continent had adopted the use of metals but it had not developed many of the techniques that accompanied the second Agricultural Revolution of the earlier Bronze Age, namely, the intensive agriculture that involved the control of animal energy in ploughing and the control of water for irrigation. Productivity was and remains low, and the limits of the potential surplus discouraged the kind of attention that people, especially elites, could give to aesthetic matters. But the problem was more complicated than that because even wild flowers were little used compared to leaves, bark and roots, and that seems in part a question of safeguarding flowers as the harbingers of fruit, grain or berries, which was also a moral matter.

Asia was quite different from Africa. There flowers were actually cultivated for use as offerings to the gods, as festival decorations often connected with prosperity, as adornments for the living. Their representations played a prominent part in the great tradition of Chinese and Japanese painting, as well as on furniture, on carvings and in Buddhist temples. In Africa I have never witnessed flowers used for these purposes in traditional situations, though certainly changes are now occurring rapidly. Instead offerings to local gods were of food, drink or blood sacrifice, for which flowers in the Indic religions were an explicit substitute, representing one aspect of the rejection of the taking of animal life, just as that in turn represented in Abraham's case the rejection of the deliberate offering of human life.

In contrasting the use of cultivated flowers in Europe and Asia with their absence in most of Black Africa, except for the East African coast under Asian influences, I was struck by the fact that it was not only in Africa that the use of flowers had little of the attraction for human beings that is often seen as universal. Even in Europe and Asia there was some ambivalence and at times a rejection. For example, the intensive flower culture of the Ancient Mediterranean, especially in Rome, was viewed by many moralists as seriously flawed. Firstly, it was part of a culture of luxury (which the exploitation of nature for food rarely was in quite the same way) and hence of differentiation (the rich enjoyed flowers while the poor who grew them lacked the basic comestibles). Secondly, the production of flowers, especially in hothouses, was seen to be forcing nature into unnatural paths.

These trends were not dominant during the Roman period. But they were present and vigorously taken up by Christians, who also accepted the idea, the Judaic idea, that the offering of flowers to gods or to men was a pagan practice; the omnipotent God had no need of material gifts, only of prayer.

As a result of this ideological change and of concomitant economic factors, the culture of flowers in Europe experienced a drastic downturn in the Dark Ages. Not only the growth and use of flowers for religious purposes were affected, but also secular life too. That downturn was experienced in representation as well as reality, and had its effect on developments in botany, especially in comparison with the contemporary East, which was in many ways more advanced. Only with the high Middle Ages did the situation change in a major way, with the return of floral decoration to Gothic sculpture and in ecclesiastical services, and later with the writings of the German botanists of the fifteenth century.

But there was to be a subsequent rejection in the Reformation, especially by Puritans, who reverted to many of the ways of the early Church and restricted the use of flowers, not only in the meeting house and the burial ground. Such a heritage of denial lives on, not only in New England. Visitors to Europe are often struck by the staggering contrast between compact, colourful, much visited Italian cemeteries and the vast, deserted urban graveyards of North America. Moreover, the penetration of the Church into everyday life meant that even the garlands on the maypole, erected by one Thomas Merton (author of *The New Canaan*) in Mary Mount, Mass., in 1637, were likened by Governor Bradford (of the Plymouth Colony) to the offerings made by erring Israelites to the Golden Calf. That was one of the factors that made America, at least until relatively recently, a land of thin rather than thick rituals, not only in a floral sense but in others too.

Despite this setback at the time of the Reformation and in some other revolutionary situations, the culture of flowers in European societies since the Renaissance has experienced a remarkable expansion. That is still proceeding. With overseas conquests, new flora were brought back to Europe in large quantities, resulting in an elaboration of their classificatory schemata as well as of their gardens and symbolic structures (Atran 1990). World domination exported all of those features to other parts of the globe (Grove 1995). With the increasing ease of transport a world market was developed in cut flowers, so that today red roses nightly make the trip from Bogota, Colombia, to the United States and the Netherlands, from where they are distributed throughout Europe and even Asia. Today the production of flowers is shifting from the glasshouses on the outskirts of major Western cities to the farmlands of tropical countries, where they can be grown without the expenditure of fossil fuels on which the northern industry depends in the colder seasons. It is true that ambivalence, even opposition, is displayed by some critics, who would prefer to see people growing grain rather than cultivating geraniums. But such concerns have not stopped the expansion of the use of flowers as commodities that has brought some obvious benefits to the Third World. You take our grain, we take your roses, to paraphrase an epigram of Martial.

In Europe this expansion has proceeded from the late Middle Ages in what might be thought a Whiggish manner, linked to modernisation. There are even those cultural historians who see the English garden and love of flowers, a comparatively recent phenomenon, as an indication of a different 'mentality' from others on that or any other continent, even of a new attitude to nature. They also implicitly link such achievements, like those of the Romantic poets, with the potentiality in England for becoming 'the first industrial nation', the spearhead of modernity. But while there were important developments in the culture of flowers in England, Europe and the West generally, we have to interpret these against the wider background of the great falling off that had taken place following the Roman period. That decline heightens the impression of dramatic cultural advance in the modern period, whereas in fact much of this burst of activity involved catching up with the cultures of the East, indeed with the past of Mediterranean Europe, before it suffered from doubts about the use of flowers under early Christianity. When this burst was viewed against its earlier past, a 'new' attitude towards flowers might be said to have emerged in Europe. But it was not a new attitude, a new mentality, a new view of nature, in any global sense. Both the love of flowers and the ambivalence about flowers had been present earlier in other cultures of luxury that preceded the shift to the late industrial cultures of affluence, of mass consumption. We find similar doubts expressed in China by philosophers anxious about the poor, in folk-tales worried about forcing nature, and during the Cultural Revolution, in criticism of luxury cultures and concern about filling the peasant's rice bowl.

Turning back to Thomas' *Man and the Natural World*, I argued that both anthropological and historical efforts have been weakened by a failure to take into account what the other half were doing. Anthropologists tended to see nature and culture as too harmoniously related in the simpler societies, overlooking evidence of the kind of ambivalence and even guilt that are often seen as attached to later societies. Modern historians tended to see new feelings towards nature emerging in their chosen period, whereas some implicit realisation of the basic problem of control and exploitation is certainly present in simpler societies, both in the past and in the present. There is a second point which emerged in my discussion of the cultural history of flowers. For many historians their view of development, of progress even, is closely tied to notions of the Enlightenment, of capitalism, and hence often enough of England, Europe or the West. Important events happened in that country and that continent since the Renaissance. But as I argued in dealing with flowers, and the same is perhaps more widely true of attitudes to nature, part of what from a local point of view seems to be a rapid advance towards the modern, was in fact a catching up with other great traditions, earlier as well as wider. We cannot understand what is happening in the modern world, especially the East, if we remain committed to a Weberian, Marxist or folk view about the deep structure of East–West differences. Those misunderstandings may not affect all our work in any direct fashion, but they do so indirectly because of the inevitably ethnocentric academic tradition in which we have been raised.

Particularly towards flowers we found ambivalent attitudes, especially in societies with advanced agriculture, with stratification, with writing and with cultures of luxury. Under certain circumstances, religious or revolutionary, puritanical or socialist, objections to their use may become dominant, as we saw was also the case with the use of animals for human consumption. Such ambivalences have both a continuing and a changing dimension; for that reason we cannot readily describe them in terms of changes of mentality. They are new feelings, sentiments or attitudes only in a specific context, not in the broader picture of comparative history, sociology or psychology. They were available to and often expressed in

Oriental civilisations, and only superficially have anything to do with the growth of the market, the division of labour, the industrialisation of production that we refer to as the development of capitalism and that we link with the rise, indeed the Uniqueness, of the West.

There are *other* changes, not in the structure of sentiments, but in use, symbols and marketing, that are linked to these wider developments in economy and society. It is the job of comparative history and comparative anthropology (or sociology) to explore which is which. But this cannot be done from the perspective of one time and place, nor yet from one discipline. The Uniqueness of the West can only be determined by looking seriously at the *other* as well as at ourselves.

Chapter 13

CREATION AND EVOLUTION

When invited to give the Frazer lecture, one of my distinguished predecessors remarked to me that the main problem was to find enough good to say about his work to fill the hour. That has never been my problem. Perhaps because I belonged to an alternate rather than an adjacent generation, so that Frazer was a benign grandfather rather than an authoritarian father. Perhaps because I was led to him by literary studies, by the notes to T. S. Eliot's great poem, *The Waste Land* (1922), for Frazer made a deep impact on the wider intellectual scene in the way that has not been given to any subsequent anthropologist writing in English. Eliot remarked that one work 'has influenced our generation profoundly; I mean *The Golden Bough* . . .'. And that takes its place alongside Dante, Baudelaire, Webster, Ovid and many others as a source of imagery and allusion. Perhaps because, as a result of this reference, I read *The Golden Bough* (1911–15 [1890]) as a prisoner of war, and it was one of the factors influencing me to take up anthropology back at the University. In any case I have always regarded Frazer as a major scholar and often found much of interest in his work. The generation of my predecessors, and many who followed, derided 'the comparative method', not only Frazer's but any other, preferring to carry out intensive fieldwork and to make their comparisons by stealth rather than openly, or perhaps thinking that a study of their particular tribe could provide the answers to all the questions one could reasonably ask. That was the period of fieldworker authoritarianism. I am wholly in favour of fieldwork but to insist that it is the sole avenue for enquiries about the social life of humankind has diminished anthropology both as an intellectual enterprise and in its relation with the outside world.

In recent years my own work has occasionally been referred to as

Frazerian, usually in a pejorative way, for two reasons. Firstly, to suggest that anthropologists should be concentrating on their fieldwork, just as historians should not stray outside their own documents. For some enquiries that suggestion might constitute sound advice, but its value clearly depends upon the question in hand. If that question has to do with, say, the nature of human cognition, then to limit one's enquiries on rationality to one group raises profound difficulties. In any case, the notion that to adopt one method (intensive research) implies the rejection of others (extensive enquiry) may be excusable as a polemic, to alter the balance of academic power at a particular moment in time; as a recipe for accumulating knowledge it is disastrous.

The other direction from which criticism has come has been the reaction to what has been described as Frazer's 'intellectualist' approach, which so many since Durkheim have rejected in favour of a symbolic interpretation of earlier beliefs, a search for deep structure or meaning while rejecting the surface meaning as 'absurd'. Once again I have no quarrel with the search for so-called deeper levels, but meaning to the actor, the intellectual meaning of such beliefs, is an essential, indeed primary, component of any understanding. For the constant 'why' questions also crop up in an oral society as they do in our own, even if less insistently.

We have recently seen psychologists taking up the Frazerian classification of sympathetic magic, which some have regarded as laws of thought (Ruzin and Nemeroff 1990). That is a remarkable reversal of the disdain in which such notions were held by many anthropologists in the following generation. It does not need me to try and rehabilitate Frazer. His importance is evident from the influence he had on the literary, the popular as well as the scholarly worlds. I want to insist that even today ideas are to be found in his work that can be profitably followed up.

The pendulum has definitely begun to swing back regarding 'intellectualism' too. Frazer raised these cognitive questions which Durkheimian sociology set resolutely aside. There were some gains in restricting the field. In praising Radcliffe-Brown's approach to the study of ritual in the 1950s, Fortes pointed out that it was not what beliefs expressed in the symbolic, or intellectual, sense that preoccupied him but what they did in defining social structure; the main issue is not 'the ostensible purpose of a totemic rite . . . which we know to be futile . . . but the contribution made by the rite to the "maintenance of that order of the universe of which man and nature are interdependent parts"', that is, the 'maintenance of the "network of social relations binding individuals in an ordered social life"' (Fortes 1955: 27). Even 'higher religions', as Srinivas' study (1952) of the Coorgs shows, could be examined free of 'the crippling trammels of theology, metaphysics and philology and brought within the realm of social science'. This approach, he claims, frees the study of religion from the recourse to conceptual history and from 'unwarranted assumptions about the working of the mind and emotions of a hypothetical savage'. That does not mean, he goes on, that other frameworks are irrelevant. But to mix them results in confusion, and in any case, the approach he advocates constitutes 'the indispensable first step in the scientific study of ritual customs and institutions in all societies'. Perhaps. But it is certainly time we took steps other than the first, and it is gratifying to see that is being done by French scholars such as Sperber, Atran and Boyer, who have begun again to look at cognitive 'universals' and to account for them in a broadly Chomskian manner as built-in to the human mind. The approach I want to put forward here is somewhat different from theirs, but it is offered to deal only with a certain range of problem, not with built-in universals of the kind these authors are tackling but related to what I see as widespread contradictions not built into the mind but arising from the situation of language-using animals, some universal, some confined to a range of societies (for example, what I call luxury cultures) that raise a kernel of doubt, ambivalence, for some actors about a particular belief or procedure and lead in a generative way to the search for an alternative.[1] The seeds of these cultural changes are embedded within internalised cultures.[2]

To discover the distribution of such cognitive elements one has to turn to comparative research. A comprehensive study by the Manuels, *Utopian Thought in the Western World* (1979), begins with the statement that dreams of the Blessed Isles are found in all cultures. If that were true, it would be an interesting fact about human culture, about capacities to understand the world and possibly about the human mind, of which some might wish to claim it as an in-built feature. Clearly one can only test the proposition by comparative research (if you like, of a Frazerian kind). It is

---

[1] On the notion of luxury, see the various references in the collected works of Marx.
[2] I use the words 'ambivalence' and 'contradiction' here in a way that carries no specific psychodynamic or Hegelian significance, though I think there is a relationship with those usages. Tension would at times be preferable than contradiction. The ambivalences may be temporarily resolved by paradoxes or in other ways, but the potentiality for change rests embedded in the situation.

of little use examining intensively one village, one group, one society, in order to perform 'a critical experiment', since presence in any one would tell you nothing about the distribution of this notion in the whole range of human societies. Only a survey could do that.

What one is likely to find from such an undertaking is not universality but, rather, a widespread distribution in certain regions or in certain types of society. That distribution is likely to be interrupted. In this instance few African groups would appear to have notions of Utopia; in the strict sense, those are more characteristic of Bronze Age (or post-Bronze Age) societies. So the problem of explanation for this kind of manifestation (though it may be considered to belong to a wider category of such beliefs with universal implications) can take neither a universalistic (non-cultural) nor a particu-laristic (local cultural) form, since a group of societies appears to be involved. Any explanation has rather to be phrased in terms of the inter-action between potentialities and environment, that is, the potentialities of cognition, of the understanding of the world in relation to certain cultural and material environments.

In *Folklore in the Old Testament* (1918), Frazer opened up a number of topics for discussion on subjects that have attracted many subsequent anthropologists (including Schapera, Fortes, Leach and Douglas). To me his chapter on 'Jacob's Marriages' was very insightful and provided a lead into examining the relation between marriage, property and inheritance in the Near East, especially with regard to women (Goody 1990, chapter 11). In this chapter I want to turn to his discussion of the ways that so-called 'primitive peoples' have viewed the origin of the world, and then to discuss these wider data in terms of my own field research, as well as in the light of cognitive processes of understanding.

Frazer looks at a large number of stories about the origin of the world, which he divides into two groups relating to 'creation' and 'evolution'. These he sees as two alternative methods of accounting for the emergence of mankind. Either there was a sudden cataclysmic creation of man as a sep-arate species or there was a gradual process of differentiation from other living creatures. He concludes,

> The foregoing examples may serve to illustrate two very different views which primitive man has taken of his own origin. They may be distinguished as the theory of creation and the theory of evolu-tion. According to the one, the human race was fashioned in its

present form by a great artificer, whether god or hero; according to the other, it was evolved by a natural process out of lower forms of animal or even vegetable life. Roughly speaking, these two theories still divide the civilized world between them. The partisans of each can appeal in support of their view to a large consensus of opinion; and if truth were to be decided by weighing one consensus against the other, with Genesis in the one scale and *The Origin of Species* in the other, it might perhaps be found, when the scales were finally trimmed, that the balance hung very evenly between creation and evolution.

(Frazer 1918: i, 44)

In fact things are not as evenly balanced as he suggests because the evolutionary tendency is not as clear-cut as he asserts. Of the thirty stories which Frazer selects as demonstrating evolutionary beliefs, in only five is it stated that the idea applies to the tribe, the people, the major designated group, as a whole. In the other cases it is quite specifically particular clans or unilineal descent groups which trace their ancestry to particular animals, one aspect of totemism. Indeed, the very tracing of this line serves to differentiate the clan segmentally from similar groups within the society, not to associate themselves with the rest of mankind as is the case with the doctrine of evolution. It might be the case that some of the tribes (the ethnic groups) mentioned do differentiate themselves in such a way from their neighbours, by reference to certain animals with which they establish an identity. This association can take the form simply of a prohibition on killing the animal or upon eating its flesh, that is to say, of hunting or food taboos. In such a way, Jews were distinguished as a socio-religious grouping by reference to their rejection of the flesh of the pig without involving any notion of descent. One early bishop declared that Christians do not eat horses and were distinguished by that (see chapter 7).

Such distinguishing prohibitions of clans tend to be given a short narrative framework, just as the characteristics of many animals are often set within the frame of an explanatory tale, a sort of *Just So* story. The particular association between social group and animal may be seen in terms of descent or else in terms of friendship; in the latter case the obligation is to help preserve some being who has earlier assisted an ancestor. Among the LoDagaa, patrilineal clans are associated with a range of prohibitions of many kinds. Where these concern animals, the explanatory tale recounts how the original ancestor of the clan found himself in difficult circumstances and was assisted by the animal in question. That is a common theme in West African 'totemic' beliefs. But sometimes I have also heard members of a clan claim the member of the animal species itself as an ancestor or a 'brother' and refer to it by a kinship term.

Note that such a belief in descent from animals is not for them inconsistent with the idea of man's creation by a High God. In other words, Frazer's alternatives are not in fact alternatives, for these beliefs may, and indeed frequently do, exist side by side in different contexts. Not only among the LoDagaa but in many parts of Africa beliefs of a 'totemic' nature are maintained at one and the same time as a theory of creation. The radical incompatibility exists only within Frazer's frame of reference, which assumes the desirability of a homogeneous world view. The fact that they can coexist, however, may raise problems of cognitive contradiction.

Frazer himself points to examples of the coexistence of these beliefs among the Australian aborigines. He writes:

> In a sense those speculations of the Arunta on their own origin may be said, like a similar myth of the Samoans, to combine the theory of creation with the theory of evolution; for while they represent men as developed out of much simpler forms of life, they at the same time assume that this development was affected by the agency of two powerful beings, whom so far we may call creators.
>
> (Frazer 1918: i, 43–4)

Indeed, Frazer saw the savage Arunta of central Australia as having 'a similar theory' to the civilised Greeks of Sicily, as propounded by the Greek philosopher, Empedocles. 'Both represent groupings of the human mind in the dark abysses of the past; both were in a measure grotesque anticipations of the modern theory of evolution' (Frazer 1918: i, 44).

In contrast to Frazer I do not assume that beliefs in creation and evolution are alternatives, but that the notions behind both are an essential feature even of oral societies, though ones that raise cognitive problems. Each culture is bound to offer some explanation of the emergence of the human species because people raise that question; it is posed by the very process of what Eliot referred to as 'birth and copulation and death'. The answer has to recognise that there are some points at which humanity is continuous with the animal world. Monkeys look like us; other animals act like humans and vice versa. They fall in the same category of living things to which anthropomorphic notions are often appropriate: they eat, we eat; they walk, we walk. In addition there is the symbiotic relationship of man and domesticated animals. Beyond that there are quasi-mystical notions that inspire many animal lovers among us. In one sense, as Heckewelder wrote of the American Indians in 1819 but which is a more general attitude, 'all animated nature, in whatever degree, is in their eyes a great whole, from which they have not yet ventured to separate themselves'.[3] This was the aspect of totemic beliefs that was emphasised by Durkheim and by Radcliffe-Brown.

It has been suggested by psychologists, and accepted by the important group of cognitive anthropologists I mentioned, that we have a built-in capacity to recognise living kinds, as distinct from artefacts. Certainly there is widespread acknowledgement of the relationship of humans with animals. Man is patently kin to the beasts. And it is not only the theologians of Western Europe who have considered the problem of whether animals have 'souls'. At the same time, the social organisation of humans is so much more complex than theirs that from this point of view human life is of a different order. To such an extent does it differ that he or she has perhaps been created independently by an omnipotent being. The structure of the pre-Darwinian situation is such that it may best be satisfied by two sets of beliefs which operate in different contexts, that of creation and that of evolution.

An emphasis on the distinction between men and animals is a feature of many cultures (Ruzin and Nemeroff 1990: 216). Hence the value of animal names as forms of abuse for fellow humans (Leach 1964) and the development of 'manners' viewed as suppressing all that is animal (Erasmus 1549; Elias 1994). Yet an ambivalence remains. In the memoirs of my LoDagaa friend, K. Gandah, he tells of his horror in seeing the blood flowing from his dying brother, and then remarks, 'But we are all animals', thus expressing both the separation and the identification; his brother was distinctly human yet blood flows through the veins of all living beings and gives them life (Gandah 1998).

There is also another aspect of human experience that encourages us to think both of creation and evolution. At the level of the individual we find

---

[3] Rev. John Heckewelder, 'An Account of the History, Manners, and Customs of the Indian Nations, who once inhabited Pennsylvania and the Neighbouring States', *Transactions of the Historical and Literary Committee of the American Philosophical Society*, Philadelphia, 1819, pp. 245, 247, 248, quoted Frazer (1918: i, 32).

these two notions manifested in his or her personal development. Human beings *evolve* from childhood to old age in a continuous process, the basis of the developmental cycle (Fortes in Goody 1958). But children appear to come into existence by a sudden act of creation, by the almost magical act of childbirth, so vividly expressed in many early Renaissance paintings where the Virgin Mother worships her own creation.

Such a dichotomy with its accompanying ambivalence (they are different but the same) is characteristic not only of oral societies. Although most contemporary Europeans accept their affinity with the apes, they are nevertheless concerned to emphasise the uniqueness of the human species (that is, its 'humanity'), a notion that is embedded in the study of 'culture' itself. Social anthropologists attempt to define 'culture' in such a way as to exclude animal societies. Think of the strongly adverse reaction by many of those academics not only to sociobiology but to all biological explanations or even to considering data on animal societies. They put their stress on the dividing line although it is far from evident that their criteria (learned behaviour, even the use of language and tool-making) are in fact unambiguously applicable only to humans. Much philosophical and psychological thinking about mind and consciousness, following the lines of the widespread body–soul dichotomy, appears to have its roots in the same problem. In talking to a well-known zoologist the other day, I spoke of the standardised gestures of certain monkeys as a sign-language. He corrected me, 'I wonder if one can use that term if consciousness is not present'. He may well be right. In any case the dichotomy which confronted other societies, confronts ourselves, being embedded in the structure of our situation. Rationalism and science do not overcome the problem. There remains the matter of identification in some contexts and separation in others.

Frazer was unwilling to entertain the possibility that these alternative views were both part of the same group's understanding of the world, existing as potential cognitive contradictions in the same society or individual. He looked for homogeneous rather than divergent ideologies, if possible those going back to common roots. Using examples from other societies, he proposes a rearrangement of the Genesis story of the Creation, wherein God offers mankind a choice between eating of the tree of life (immortality) and of the tree of death (in fact, knowledge which would lead to death). In his view that emendation corresponds better to 'the true original story of the Fall of man' in which the creator would be placed 'in a far more amiable light', freed from 'that suspicion of envy and jealousy' present in Genesis. A less idealistic approach would not try so hard to seek a homogenised version; the divergence we find rests on cognitive contradictions in the human situation combined with the generative potential of myth.

Let me pursue the theme in relation to my own field data. Among the LoDagaa of northern Ghana, an account of the creation of their world, their cultural word, is given in the course of a recitation told during the long initiation rites to the Bagre society. The Bagre recitation is not a 'fixed text', though it has recurrent elements as well as changing ones. Variations are constantly taking place leading to a divergence of versions. Together with K. Gandah, I have made a number of recordings, transcriptions and translations, details of which are given in the accompanying table to guide the reader through the material. The Bagre performance always consists of the White (largely an account of the rites) and the Black (the origin of man's culture). The Lawra Bagre takes a substantially different form.

Versions of the Bagre

Chaa Bagre, 1972 [Goody 1972a], Oxford (dictated 1951) Black/White
Chief's house (Naayili), 1981 [Goody and Gandah 1981], Paris (recorded 1969) Black/White
Baaperi (Naayili), unpublished (recorded 1969) White (3 versions)
Lawra Bagre, unpublished (recorded 1974/5) White
Yikpêê (1) Bagre, unpublished (recorded 1974/5) White
Yikpêê (2) Bagre, unpublished (recorded 1974/5) White
Gomble Bagre, unpublished (recorded 1978/9) Black/White
Biro Bagre, unpublished (recorded 1978/9) Black
Ngmanbili Bagre, unpublished (recorded 1978/9) Black

Membership of the Bagre offers benefits of a curative kind. More than that, during the first phase of the initiation the neophytes are killed off by consuming a medicine which is then used to revive them. They are promised freedom from earthly troubles and from mortality itself, since the medicine conquers death. However, in the second stage of the proceedings (the Black Bagre), these promises held out to mankind are shown to be false. Death and sickness remain in the world despite all humanity can do. The proffered relief is not entirely illusory, for we have to continue to do what our ancestors did before us (lest the outcome be worse) without much hope of improving our lot. Once again there is contradiction, for we find both illusion and disillusion. Moreover there is a clear recognition that not everybody will accept the account offered to the initiates. In the Lawra Bagre of 1974, on the morning of the Bagre Dance (Second Day), the speaker announced: 'There are some fools here, who are making a noise, they'll say it's a useless thing. But we know it is our heritage' (Lawra Bagre, I. 277). We perform whether or not we believe because it is our culture or custom. And that same acknowledgement of scepticism applies to God himself: 'The one they call God, who has ever seen Him come down to stay?' (Lawra Bagre, I. 315).

There is even a problem about the heritage, tradition, about what is transmitted or handed over culturally. This has been passed down to us by our ancestors whose representatives are the present-day elders who, as Speakers, recite the myth. In the Black Bagre (1982), when the first man is in trouble, the Bagre god tells him to consult the elders:

Where are the elders?
Turned into maggots,
burrowing into the ground

(ll. 25–8)

In other words they are no longer around, nor are their like, and we ourselves have to do as best we can, though that is never adequate. The Ngmanbili (Black) Bagre puts it this way:

The matters of old
who can know them?
Alas, alas,
it is God
who created us
and who punishes us.
Our forefathers' matters,
who can know them,
sit and know them?

(p. 20)

The hopelessness, the impossibility that one person can know all, means that others have to help in the recitation:

Can I know
the matter of God?

One single person
cannot
know all,
know it completely.

(pp. 26–7)

An individual Speaker is dependent on the help of friends but, above all, on his predecessors who knew so much about these things – but not everything, even in their case. So his version is bound to be imperfect. The Speaker in the Biro (Black) Bagre admits:

I cannot know it,
but fumble along,
for they did not know all.

Even the specialists, the Speakers, only fumble with ancient things, with traditional knowledge. The Gomble (Black) Bagre opens in a similar fashion:

They knew this matter
then one day,
they turned to maggots,
burrowed into the earth
and left it for the children.
The children continued on,
and fumbled with it.
They are here
and I'll tell you
I cannot know all.

(ll. 15–24)

Right throughout the Bagre is the insistence that, although man performs,

it is God's matter
naangmin yelo
that none can know.
nir ka bi.

The mystery surrounding man's problems remains in the hands of God. The Bagre god himself is seen as the offspring of the High God, and it is he who comes down to visit the Bagre house and shrine during the course of the ceremony of Bagre Eve. So in the rites too, it is God's path (*Naang-min sori*) they follow.

On the other hand, God's path is never altogether clear, and not only to human beings but to other supernatural agencies as well. In the first published Bagre (1972) the beings of the wild try to distract man from that path and are criticised for doing so. The High God is more or less exempt from overt criticism of this kind, but that does not go for his 'children'. Attitudes are often more distinctly ambivalent towards the other divinities. That version begins by calling on the Bagre god, 'In the beginning was god . . .', who is then addressed as

the thieving god,
the lying god,
the troubling god.

(ll. 8–10)

In the version published in 1981, the god is again insulted.

I rebuked him,
as the lying god (*ngmin gagaara*),
the thieving god.

(ll. 10–12)

When the god objects to being treated in this way, the speaker changes his tone.

So I praised him,
as the god of fertility,
the god of farming,
the god of the criss-cross marks [painted on the initiates],
the god with a good heart

(ll. 18–22)

In other words, it is not simply that humans appeal to the gods for their help; the gods themselves cause trouble. They promise what they cannot deliver (the lying god) and they require us to produce enormous amounts of food for the performances (the thieving god).

It is this kernel of doubt that gives rise to important variations, since it suggests the need to turn to the alternative possibilities already potentially present in the situation. And the kernel of doubt exists because the notion of a Creator God and of other divine agencies that are able to help us runs counter to human experience that suffering continues to exist, despite the goodness and omnipotence of God. In other words, the problem of evil that haunts theology also worries the LoDagaa and many similar cultures. That is not only an intellectual problem. The persistence of disease demands we seek other solutions to the ones that have failed us in the past, and sends us off on a quest that is a continuing enquiry into this world and the next.

Let me turn from these contradictions and ambivalences revealed in the Bagre back to the problem of creation and evolution. The Bagre is not really a creation story. It does not account for the physical universe, for the creation of animals, or even from one standpoint for the creation of mankind, for it begins with two men already in trouble. On other occasions people will say 'Na-angmin ir ti, God created us', using the verb for a potter creating a pot out of clay. As an explanation the same notion could be applied to rivers, to supernatural beings, probably to everything that exists. However, the Bagre is specifically about the creation of man's culture, including his (biological) knowledge of procreation.

In the 1972 version, the younger of the original two (brothers?) is troubled and starts off on a quest. He comes to a river which he is shown how to cross by a being of the wild (a water being). On the other side

> there was an old man
> with a pipe

(ll. 106–7)

and his dogs. The old man asks him what he wants. He replies

> that the affairs of God
> trouble me greatly.

(ll. 122–3)

Note that God is specifically the High God, not the Bagre god of the opening passage, and from what comes later the old man appears to be God himself, who asks:

> 'What can I do?'
> The affairs of God
> bring great suffering.

(ll. 126–8)

The beings of the wild then call the younger man to the woods and show him how to make food from guinea-corn, how to make fire, then to smelt iron ore and forge a hoe blade, and how to farm. The earth and the rain together make a tree grow and he is told to climb up to God's house, with the help of the Spider and his web. The Spider is a very central figure, a mediator between man and God, with the web serving as a ladder in many African folktales. In Heaven (literally, God's country) he sees God.

> The old man
> was lying there,
> they saw him
> on a cow's hide.
>
> (ll. 505–8)

> He is surrounded by
>
> a huge dog,
> with a leopard
> and a lion,
> and an elephant
> and a duiker
> and a hippopotamus
> in a small pond.
>
> (ll. 513–19)

God called our ancestor over, took some earth, pressed it together, called a young girl, told her to take a pot and some okro. He chewed the okro, which contains a sticky semen-like fluid, and spat it into a container (representing a vagina). The young girl is asked to pour the fluid over the earth into which the man then has to plunge his left hand (his penis?). A fly and his mate shit on top and after two days a tom cat and his mate scrape at the earth to reveal a child. That was Creation but it was also procreation. For the man and girl proceed to quarrel over the ownership of the child. The conflict is between individual possessions and sexual reproduction which requires a couple, as we later see.

God's wife, 'a wise old woman', is called over to help the girl in her post-natal tasks, including the ejection of the after-birth. The girl is then told that the child came from her own belly, apparently disconfirming its creation by God. The child (a boy) grows up but the quarrel with the father resumes. So the old lady takes them both back to God, who provides a manifestly sexist test of pissing down a tube to decide the ownership.

Clearly the woman has greater difficulty and it goes in favour of the man, who later tries to tell the child he has no mother. But the child rejects his answer, again stressing the duality of parenthood against paternal or patrilineage claims and saying:

Have you seen anyone
who has no mother
and yet has a father?

(ll. 1442–4)

Following this incident the beings of the wild continue their instruction and show him how to make a bow and arrows and how to shoot. From this all culture came, from outside supernatural sources that ultimately went back to God. It was the beings of the wild who

came out and took him
and led him off
into the woods,
where they showed him
many things,
they taught him everything
except about death.

(ll. 3024–30)

Then the younger one, who had gone off on the quest, taught the rest of us

how to hoe,
taught us
how to eat,
taught us
how to brew beer
taught us
how to grow guinea-corn,
taught us
how to kill wild animals.

(ll. 3035–43)

But we had really learnt from God mediated by the beings of the wild.

In the 1981 version the account of the origin of things is very different. The recitation opens with a man and a women quarrelling about their lack of possessions. The exchange of reproaches comes out even:

'What sort of a wife
has no water pot
and no calabash?'
(The woman replied:)
'What sort of a man
has no hoe,
has no axe?'

(ll. 41–7)

They decide to build a house, and the man makes bows and arrows which he sells in the market place. Following this, the listener is introduced to the gamut of basic cultural processes, the brewing of beer, the firing of pots, the hunting of animals, the making of brass ornaments. The man builds a smithy, makes charcoal, smelts iron; he weaves mats, makes poison, builds a boat. He goes down to the riverside (l. 1798), as at the beginning of the 1972 version, and there he encounters some curious people (probably 'the beings of the wild with their red hair'). This is the only time the beings of the wild, who play such a central part in the earlier version, are mentioned. Indeed, the whole visit to God's house has disappeared, although there are some passing references. The man goes across the river (which is presumably the River of Death dividing this world from the next) and immediately encounters the male cat who in the earlier version revealed 'God's child':

The male cat
begat its kittens,
you see him,
he went along
to look at them.
It leapt right up,
leapt into the sky
with the kitten on its back.

(ll. 1824–31)

He sees the male cat begetting its kittens, picked them up and 'came down' with them to the riverside where he meets the beings of the wild (l. 1857). That is all there is of the journey to Heaven – in this case a movement up and down, but with no reference to God or his part in creation, and no discussion of the role of the beings of the wild. I have noted before that some versions are much more theocentric than others. Here all non-human action is peripheralised (except that involved in the performance of the Bagre itself). In this version, 'man makes himself'. There is no exogenous process of creation. I would add that the parts of the recitation that relate to the ceremony itself (the White Bagre) are recognisably similar. But not the Black, which differs about these fundamentals. Indeed, we see in the Bagre not specific arguments about the role of deity but differences in approach which in other circumstances many have interpreted as representing distinct stages of development. Weber distinguished religions as theocentric or cosmocentric; here we have an alternation between the two, without any long-term developmental implications.

How do we account for these enormous differences, whose presence must modify ideas about the fixity of such cultural beliefs? Let me point to the close resemblance in the opening lines and in the notion of a quest, a search for the main techniques, the basic knowledge, required by the LoDagaa to conduct their lives, food, farming, hunting, crafts and (in the first published version) procreation. But the way this is achieved is quite different. In the earlier instance, one of the first men seeks knowledge from God and from the beings of the wild, who have themselves been taught by God. From the latter he learns the techniques, from the former how to create life itself, although that is ambiguously presented. For the creation of life, while apparently shown to man by God, is also a human activity, and the snakes of the forest later teach the woman independently how to procreate in an earthly manner.

The Biro and Gomble recitations (1978/9) resemble each other in their content except that the latter is twice as long (the transcription occupies 49 pages as compared with 23). They seem to combine aspects of both the creation of the world and man's invention. Each begins in the same way, with references to the stars in the sky (the only LoDagaa context I know of in which these are discussed), to the animal kingdom, and then to God's gift of a hoe to the man and woman who were already living on earth. He gave this because they were cold, sleeping under the rain without a roof. Using the hoe they build themselves a house, a procedure that is described in detail. God also gave him some reeds (p. 7), possibly to make a mat. In any case they copulated together on a mat after quarrelling about who should come to whom, which seems to have angered God, possibly because they were engaging in the act of creation reserved for him alone. In any case the woman later denied that she had taken part in intercourse, and the man hung his head in shame; each had 'spoilt' the other (as in adultery). A child is subsequently born and the new mother is instructed what to do by an old woman. As in the 1972 version the mother and father then quarrel about the ownership of the child. The woman makes some beer and provides her son with a bow but it doesn't work. So the father makes one instead, emphasising his role in the gendered division of tasks.

In these two versions of the Black Bagre God is constantly coming down to earth. In the first one he gives a hoe (handle) to the man and woman, who are conceived as lacking the basic means to sustain life; in the Gomble recitation a hoe is given to the man in a more gendered way (though women do sometimes have small hoes for vegetable farming). There is no voyage to God's country and man does a lot for himself.

One aspect of creation (as of procreation) is related to the question of gender. Difficulties arise between male and female roles. In many societies male dominance in a wide range of social affairs, including leadership in politics and war, suggests not only that God is male but that man should be the first object of creation. In the Hebrew Bible, Eve is then created out of Adam's rib. But the central problem for humanity is that man is a progenitor, he does not give birth and physically create in that sense. That role belongs to woman. So there also has to be a switch of gender (engendering) emphasis between the male and female, between creation and procreation. We have seen that the 1972 version relates how in the beginning there were two men (possibly brothers). A woman, referred to stereotypically or formulaically as 'the slender young girl', is not involved in the first act of creating a child, which God effects out of a mixture including clay. Neither is the man, though they both are implicated symbolically and quarrel about the ownership of the child that has been created. Later on when more children are required, humanity is brought more squarely into the picture. The beings of the wild take the woman to the woods where she sees snakes copulating. They show her what to do, and she returns and explains to her husband how enjoyable it is, so they then set about producing a family. The duality of parenthood and parental responsibility is constantly stressed; even if men otherwise play a dominant part in the acquisition of culture, in this act of creation, procreation, both participate equally .

Just as we have the alternatives of the Big Bang (creation) and the Expanding Universe (evolution) at the level of initial creation, so too man's culture can be seen as either given by God or invented by man himself. I want to suggest that however else they can be interpreted, these accounts have to be understood 'cognitively', that is, as ways of understanding the world, each of which poses a problem. They are not absurd, as some structuralists have suggested, forcing us to go searching for a deep structure on that account (though there may be other reasons why we should do so). The surface meaning, the meaning to the actor, is the first important level to examine. Moreover that surface meaning is not single-stranded. These versions I have discussed all emanate from the same neighbouring group within a few years of each other. The way that myths vary over time and space, when most accounts suggest their longevity, indeed perpetuity, is a problem I have touched upon elsewhere. Here I have tried to draw attention to the diverse ways of understanding the world that they display, as each particular version poses problems and contradictions which may lead people to take up or generate an alternative position.

From one perspective that diversity is, I suggest, part and parcel of humanity's encounter with the universe. Regarding the difference between the gift of culture from God or its origin in human invention, universal experience teaches both that humans are capable of creating artefacts (with the potter's clay, for example) and that in other cases they are faced with what has already been long created (language, for instance) and perhaps which, like growing things, they cannot themselves create. It touches upon the distinction between inherited and acquired property or knowledge. The different positions achieve their expression in various versions of the Bagre. Man is dependent on the gods but he also has to stand on his own two feet.

What we find included in these accounts are alternatives to the problem of origins. In the 1972 version, God creates a child for the first people (the younger one and his wife) while the beings of the wild show him the other processes humans need to know about in order to survive. In the other recitals God is present as a force, the ultimate force, and he provides the first man and woman with a base to build a house. But he may do little else. While there is no doubt that he is the Creator God, there are alternative views about what he creates. In other versions, it is much more a case of man making himself by discovering the right way; in other words, they take a developmental or evolutionary view of culture. That is only one way in which the versions vary – the story they tell is different in many others, although all are concerned with the origins of things, and specifically of man's cultural equipment.

At one level these variations have to do with the nature of the transmission and creation of long oral recitations (the two processes are in fact always one). But the different content of the versions indicates not simply variants on a theme, but the presence of alternative approaches to topics. Creation and evolution coexist, with God playing a varying part. While all knowledge comes from him, it is not entirely comprehensible by humans, who are always in the situation of possessing imperfect information. That is why even what we must believe in (for instance, the Bagre) is deceptive knowledge; it fools us, as do other divine agencies. The beings of the wild deceive us, so too does the Bagre god, who is a lying god.

I argue that this aspect of oral cultures should make us rethink our ideas about them. Intellectually, cognitively, they are much more dynamic than is often thought; that should be clear from the degree of divergence in the versions of the Black Bagre (as compared with the White, which is tied to external ritual procedures). That situation has been obscured partly because fieldwork has often confined people to taking a slice of time, one performance of a ritual, one recitation, to characterise something called a culture which exists by definition over time. Repeated observations over time together with the use of the tape recorder have changed all that; creation and evolution coexist as alternative possibilities, not necessarily in one version but in several recited over time. That is as true of other cognitive notions.

This view of myth and of the world views of simple societies cuts across Horton's perception of them as closed rather than open societies, and even more across Habermas' idea that, because of their totalising power, validity claims are out of place. It is true that beliefs are not subject to the tests that are characteristic of modern science (as is true of many of our own). Contradictions may be tolerated to a greater extent (partly because in oral cultures they are more difficult to detect). But they do exist implicitly and sometimes explicitly, leading to questions and then to changes in culture. No society is ultimately closed, although degrees of openness vary. Myths are rarely if ever as totalising as Habermas suggests; there are always some exit routes opened by actual or potential contradictions. Moreover, validity claims can be and are applied to supernatural agencies; there are gods who fail as well as ones that succeed, and those who fail may be abandoned in favour of others. Mythical or culturally standardised world views are not immune from internal criticism, from 'communicatively achieved understanding', from 'rational enquiry', from reflective assessment as well as from dogmatism.

Habermas takes up the subject of the mythical world view which was the starting point for the analysis of religion by Weber. From that point a process of rationalisation in religions was seen to begin which, as Tenbruck remarks, takes an evolutionary trajectory. Supernatural powers began by being immanent in things, then beings emerged that lay behind those things; that situation in turn gave way to personal beings, then to a monotheistic High God, subsequently to a judgemental deity, later to emissary prophecy and finally to the Protestant doctrine of predestination (Habermas 1984: 196). Apart from the ethnocentric culmination in Protestantism, the proposed sequence, which reminds one very much of Tylor's attempt in *Primitive Culture*, is quite unsustainable. Most if not all religions begin with a concept of a creator God; there is minimal evidence for this evolutionary schema.

As a result of this rethinking, the process of cultural transmission has itself to be reconsidered. It seems to me clear that whatever weight we give to built-in factors (and these have to be individually demonstrated), we must also allow for cultural reproduction of the classic kind as well as for its internal problems, worries, which lead to the adoption of alternative attitudes. In other words, the world view includes a kernel of doubt, creating a potential ambivalence about any particular solution. The source of that ambivalence may lie in the beliefs (or categories) of a particular culture; it may lie in the situation in a particular range of societies, for example in luxury cultures that generate their own critique; or it may lie in the human situation itself, as in the killing of other human beings, which may be regarded as threatening life itself as well as defending it. Or with the origin of the world and the aspects of creation or evolution, good and evil, men or gods.

Let me return to the problem of cognitive universals. I have argued in favour of the rehabilitation of the intellectualist approach that assigns cognitive meaning to the actors. I have also argued in favour of the recognition of transcultural features, including universal ones, which demand explanation. Evolutionary explanations can easily go too far, in imposing sequences that are invalid from an empirical standpoint. An alternative is to see universals (or widespread factors) as built-in (or as the result of built-in constraints). While not denying their existence, many significant features arise, in my view, from the situation in which language-using beings find themselves. Some of these situations give rise to propositions, attitudes, beliefs, that contain internal contradictions or display contradictions with regard to their referents. That in turn raises ambivalences, or a kernel of doubt, in the minds of the actors, and may provide the impetus for shifting to another belief (as with images), or for incorporating that ambivalence in rituals (as with homicide) and in contextualised beliefs (as with creation and evolution).

One final point. Frazer never undertook fieldwork, and his brand of comparative research has become unfashionable. My teachers too were against something called the comparative method, yet they all undertook some forms of comparison. Post-modernists, locked in their own self-questioning and the intimacy of their encounters, have other objections. But all undertook some form of comparison if only because they are using English to present, say, Jain or Asante ideas. Just as many problems in field research require us to take a longer timespan into account (not necessarily for every practitioner but for the ensemble), so too there has to be interaction between local and comparative knowledge. For culture is a fact not of one society but of all, and many of its aspects one cannot study without openly acknowledging the interplay between the particular and the general. Field study must be set in a wider context not necessarily of comparative work but of comparative questions.

Chapter 14

CIVIL SOCIETY IN A COMPARATIVE PERSPECTIVE

'Civil society', does it exist? As a concept developed in the West, certainly. It arose first in Ancient Greece, and was elaborated in the Enlightenment, to characterise in a favourable light one's own institutions (or society) in contrast to those of others. The 'other' varied, but included both barbarians and despots. In the eighteenth and nineteenth centuries these 'uncivil' societies embraced past autocrats and present orientals whose societies were thought to have been unable to develop in the manner of Western Europe. After a period of neglect, the term has recently been called back into use in political discourse.

In the present period of post-Cold War adjustment, 'civil society' carries, as earlier, a heavily normative burden. It is what we in the West have and wish to see developed not only in Eastern Europe but in the East more generally. Like the associated notions of democracy and representation, of law and freedom, especially as they apply to the market, its absence in the East is seen as having impeded the earlier process of modernisation, and even now as restricting the exercise of human rights. We can recognise its contemporary role as a battle-cry. But does it carry any serious weight in the comparative analysis of political systems as distinct from representing a theme in Western political thought?

I want to discuss briefly the concept of civil society in relation not so much to political philosophy as to sociology, anthropology and history. Then I consider whether, despite its use to denigrate the other, it can serve any useful purpose to analyse the West, the earlier or the later East, or even, in view of the very different conditions that pertained, Africa. But first let me attempt some elucidation.

The Aristotelian conception of the unity of society and the state, or of civil and political society, has been contrasted with the disaggregation of civil society and the state in the early modern period. Aristotle saw civil society as 'a domination-free association of peers who communicatively and publicly establish their goals and norms of action and who regulate their interaction through principles of justice' (Cohen and Arato 1992: 122, in Honneth *et al.* 1992). Every phrase in this description calls for an extended commentary, which is why it is difficult to align with any social data. Suffice to say that it adds up to a highly idealistic ideal type of democratic control.

The early modern conception has been seen as taking the form either of stressing pluralistic normative integration or of postulating individualistic, utilitarian forms of action. Durkheim and others followed the first course, neo-conservatives the second. In both we are faced with the problem of timing similar to that found in the case of national law. Many see this as a doctrine originating in the seventeenth century; Lévi-Strauss and others find it already present in Aristotle, though it was fully harmonised with 'civil society' by Aquinas. That is the background of the phrase from the standpoint of 'conceptual history'. We should add an alternative starting point that has been developed among those intellectuals connected with contemporary 'social movements' such as Solidarity in Poland. 'Civil society', like human rights, is what authoritarian regimes lack by definition. It is what the Greeks, the Enlightenment and the West today has; it is what despotic governments, whether in the past or the present, in the here or the elsewhere, do not have.

In its early modern aspect, the notion of civil society has been seen as linked to the European society of that period. Habermas

> outlines the emergence during the eighteenth century of a new sphere between private life and public authority under the old name of civil society (*Zivil societat*) or simply society.[1] That represented a new type of 'publicity' (*Offentlichkeit*) based in principle on the autonomous voluntary association and reasoned communication of free and equal individuals.
>
> (Cohen and Arato 1992: 129)

---

[1] Marx's use of 'civil society' refers to Hegel and the Enlightenment: 'The material conditions of life, the sum total of which Hegel, following the example of the Englishmen and Frenchmen of the eighteenth century, combines under the name of "civil society", that, however, the anatomy of civil society is to be sought in political economy' (Marx 1958: 181).

That activity was located at the level of the social, a public sphere which penetrated the state through the parliamentary principle, dissolving the absolutist's *arcana imperii*. And it formed the subject of Locke's enquiries into the development of new political forms. In other words 'civility' enters into social and political life through the intervention first of voluntary associations and reasoned discussion, then through the modification of the monolithic powers of the state by the medium of parliament. In other words, the notion is associated with a long-term 'civilising' of political and indeed societal relations which is seen as resulting from pressures from 'non-government organisations' on the one hand and from public opinion on the other.

It is superfluous to note that these discussions are deeply embedded in Western political theory, Western philosophy and Western social science. They embody concepts developed in the course of Western intellectual history, often as political instruments. But let us turn to questions that bear not so much on the intellectual history of the concept but on its possible use as an analytical tool for comparative purposes. I begin with a general remark which relates to the separation of society and polity implied in the usage itself. In the Parsonian model, the polity is neither distinct from nor coincidental with society; it is part of a wider whole in the sense of the social system. The alternative assumption results from the looser usage of some specialists. Economists, for example, call 'social' or 'cultural' anything that is incapable of being analysed within their particular framework; 'society' somewhat arbitrarily denotes 'the rest' or 'the other', as in the phrases economy and society, religion and society, or family and society. For Parsons and for most anthropologists the polity is a sub-system of the social system, though one which often displays a certain dominance in social life because of the state's role in territorial relationships, in the control of physical force, and in law-making and government more generally. But not all societies possess centralised institutions or state organisations of this kind. In these other cases, to suggest that the polity implies the state and can be separated from a notion of society would clearly be nonsense.

The Western orientation embedded in the notion of 'civil society' is not of course necessarily an impediment to its use. Natural science has thrived upon its Western base. However, in the case of the social sciences and the humanities acute problems do arise with such ethnocentic terms. I have referred to two main usages of the concept of civil society: for short, the Greek and the early modern. For Habermas the decisive break came with the Enlightenment, that is, with the further development not only of democracy ('communication of free and equal individuals') but also of rationality, since that communication has to be 'reasoned'. In other words, we cannot divorce this argument from the claim that a new form of rationality was developed in the West, a form that Weber called the 'rationality of world mastery'. Others (for example Gellner 1992) see this development not as an altogether new form of rationality but as the more thorough-going application of an already existing variety, inherited from Aristotle, elaborated to the limits by Descartes with his famous formula: I think, therefore I am. But in either case that rationality is considered to result in the Enlightenment and the development of modern knowledge systems, especially in the natural sciences, though it also took an economic form intrinsic to the development of capitalism, industrialisation, modernisation.

I do not reject the Enlightenment idea of a long-term progression (even 'progress') towards 'civility', the kind of progression that Elias has discussed in Western Europe at the level of spitting and other bodily functions. But such a development of restraint and 'manners' is not limited to Western Europe, is more diversified than that scheme suggests, and is less deeply rooted in the psyche and the society than the word itself implies. 'Civilised' is more appropriate as a technical archaeological concept than as a moral one. It does not require much ransacking of the memory to recall the acts perpetrated some fifty years ago by those who claim Goethe and Beethoven as their cultural ancestors, and who pride themselves today and yesterday on their civility. Or the more recent horrors done in the name of the great Khmer civilisation of Ankor Wat. Or the contemporary atrocities committed by inhabitants of that centre of Balkan civility, Sarajevo. The history of all civil and civilised societies, especially imperial, colonial and immigrant ones, is blood-stained in similar ways.[2] There is no straightforward unilineal shedding of the 'uncivil'.

It is obvious that the past three hundred years has seen major developments in the West in the importance of parliamentary government (and of electoral systems of choosing representatives) as well as in secularised knowledge and in the economy. However, there is a problem in describing

---

[2] I do not wish to suggest these horrors did not differ in magnitude, in intensity or in ideology, or that there was nothing specific about the Shoah or about ethnic cleansing. I am talking simply of the limitations in referring to societies as 'civil'. See Geras (1997) on Mandel and the holocaust.

these events as well as in explaining them if they are dealt with at the level of the birth of democracy, or of rationality, or of civil society. That is the case whether we are dealing with Athens or with the Enlightenment. Take democracy. Contrary to much received opinion, representation of a kind has existed in many other forms of government, possibly in all, in ships of eighteenth-century pirates as well as in tribal chiefdoms. What we have experienced more recently is its extension, elaboration and formalisation in the nation-state, first, in the West (though not in its colonies), then elsewhere. There are of course many differences in the forms of representation and in their efficacy; compliance with authority, clearly a variable, has been reduced in significant ways in the modern West, but the difference is a matter of degree; representation of people's interests did not begin with the Enlightenment, though it was certainly extended.

The same can be said of the application of rationality to economic and 'cultural' activities, as seen in the development of the economy and of knowledge systems. As far as economic development is concerned, Indian and Chinese participation in the ancient trading systems of the eastern oceans certainly required the application of 'rational' techniques. Regarding knowledge systems, parallel techniques were as clearly utilised to create the encyclopaedias of Sung China as the *summae* of medieval Europe. Neither the abilities nor the capacities (I see the first as biological, the second as cultural) to carry out 'rational' actions were absent in the East, and it is Western myopia that looks upon the world in such a paternalistic light – or rather in the absence of light, as the Unenlightened, those whom the Enlightenment never reached. That myopia also applies to the concept of civil society, for here too is an institution that the West claims to have invented at a certain (disputed) moment in time and which others did not or could not develop. Once again, the idea has taken root by selecting a specific historical situation in the West, important in terms of world history, and attributing to it some very general qualities. Indeed, there is a kind of moral evaluation attached to the very concepts of civility, rationality and enlightenment, qualities that are seen as contributing to the so-called European miracle and that are necessarily unique to the West. That approach makes for an ethnocentric and suspect social science which does little to clarify the analysis of the undoubted achievements that took place at that time, but which must be seen in the light not only of those of ancient Greece, but of those of earlier Mesopotamia, of the Arab Near East and of Tang and Sung China. In each of these periods, achievements have to be accounted for not in terms of the attribution of permanent general qualities (for example mentalities) which others are held not to possess, since the achievements represent at best a temporary advantage which is about to be lost or overtaken, but on a more specific basis. Not in other words by 'rationality' as a unique possession, but possibly by 'rationalising', by specific techniques of logical operation that are more contextually dependent.

Whereas, in Western thought, whether rationality is seen as having had its birth either in Ancient Greece or in the post-Renaissance West, it is by definition a European product which is then offered to the rest of the world. For Weber Western rationality was 'the rationality of world mastery', just as for Habermas and many others the emergence of this feature at the time of the Enlightenment has an explanatory value in accounting for contemporary Western achievement, in contrast not only to its earlier past but to the non-European societies who failed to make the break at all.

The third use of the notion of civil society as emerging in 'social movements' carries a similar moral evaluation that places it equally on the side of the angels. There it can be seen as one of the major 'weapons of the weak', allowing individuals and groups to battle with 'the state'. That possibility is almost universally welcomed, whatever the government (except of course *by* the government, for whom political action of this kind may be 'counter-revolutionary' or just disturbing, that is, seen as creating a disturbance). Civil society then becomes attached to the notion of civil liberties, of human rights, embodied in formulae such as 'liberté, égalité et fraternité' which revolutionary social movements embrace and which the state, even the revolutionary state, tends to reject or at least to compromise. Put in this way, the notion of civil society again becomes a Western attribute, since the 'despotic' societies of the East were not thought to allow such opposition to develop.

The use of these concepts is clearly linked to nineteenth-century (and earlier) discussions about those 'other' societies which displayed 'traditional' types of authority and had absolutist regimes, even Asiatic forms of dominance where no interference was brooked with the decisions of the ruler. This kind of Alice in Wonderland 'off with their heads' view of Asian regimes lay at the back of the many references to static, stagnant, despotic, autocratic, absolutist governments. Nor was the idea confined to Marx and Weber. In the earlier eighteenth century, Europeans had sometimes used the East to promote Utopian notions. Tacitus had done this with the Germans, so did the Jesuits with China, and the British with the village community in India. However, the rapid growth of knowledge and the onset of industrialisation created a gap between West and East, leading to a radical devaluation of the latter. It was no longer purely ethnocentricism or xenophobia that was involved; there was an evident superiority in knowledge systems and in the economy that called for an explanation.

Enshrined in many European discussions of the Indian polity was the notion of the obstructive, indeed destructive, role of the supreme power of the ruler. In the mid eighteenth century the British author and administrator, Robert Orme, wrote of his autocratic power, especially in the legal domain. He called the government 'despotic' partly because of a misunderstanding about land tenure. 'All the lands in kingdom belong to the King', he declared. In fact this arrangement was little different from the claims made on behalf of European monarchs, and referred to certain over-riding political rights possessed by the ruler which were closely related to his claim to collect taxes and extract services. Others have attributed the failure of India to develop a capitalist system to the power wielded by the monarch and to the consequent insecurity and status of merchants whose property might be confiscated at any time, and who therefore preferred to keep their wealth in jewels rather than to invest in production; in fact many Jains, an important merchant group, would not put money into agricultural land in India for the religious reason that farming involved the taking of life. Royal interference in production and exchange played its part but that was not unknown in Europe; for instance, in 1505 the King of Portugal declared a royal monopoly over the spice trade. It is true that Eastern governments tended to be more centralised than the feudal ones of the West, which were more locally centred after the decline of the Roman Empire. But these arguments of Western scholars were partly dependent on the idea that 'law' did not exist in Asian societies; that despotism was arbitrary and inimical to the predictability of law. Without law there was a Hobbesian state of nature in which commerce and industry could not flourish and which was diametrically opposed to the order of a 'civil society', though it should be added that for other writers, such as Locke and Rousseau, the state of nature was not violent but pacific. Moreover, the rapacity and the despotism of Eastern rulers has often been exaggerated while that of the West underplayed. Extensive trade did develop in India, and merchant groups flourished from an early date, as we see in their strong support of Buddhism and Jainism from the sixth century BCE.

Of the legal situation in India Orme (1805: 403) wrote that 'a government depending upon no other principle than the will of one, cannot be supposed to admit any absolute laws into its constitution; for these would often interfere with that will'. The notion of 'absolute laws' is connected with their universal application to all citizens. But it is also linked to the idea that civil society and perhaps natural law itself, like the rights of man (human rights), are applicable to all societies. Such extreme universalism runs into conflict not only with extreme cultural relativism, which regards different legal and social systems as essentially incomparable, but also with a view that sees different types of legal or jural arrangement as being appropriate to certain regions, levels of development, or categories of society. That view would allow for greater flexibility than, say, the idea that representative government or even democracy must necessarily take one of the forms developed in the West to warrant the name. The contrary was recently argued by the former prime minister of Singapore. He complained that because of the trade surplus that Asians had with the United States, they were subject to pressure, especially from human rights groups, when, for example, Singapore decides to hang drug smugglers or cane a miscreant. These protests he described as 'a little bit of one-upmanship – "We are a superior civilisation, come up to our standards."' But he insisted there is 'nothing universal about human rights. We will change in time but so too will Western norms, for they are not universal' (*The Straits Times*, 29 November 1993). While laws are not infinitely variable, neither are they absolute in this sense of being universally applicable.

The idea that Eastern societies were not just different but different in basic ways that prevented them from 'modernising' was crystallised in Marx's concept of oriental government, associated with the static, oriental mode of production. This theme was developed by Wittvogel in a well-known study, entitled *Oriental Despotism* (1957). Weber saw these societies as characterised by 'traditional' authority and as lacking the legal rationality of Western bureaucratic systems. The details of their arguments need not concern us here. What is clear is that they took over notions of the East that dwelt upon the autocratic nature of authority, whether of the king or of the family head, and contrasted with the 'democratic' systems of the West, characterised by pluralism, by checks and balances, by countervailing institutions, by parliamentary assemblies, and by juries in which the populace were represented. In fact at an earlier period, between c. 600 and 321 BCE, India had had a series of 'republican' institutions in addition to the orthodox monarchies. These republics are said to have originated either in 'tribes' (presumably acephalous peoples) or in refugees from the kingdoms themselves. As so often, the kingdoms rose in the rich Ganges plain while the republics (or 'tribes') were found in the hill areas. There they had elected leaders and instituted voting procedures (copied by the Buddhists) and assemblies; it was these latter areas that gave birth to the heterodox religious movements of Jainism and Buddhism that broke away from Hinduism and the caste system (Thapar 1966: 53).

Even the states were not as despotic as the West thought. If we look back at Orme's account we will see that he is struck by a contradiction. For 'if the subjects of a despotic power are everywhere miserable, the miseries of the people of Indostan are multiplied by the incapacity of the power to control the vast extent of its dominion' (Orme 1805: 400).[3] So the limitations of the mode of communications constrains the practice of despotism. As a consequence, there was a significant area of free play, of plurality, between the private and public worlds.

It was the same in China. We hear much from modern social scientists about 'the reach of state', 'the emperor in the village'. Undoubtedly the impress of the state made itself felt to a greater extent and over a greater area than in India, which was politically more fragmented. The penetration of a written corpus was everywhere profound, from the political as well as the general 'cultural' point of view. In China the polity deliberately took control of the religious system and encouraged a tradition of secular writing, whereas in India, religion and polity (the Brahmin and the Kshatriya) were more directly opposed, especially for Hindus under the long period of Muslim rule. Nevertheless state power had its limits in China as in India. One indication is the fact that from the end of the fourteenth century to 1893 there existed an imperial ban on emigration and overseas travel. Nevertheless, during this period millions of Chinese established themselves beyond the edge of the southern coasts (Wang Gungwu, introduction to Ng 1983). 'Despotic' rule did not stop them settling in Nanyang, in the regions around the Southern Seas.

Earlier notions about Eastern despotism have been modified not only for the mechanical reason that the reach of the state could never remain absolute over long periods. Recent work by historians and other social scientists has brought out the civil aspects of that society. These studies are well

---

[3] Other accounts took a more sympathetic line, including the seventeenth- and eighteenth-century ones of China that were influenced by the reports of Jesuits, but this was the line pursued by later Western social theory.

known to specialists but have made little impact on Western social theory. The latter clings to Weberian notions of traditional patrimonial authority which fit neatly with ethnocentric folk models about the Uniqueness of the West. The newer data challenge such assumptions. For example, Scott's work on 'weapons of the weak', on resistance to authority, as a general feature of advanced agricultural societies was carried out in south-east Asia and later generalised from there. In many parts of Asia, historians have studied collective movements against authority, for that certainly did not go unchallenged. Here I want to focus not on acts of rebellion but on the positive sense of plurality and civility that one gains from reading, for example, accounts of Edo in seventeenth-century Japan, or of the coastal Chinese city of Hangzhou at the time of Marco Polo in the late thirteenth century, which one recent commentator described in the following terms:

> The city was noted for its charitable institutions as for its pleasures. There were public hospitals, nurseries, old people's homes, free cemeteries, help for the poor, and state institutions from which the officials benefited more often than the poor. The poor were sometimes the object of private charity on the part of the rich merchants who wanted to make a name for themselves by doing good works.
>
> (Balazs 1964: 99)

Charity and its accompanying institutions was not a prerogative of the West; once again it was a feature of the socio-economic stratification of urban social life.

At this time Hangzhou was the southern capital of China with a population of between 1,000,000 and 1,500,000. The city of Hankow (or Wuhan) developed much later, but it too raises the question of civil society. Discussions of modernisation in the West recognise the critical role played by the city in this process. This special form of urban life is seen as providing the necessary conditions for the emergence of the idea of freedom and the equality of individuals before the law, as well as of the free alienation of property. In Europe these developments were held to have hastened the passing of feudalism with fundamental results both politically and intellectually, but that continent was not alone to experience these ideas.

> Politically, it left a heritage of democracy ... as well as the concept of a corporate political body with a clearly demarcated public

sector in terms both of budgetary accounting and professional civil service. Intellectually, it fostered the primacy of rationality, both in legal procedure and in an economic focus on calculability of returns on investment – in Weber's words, the medieval urbanite was well 'on the way to becoming an economic man (*homo oeconomicus*)', . . . laying the groundwork for early capitalism.

(Rowe 1984: 3)[4]

Western social theorists saw the type of city that promoted this development as first emerging in medieval Europe, beginning with the relatively independent *commune* that appeared in northern Italy during the course of the eleventh century. From there the institution soon spread to France, Germany and the Low Countries. That was the thesis of Henri Pirenne in his work on *Medieval Cities* (1925) and it formed the basis of Max Weber's essay on *The City* (*Die Stadt*) (1968). A commune of this kind was more than an urban settlement; according to Weber it was marked by the dominance of trade-commercial relations, a court with at least partially autonomous law, and a government with some room for independent action. For its inhabitants required some liberty.

For Weber, Eastern towns, and specifically those in China, failed to meet these criteria; nor did European towns before the eleventh century. Neither had succeeded in making the passage from traditional to rational. On the political level he saw the heavy central administration as allowing little autonomy; the town's role as a garrison or 'princely city' was more important than as a market. It was a centre of 'rational administration' rather than of commerce, where the inhabitants continued to identify with their native places and with their families rather than with the town itself. In the town they were sojourners, temporary visitors. 'All communal action there remained engulfed and conditioned by purely personal, above all by kinship relations.' So these settlements, vast as they were (and in the second half of the nineteenth century Hankow was among the largest in the world, just as Hangzhou had been in the thirteenth), lacked a notion of citizenship and any way of enforcing 'contractual autonomy'. The existence of clans and guilds served only a segment of the population, pointing to the absence of either a *polis* or a *commune*, or, if one extends the notions, of a polity or a community.

---

[4] My account is derived from this excellent study of Hankow in the nineteenth century.

The ideas of Weber were accepted not only by Europeanists. For example, the notion of the particularistic character of Chinese economic behaviour was taken up by the sinologists, Levy and Feuerwerker, that of the failure of urban development by Balazs and Eberhard. The latter saw the possibility of industrial development in the Sung as inhibited by the structure of the town, while the former characterised the government as despotic, with the town overly dependent on the countryside.

Conclusions of this kind have been radically altered by more recent work on China, especially on its urban life. Skinner (1977) has called attention to the hierarchy of commercial central places, which in various respects was distinct from the hierarchy of administrative ones. Elvin (1974) has pointed to the non-administrative structures of social and political power within large urban centres like Shanghai. Rowe's detailed study of Hankow shows that guarantees of contracts were provided by the administration, and that Chinese firms used 'principles of rational capital accounting' in 'a rational, orderly market'. The importance of guilds as 'proto-capitalist corporations' and the existence of other voluntary associations helped Hankow to escape 'heavy-handed bureaucratic domination' (Rowe 1984: 10). In other words, Chinese cities were not as monolithic as had been supposed, leaving room for the development of trading and commercial relations as well as providing an opening for the adoption of Western industrialisation and Western knowledge.

The erroneous view of the Eastern city has also been challenged for India, at least for Ahmadabad, one of whose historians, Gillion, has written (1968: 5):

> The traditional cities of India are most often viewed through the eyes of Bernier and other European travellers who visited the Mughal court, and in the light of Weberian and Marxist analysis. They are contrasted with the self-governing towns of medieval Europe with their charters, esprit-de-corps, united bourgeoisie, and independent military power. They appear to be disunited, often ephemeral conglomerations of subjects, dependent on the court and the military official elite, and prevented from free association by caste rivalries and other religious constraints. But Ahmadabad was, to some extent, an exception. Here was a city with a corporate tradition and spirit, an hereditary bourgeois elite, and a history of financial, commercial, and industrial activity ...

Its wealth came from trade, industry and handicrafts, which were independent of the patronage of a single court; its merchants and financiers made up a distinct social strata, wielding considerable power through the institutions of the city head (*Nagarseth*) and the *mahajans* or guilds. If it did not enjoy urban autonomy on the European model, 'the government of the city was responsive to their wishes'. The later history of Ahmadabad represents 'the transformation of an important traditional centre of trade and industry into a modern industrial city, under the leadership of an indigenous financial and mercantile elite'.

Changes in the view of some Eastern cities have led to a revaluation of East–West differences. Rather than treating the East and the West as following totally different trajectories in the medieval period, the feudal road on one hand and that of 'Asiatic exceptionalism' on the other, recent accounts (for example Wolf 1982) suggest that we should think of two varieties of a single configuration, the tributary state. Such an approach has the advantage of recognising the common roots of both East and West in the Bronze Age, with its Urban Revolution (as Childe called it), bringing political science closer to the findings of prehistory.

In this perspective we should find similar but not identical regimes developing in both parts of Eurasia, so there is no longer any call for the radical distinctions found in the writings of Weber, Marx and many other thinkers. A parallel criticism applies to 'world systems theory', where 'the other' is always peripheral to the European centre. But this was hardly the situation in the early medieval period when the major region for manufacturers, trade and knowledge centred on China and India, nor yet in the thirteenth century when the Muslim Near East achieved a dominant position in the world's commercial networks (Abu-Lughod 1989). The same criticism applies to the 'critical theory' of Jürgen Habermas, which places so great an emphasis on the role of the European Enlightenment in the development of systems of knowledge, and of 'civil' (and 'civilised') society, to the neglect of the major achievements of earlier China and elsewhere. This is an area where critical theory has not been critical enough, largely because it has not taken a sufficiently global point of view.

In the pages that follow I want to suggest that most Western analysts have not only got it wrong about the East (and hence necessarily about the West, since one is seen in opposition to the other), but also about a wide range of other political systems. For whether or not we find in these other societies an explicit discussion on the Western model of law, of representation, of a 'civil' way of life, something of these features can never-theless be discerned even in those African societies that have minimal forms of government ('tribes without rulers'). At the same time the 'states' that possess centralised institutions are far less 'despotic' and far more 'civil' than is often allowed.

THE CIVIL SOCIETY IN PRECOLONIAL AFRICA?

In Africa we find polities of two broad kinds. Let us consider West Africa. One kind was characterised by an ordered hierarchy of chiefs, at the top of which stood a paramount, vested with varying degrees of 'power'; the other was characterised by masters of the Earth, Earth priests, or custodians of the Earth shrine (as they are variously called). The former (centralised) also had their priests, and their chiefs had magico-religious powers, while the latter (non-centralised) had clan elders and even some embryonic or absorbed chiefs who exercised a very limited authority. Nevertheless, the distinction between these different forms of polity was clear enough to the participants. It was also a distinction that was central to the analysis of *African Political Systems* offered by Fortes and Evans-Pritchard in their seminal collection bearing that title (1940); they called the former (Type A) 'states' (or 'primitive states' in Kabery's subsequent study), and the latter (Type B) acephalous (headless) or segmentary peoples; I myself often refer to the latter as 'tribes' for convenience. In Africa these two types of polity, states and tribes, existed in tandem; they were not simply evolutionary stages that replaced one another (though over the longer term that did happen) but were present side-by-side and articulated in a regional frame-work. Between the states lay acephalous structures, which were not simply remnants of earlier social formations but often stood in opposition as well as in juxtaposition to their neighbours. In areas that were difficult of access, like the Bandiagara scarp in Mali inhabited by the Dogon (on whom so many earlier French anthropologists cut their teeth), or like the Scottish Highlands, the Albanian hills or similar regions in India and China, these peoples often deliberately avoided state power. Some communities escaped from the clutches of the state as the result of a self-imposed exile following a failed attempt to take over a kingdom (absorbed chiefs), others through the gradual decay of central power, and yet others perhaps as the result of an active search for an alternative life-style. In any case they often prized what we would call their 'freedom', a liberty not guaranteed by law in the formal sense but by customary sanctions; the law of the law court is only one of several possibilities for running a community, and one that is inevitably associated with states.

It was not only true in Africa but elsewhere too that some peoples appear deliberately to have chosen a non-state existence. The Yao are described as a minority people, living in Guangxi, Guangdong, and other provinces in south and south-west China. This name was given by the dominant Han to peoples living in mountainous areas, and hence difficult to control, absorb or educate (Fei Xiaotong 1991). They speak not one but a variety of languages belonging to the Sino-Tibetan group, and know themselves by a number of different names. They seem to be indigenous, hill-dwelling agriculturalists and no doubt some of them are just that. But recent research suggests that some of their ancestors were settled in the plains around Lake Dongthing in the middle basin of the Yangtze River. They took to the hills in order to avoid having to give corvée services to 'reactionary rulers, and preferred instead to enter the primitive forests of the deep mountains and build their homes with their own hands, to protect their life of freedom' (Fei Xiaotong 1991: 17–18). In other words they opted for the civil rather than the 'civilised'.

The kind of acephalous polity that is classically represented by the pastoral Nuer of the southern Sudan has been described as leaderless, law-less, feuding: in short, anarchic. It lacked the very criteria of sovereignty as understood by generations of political philosophers in the West. And not only in the West; it has been the view of states and their members everywhere – in China, India, in the Near East – that such peoples represent disorder.

The major contribution of Fortes and Evans-Pritchard was to bring about a reassessment of this view. Some earlier anthropologists had been concerned with the problem of 'law', in the broadest sense, with the way that order or a substantial measure of order was maintained in these soci-eties. It is true that in a number of conflict situations, the inhabitants would resort to self-help. But feuding was not pure violence; it was regulatory in an important sense, although it did not appear as such to states whose first claim was to a monopoly on the use of force, at least beyond a domestic level. Such acephalous polities were, as Evans-Pritchard and others have insisted, highly structured and norm-orientated. Nor was self-help their only form of sanction on behaviour; an array of others placed checks on deviant conduct. Indeed, it is clear that all human societies have to face 'the problem of order', as Parsons called it, thinking back to Spencer and to Durkheim's *Division of Labor in Society*. Order could be achieved without the external instrument of sovereigns, kings, rulers or chiefs. And as Evans-Pritchard once again showed, a very important mechanism was the segmentary (as distinct from the centralised, hierarchical) arrangement of families, villages and clans – or indeed of other kinds of social group – who acted together in some contexts and were opposed in others.

Segmentary processes involve conflict as well as cooperation, hence the importance of the feud. In African states, disputes were regularly taken to the chief who represented the community to the outside (as *dux*) as well as giving judgements within (as *rex*). Their presence penetrated right down to the family level, for while revenue was rarely raised by regular taxation, subjects had obligations to work on the farm of the rulers, who also collected contributions from each litigant in court as well as from travellers passing through the kingdom. His presence made itself felt in many ways, though the extent of what has been called 'the reach of the state' differed between kingdoms, partly as a function of the distance of the periphery from the centre, partly through variations in the ability to command force, partly for other reasons.

How did civil society manifest itself in these different regimes, firstly, in the rule of law and indeed of 'justice', of human rights, and secondly, in the existence of plural sources of power? Acephalous polities are inevitably pluralistic, with decision-making resulting more from discussion than from command. A limited authority rests with a number of institutions, secret societies, age sets, local groups. It is also true that the lineage or clan is frequently dominant at a local level. As a result it is difficult to escape from specific decisions or from customary agreements, for these are sustained not simply by a minority of elders but by the community in depth. Law in the most general meaning of that word, 'lawful behaviour', is therefore widely observed and respected.

Such societies lack not only formal law but a formal polity in the original, restricted, sense of that word. There is not a lack of governance but a lack of government, meaning a governing body of a centralised kind. In other words there is little or nothing to which 'civil society' could be opposed.

However, the states of Africa do possess a central government that is organised around a paramount and his subordinates, advisers and counsellors. Despite the prevalent image of autocratic chiefs extracting unquestioned obedience from their peoples, this kind of Austinian situation is very rare. In the kingdom of Asante in West Africa the paramount was described as 'he who speaks last'. In Gonja, to the North, the paramount was even more remote; I have called that polity 'an overkingdom' on the ancient Irish model, since he reigned rather than ruled. Quite apart from the shadowy nature of the rulers, even at the divisional level, power of an important kind lay in the hands not only of subordinate chiefs, responsible to their subjects; it also belonged to organisations of 'young men' who were specifically not chiefs, and of a multitude of religious functionaries whose appeal was to forces outside the polity itself. But there was a very important 'estate' of Muslims who followed a different set of rules, legitimised by the Prophet and the Holy Book, and who carried on wide-ranging commercial activities. These involved trading with merchants outside the kingdom, so that they had a different set of social relationships as well as religious, spatial and temporal ones, from the ruling dynasty or estate. It is true that they married frequently with members of that estate, and that from many points of view the kingdom as a whole was culturally homogeneous. But they possessed a certain degree of 'independence' because of these outside links, both with Allah and with other groups of Muslims, through whom they might exercise their influence with external powers to intervene in the affairs of the kingdom.

In conclusion, among the acephalous peoples of Africa, as in the hills of China, we find evidence of populations who prefer to place themselves as far as they can from the power of the state. Some may be said to choose a measure of political freedom, but their existence betrays little of the anarchy and disorder often attributed to them by outsiders. Order exists even in societies marked by what Durkheim called mechanical solidarity. But the existing sanctions were not as oppressive as he made them sound. Even in the simple states and acephalous societies of Africa, there is some space for manoeuvre between the personal and the public. Public protest was more difficult than in Asia, and often took the form of 'exit' rather than 'voice', as it frequently did in Europe. Nevertheless 'commoner resistance' did exist and acted as some kind of restraint on oppression.

The case of Africa is very different from that of the major societies of the Eurasian continent. In the latter, they had all benefited from the agricultural developments of the Bronze Age, which were accompanied by the emergence of complex urban communities, based on advanced agriculture, with a high degree of specialisation and the use of writing. It was under those conditions that 'civilisation' first developed. While the Greeks clearly elaborated the notion of 'civil society' in the most literal sense, both its uniqueness and the particular virtues of the European commune (especially in preparing the way for economic advance) have been greatly exaggerated. That is also the case with the idea that the Enlightenment established a special form of rationality or of civility that lies behind Western achievements. Achievements there were, but they need to be looked at from a global perspective, not one resting on the thoughts of Western scholars alone.

BIBLIOGRAPHY

Abrahams, R. G. 1986 In-marrying sons-in-law in Finland. MS

Abu-Lughod, J. L. 1989 *Before European Hegemony: the world systems AD 1250–1350*. New York

Alessi, G. 1994 *Alla Pentola dell'Oro: cucina, cucinare, mangiare a Firenze oggi*. Florence

Ambrosogli, M. 1996 *The Wild and the Sown: botany and agriculture in Western Europe, 1350–1850*. Cambridge

Amin, S. 1980 *Class and Nation: historically and in the current crisis*. London

Anderson, M. 1976 Marriage partners in Victorian Britain: an analysis based on Registration District data for England and Wales 1861. *Journal of Family History* 1: 55–78

Anderson, P. 1974 *Passages from Antiquity to Feudalism*. London

Aran, J.-P. 1974 *Le Mangeur du XIXe siècle*. Lausanne

Arensberg, C. and Kimball, S. T. 1940 *Family and Community in Ireland*. Cambridge, MA

Ariès, P. 1960 *L'Enfant et la vie familiale sous l'Ancien Régime*. Paris

Armstrong, A. H. 1957 *Introduction to Ancient Philosophy*. London

Armstrong, K. 1993 *A History of God: from Abraham to the present: the 4000-year quest for God*. London

Atran, S. 1990 *Cognitive Foundations of Natural History; towards an anthropology of science*. Cambridge

Augustins, G. 1989 *Comment se perpétuer?: devenir des lignées et destins des patrimoines dans les paysanneries européennes*. Nanterre

Balazs, E. 1964 The birth of capitalism in China. In E. Balazs (ed.) *Chinese Civilization and Bureaucracy: variations on a theme*. New Haven

Bartlett, F. 1932 *Remembering*. Cambridge

Basham, A. L. 1954 *The Wonder that was India*. London

Bec, P. 1995 *Chants d'amour des femmes troubadours: troubairitz et 'chansons des femmes'*. Paris

Beier, A. I., Cannadine, D. and Rosenheim, J. M. (eds) 1989 *The First Modern Society: essays in English history in honour of Lawrence Stone*. Cambridge

Berlivet, L. 1966 Les responses aux accusations de moralisme. Paper given at Entretiens Franklin, Paris, June

Besançon, A. 1994 *L'Image interdite: une histoire intellectuelle de l'iconoclasme*. Paris

Beteille, R. 1987 *La Chemise fendue: vie oubliée des femmes de Rouergue*. Rodez

Biegel, H. R. 1951 Romantic love. *American Sociological Review* 16: 326–34

Birrell, A. (transl.) 1995 [1982] *Chinese Love Poetry: new songs from a jade terrace – a medieval anthology*. London

Bloch, M. 1924 *Les Rois thaumaturges*. Paris

Boase, R. 1977 *The Origin and Meaning of Courtly Love: a critical study of European scholarship*. Manchester

Bottéro, J. 1977 Les noms du Marduk, l'écriture et la 'logique' en Mésopotamie ancienne. In M. de Jong Ellis (ed.) *Essays on the Ancient Near East: in memory of Jacob Joel Finkelstein*. Hamden, CT

Boucher, J. 1982 L'alimentation en milieu de cour sous les derniers Valois. In J.-C. Margolin and R. Sauzet (eds) *Practiques et discours alimentaires à la Renaissance*. Paris

Bourdieu, P. 1977 *Outline of a Theory of Practice*. Cambridge

Bowra, C. M. 1962 *Primitive Song*. London

Boyer, P. 1994a Cognitive constraints on cultural representations: natural ontologies and religious ideas. In L. A. Hirschfeld and S. A. Gelman (eds) *Mapping the Mind: domain and specificity in cognition and culture*. New York

Boyer, P. 1994b *The Naturalness of Religious Ideas; a cognitive theory of religion*. Berkeley, CA

Boyle, M. O'Rourke 1997 *Divine Domesticity: Augustine of Thagaste to Teresa of Avila*. London

Bray, F. 1986 *The Rice Economies: technology and development in Asian societies*. Oxford

Brenner, R. 1989 Bourgeois revolution and transition to capitalism. In A. I. Beier, D. Cannadine and J. M. Rosenheim (eds) *The First Modern*

Society: essays in English history in honour of Lawrence Stone. Cambridge

Brewer, J. 1997 *The Pleasures of the Imagination: English culture in the 18th century*. London

Brown, P. 1971 *The World of Late Antiquity: from Marcus Aurelius to Muhammed*. London

Cain, M. and McNicoll, G. 1988 Population growth and agrarian outcomes. In R. D. Lee *et al.* (eds) *Population, Food, and Rural Development*. Oxford

Caldwell, J. C. and P. 1987 The cultural context of high fertility in sub-Saharan Africa. *Population and Development Review* 13: 409–37

Carrasco, P. 1959 *Land and Polity in Tibet*. Seattle, WA

Carruthers, M. J. 1990 *The Book of Memory: a story of memory in medieval culture*. Cambridge

Cart, G. 1960 *Le Paysage en Orient et en Occident*. Paris

Catelot, A. 1972 *L'Histoire à table*. Paris

Chaperon, S. 1996 *Le Creux de la vague: movements féminins et féministes 1945–1970*, 2 vols. Ph.D. thesis, European University Institute

Chattopadhyaya, D. 1959 *Lokāyāta: a study in ancient Indian materialism*. New Delhi

Cockshut, A. O. J. 1964 *The Unbelievers: English agnostic thought, 1840–1890*. London

Cohen, M. L. 1976 *House United, House Divided: the Chinese family tradition in Taiwan*. New York

Coles, J. M. and Harding, A. F. 1979 *The Bronze Age in Europe*. London

Collomp, A. 1983 *La Maison du père: famille et village en Haute-Provence aux XVIIe et XVIIIe siècles*. Paris

Colt, J. C. 1844 *The Science of Double Entry Book-keeping*. New York

Coulbourn, R. (ed.) 1956 *Feudalism in History*. Princeton

Cowell, E. B. and Gough, A. E. (transls) 1904 *Sarvadom-śanasamgraha*. London

Crawley, E. A. 1902 *The Mystic Rose: study of primitive marriage and of primitive thought in its bearing on marriage*. Revised and greatly edited by Theodore Besterman. London

Czap, P. 1982a A large family: the peasant's greatest wealth. In R. Wall, J. Robin and P. Laslett (eds) *Family Forms in Historic Europe*. Cambridge

Czap, P. 1982b The perennial multiple family household, Mishino, Russia, 1782–1858. *Journal of Family History* 7: 5–26

Dausse, L. 1993 Epoque Gallo-Romaine: l'essor des échanges. In Anon (ed.) *Echanges: circulation d'objets et commerce en Rouergue de la Préhistoire au Moyen Age.* Montrozier

Davies, N. Zemon 1985 Review of *The Development of Family and Marriage in Europe. American Ethnologist* 12

Davis, J. 1973 *Land and Family in Pisticci.* London

Delille, G. and Rizzi, F. (eds) 1986 *Le Modèle familiale européen: normes, déviance, contrôle du pouvoir.* Rome

Diakonoff, I. M. 1969 The rise of the despotic state in ancient Mesopotamia. In I. M. Diakonoff (ed.) *Ancient Mesopotamia*, pp. 173–203. Moscow

Diamond, J. 1997 *Guns, Germs, and Steel: a short history of everybody for the last 13,000 years.* London

Dietler, M. 1990 Driven by drink: the role of drinking in the political economy and the case of Early Iron Age France. *Journal of Anthropological Archaeology* 9: 352–406

Dillon, E. J. 1895 *The Sceptics of the Old Testament: Job, Koheleth, Agur.* London

Douglas, M. 1971 Deciphering a meal. In C. Geertz (ed.) *Myth, Symbol and Culture.* New York

Dronke, P. 1965 *Medieval Latin and the Rise of the European Love-Lyric*, 2 vols. Oxford

Duby, G. 1997 *Women of the Twelfth Century.* Cambridge (French edn 1995)

Dumont, L. 1970 *Homo Hierarchicus: the caste system and its implications.* Chicago (French edn 1966)

Dumont, L. 1976 *Homo Aequalis.* Paris

Dumont, L. 1983 *Essais sur l'individualisme: une perspective anthropologique sur l'idéologie moderne.* Paris (English transl. 1986)

Durkheim, E. 1893 *La Division du travail* (English transl. 1947). Paris

Durkheim, E. and Mauss, M. 1963 *Primitive Classification.* London

Elias, N. 1994 [1939] *The Civilizing Process.* Oxford

Eliot, T. S. 1963 *Collected Poems 1909–1962.* London

Elvin, M. forthcoming. Introduction to Liu Ts'ui-jung and M. Elvin, *Sediments of Time: environment and society in Chinese history*

Elvin, M. and Skinner, G. W. (eds) 1974 *The Chinese City between Two Worlds.* Stanford, CA

Engels, F. 1887 *The Condition of the Working Class in England.* London (1st German edn 1845)

Englebert, O. 1984 [1946] *La Fleur des saints*. Paris

Enjalbert, H. 1975 *Histoire de la vigne et du vin: l'avènement de la qualité.* Paris

Epstein, S. 1962 *Economic Development and Social Change in South India.* Ox-ford

Erasmus, D. 1549 *The Praise of Folie*. London

Evans-Pritchard, E. E. 1937 *Witchcraft, Oracles and Magic among the Azande.* Oxford

Evans-Pritchard, E. E. 1940 *The Nuer.* Oxford

Faure, D. 1989 The lineage as business company: patronage versus law in the development of Chinese business. *The Second Conference of Modern Chinese Economic History*, January 5–7, The Institute of Economics, Academia Sinica, Taipei

Febvre, L. 1947 *Le Problème de l'incroyance au 16e siècle; la religion de Rabelais.* Paris

Fei Xiaotong, 1991 Fifty years investigation in the Yao mountains. In Fei Xiaotong, *The Yao of South China: recent international studies* (eds J. Lemoire and Chiao Chien). Paris

Finnegan, R. 1970 *Oral Literature in Africa.* Oxford

Flandrin, J.-L. 1979 *Families in Former Times.* Cambridge

Flandrin, J.-L. and Montanari, M. (eds) 1996 *Histoire de l'alimentation.* Paris

Flew, A. G. N. 1974 Agnosticism. Entry in *Encyclopaedia Britannica*, 15th edn. Chicago

Fortes, M. 1955 Radcliffe-Brown's contribution to the study of social organization. *British Journal of Sociology* 6: 16–31

Fortes, M. 1958 Introduction. In J. Goody (ed.) *The Developmental Cycle in Domestic Groups.* Cambridge

Fortes, M. 1959 *Oedipus and Job.* Cambridge

Fortes, M. and Evans-Pritchard, E. E. (eds) 1940 *African Political Systems.* Oxford

Frank, A. G. 1993. Bronze Age World System cycles. *Current Anthropology* 34: 383–429

Frazer, J. 1911–15 [1890] *The Golden Bough: a study in comparative religion*, 3rd edn. London

Frazer, J. 1918 *Folklore in the Old Testament*, 3 vols. London

Freedman, M. 1962 The family in China: past and present. *Pacific Affairs* 34: 323–36

Freedman, M. 1963 Chinese domestic family models. *VIe Congrès internationale des sciences anthropologiques et ethnologiques*, vol. 2, part 1. Paris

Freeman, D. 1996 'The debate, at heart, is about evolution'. In M. Fairburn and W. H. Oliver (eds) *The Certainty of Doubt: tributes to Peter Munz*. Wellington

Freeman, M. 1977 Sung. In K. C. Chang (ed.) *Food in Chinese Culture*. New Haven, CT

Friedl, E. 1986 The position of women: appearance and reality. In J. Dubisch (ed.) *Gender and Power in Rural Greece*. Princeton, NJ

Furnivall, F. J. 1882 *The Fifty Earliest English Wills in the Court of Probate, London*. London

Galsworthy, J. 1922 *The Man of Property*. London

Gandah, S. W. D. K. 1998 *The Silent Rebel*. Accra

Gaunt, D. 1983 The property and kin relationships of retired farmers in Northern and Central Europe. In R. Wall *et al.* (eds) *Family Forms in Historic Europe*. Cambridge

Gellner, E. 1992 *Reason and Culture*. Oxford

Geras, N. 1997 Marxists before the Holocaust. *New Left Review* 224: 19–38

Ghosh, A. 1992 *In an Antique Land*. London

Giddens, A. 1991 *Modernity and Self-identity: self and society in the late modern age*. Cambridge

Giddens, A. 1992 *The Transformation of Intimacy: sexuality, love and eroticism in modern societies*. Oxford

Gillet, P. 1985 *Par Mets et par vins: voyages et gastronomie en Europe (XVIIe–XVIIIe siècles)*. Paris

Gillion, K. L. 1968 *Ahmedabad: a study in Indian urban history*. Berkeley, CA

Gilman, A. 1981 The development of social stratification in Bronze Age Europe. *Current Anthropology* 22: 1–23

Goitein, S. D. 1967 *A Mediterranean Society: economic foundations*, vol. 1. Berkeley, CA

Goitein, S. D. 1973 *Letters of Medieval Jewish Traders*. Princeton, NJ

Goitein, S. D. 1978 *A Mediterranean Society: the Jewish communities of the Arab World as portrayed in the documents of the Cairo Geniza*, vol. 3. Berkeley, CA

Goode, W. J. 1959 The theoretical importance of love. *American Sociological Review* 24: 34–47

Goody, E. 1982 *Parenthood and Social Reproduction: fostering and occupational roles in West Africa.* Cambridge

Goody, E. (ed.) 1994 *Anticipatory Interactive Planning.* Cambridge

Goody, J. 1956 *The Social Organisation of the LoWiili.* London

Goody, J. 1957 Anomie in Ashanti? *Africa* 27: 75–104

Goody, J. 1958 The fission of domestic groups among the LoDagaba. In J. Goody (ed.) *The Developmental Cycle in Domestic Groups.* Cambridge

Goody, J. 1962a *Death, Property and the Ancestors.* Stanford, CA

Goody, J. 1962b On nannas and nannies. *Man* 62: 179–84. Reprinted in J. Goody 1969 *Comparative Studies in Kinship.* London

Goody, J. 1971 *Technology, Tradition and the State in Africa.* London

Goody, J. 1972a *The Myth of the Bagre.* Oxford

Goody, J. 1972b The evolution of the family. In P. Laslett and R. Wall (eds) *Household and Family in Past Time.* Cambridge

Goody, J. 1972c *Domestic Groups* (Addison Wesley Modules in Anthropology, No. 28). Reading, MA

Goody, J. 1975 Religion, social change and the sociology of conversion. In J. Goody (ed.) *Changing Social Structure in Ghana: essays in the comparative sociology of a new state and old tradition.* London

Goody, J. 1976 *Production and Reproduction: a comparative study of the domestic domain.* Cambridge

Goody, J. 1979 Slavery in time and space. In J. L. Watson (ed.) *Asian and African Systems of Slavery.* Oxford

Goody, J. 1980 Rice-burning and the Green Revolution in northern Ghana. *J. Development Studies* 16: 136–55

Goody, J. 1982 *Cooking, Cuisine and Class: a study in comparative sociology.* Cambridge

Goody, J. 1983 *The Development of the Family and Marriage in Europe.* Cambridge

Goody, J. 1990 *The Oriental, the Ancient and the Primitive.* Cambridge

Goody, J. 1991 Icones et iconoclasme en Afrique. *Annales ESC:* 1235–51

Goody, J. 1993a *The Culture of Flowers.* Cambridge

Goody, J. 1993b East and West: rationality in review. *Ethnos* 58: 6–36

Goody, J. 1996a *The East in the West.* Cambridge

Goody, J. 1996b Cognitive contradictions and universals: creation and evolution in oral cultures (the Frazer lecture 1994). *European Journal of Social Anthropology* 4: 1–16

Goody, J. 1997 *Representations and Contradictions: ambivalance towards images, theatre, fiction, relics and sexuality.* Oxford

Goody, J. forthcoming. The demographic transition in Africa.

Goody, J. and Gandah, S. W. D. K. 1981 *Une Récitation du Bagré.* Paris

Goody, J. and Watt, I. P. 1963 The consequences of literacy. *Comparative Studies in Society and History* 5: 304–45

Gordon, W. 1765 *The Universal Accountant.* Edinburgh

Greenhalgh, S. M. 1987 Families and networks in Taiwan's economic development. In S. M. Greenhalgh and E. A. Winckler (eds) *Contending Approaches to the Political Economy of Taiwan.* Armonk, NY

Greenhalgh, S. M. and E. A. Winckler (eds) 1987 *Contending Approaches to the Political Economy of Taiwan.* Armonk, New York

Greenhalgh, S. M. and E. A. Winckler 1990 Land reform and family entrepreneurialism in East Asia. In G. McNicoll and M. Cain (eds) *Population and Rural Development: institutions and policy.* A supplement to *Population and Development Review*

Griffith, R. T. H. 1889 *The Hymns of the Rig Veda.* 4 vols. Benares

Grove, R. 1995 *Green Imperialism: colonial expansion, tropical island Edens, and the origins of environmentalism 1600–1860.* Cambridge

Guthrie, W. K. C. 1962 *History of Greek Philosophy,* 4 vols. Vol. 1: *The Earlier Pre-Socratics and Pythagoreans.* Cambridge

Guy, C. 1961 *Almanach historique de la gastronomie française.* Paris

Habermas, J. 1971 *Towards a Rational Society.* London

Habermas, J. 1984 *The Theory of Communicative Action.* 2 vols. London

Hajnal, J. 1965 European marriage patterns in perspective. In D. V. Glass and D. E. C. Eversley (eds) *Population in History: essays in historical demography.* London

Hajnal, J. 1982 Two kinds of pre-industrial household formation systems. *Population and Development Review* 8: 449–94

Halbwachs, M. 1925 *Les Cadres sociaux de la mémoire.* Paris

Halverson, J. 1976 Animal categories and terms of abuse. *Man* [new series] 11: 505–16

Harris, M. 1975 *Cows, Pigs, Wars and Witches.* London

Harris, M. 1983 [1968] *The Rise of Anthropological Theory: a history of theories of culture*. London

Hasluck, M. 1954 *The Unwritten Law in Albania*. Cambridge

Hawkes, D. 1989 *Classical, Modern and Humane: essays in Chinese literature*. Hong Kong

Hill, B. 1989 The marriage age of women and the demographers. *History Workshop Journal* 28: 129–47

Homans, G. C. 1941 *English Villagers of the Thirteenth Century*. Cambridge, MA

Honneth, A., McCarthy, T., Offe, C. and Wellmer, A. 1992 *Cultural-Political Interventions in the Unfinished Project of Enlightenment*. Cambridge, MA

Hopkins, K. 1980 Brother–sister marriage in Roman Egypt. *Comparative Studies in Society and History* 22: 303–54

Horton, R. 1973 Lévy-Bruhl, Durkheim and the Scientific Revolution. In R. Horton and R. Finnegan (eds) *Modes of Thought*. London

Hsieh, Jih-chang 1985 Meal rotation. In Hsieh Jih-chang and Chuang Ying-chang (eds) *The Chinese Family and its Ritual Behavior*. Taiwan

Hsu, V. N. Y. and F. L. K. Hsu 1977 Modern China. In K. C. Chang (ed.) *Food in Chinese Culture*. New Haven, CT

Huegel, Baron F. von 1931 *The 'Reality of God' and 'Religion and Agnosticism', being the literary remains of Baron F. von Huegel*, edited by E. G. Gardner. London

Hufton, O. 1974 *The Poor of Eighteenth-Century France, 1750–1789*. Oxford

Hufton, O. 1995 *The Prospect before Her: a history of women in Western Europe*, vol. 1, *1500–1800*. London

Jones, G. I. 1949 Ibo land tenure. *Africa* 19: 309–23

Kerr, M. 1958 *The People of Ship Street*. London

Khare, R. S. 1976 *The Hindu Hearth and Home*. Delhi

Klassen, N. 1995 *Chaucer on Love, Knowledge and Sight*. Cambridge

Knab, L. 1885–1902 Cheval: alimentation. *La Grande Encyclopédie*, vol. 10. Paris

Kocher, P. H. 1946 *Christopher Marlowe: a study of his thought, learning and character*. Chapel Hill, NC

Lach, D. F. 1970 *Asia in the Making of Europe*, vol. 2. Chicago

Lall Nigam, B. M. 1986 Bahi-Khata: the pre-Pacioli Indian double-entry system of bookkeeping. *Abacus* September: 148–61

Lancaster, C. S. 1979 The influence of extensive agriculture on the study of sociopolitical organisation and the interpretation of history. *Amer. Ethnol.* 6: 329–48

Lantz, H. R. 1981 Romantic love in the pre-modern period: a sociological commentary. *Journal of Social History* 15: 349–70

Laslett, P. 1965 *The World We Have Lost.* London

Laslett, P. 1969 Size and structure of the household in England over three centuries. *Population Studies* 23: 199–223

Laslett, P. 1972 Mean household size in England since the sixteenth century. In P. Laslett and R. Wall (eds) *Household and Family in Past Time.* Cambridge

Laslett, P. 1982 Family and household as work group and kin group: areas of traditional Europe compared. In R. Wall, J. Robin and P. Laslett (eds) *Family Forms in Historic Europe.* Cambridge

Laslett, P. and Wall, R. (eds) 1972 *Household and Family in Past Time.* Cambridge

Laurence, M. 1954 *A Tree for Poverty: Somali poetry and prose.* Nairobi

Leach, E. R. 1961 *Pul Eliya, a Village in Ceylon: a study in land tenure and kinship.* Cambridge

Leach, E. R. 1964 Anthropological aspects of language: animal categories and verbal abuse. In E. H. Lenneberg (ed.) *New Directions in the Study of Language.* Cambridge, MA

Legge, J. 1872 *The Chinese Classics.* Vol. 5, pts 1 and 2. The Ch'un Ts'ew, with the Tso Chuen. London

Lehrer, A. 1974 *Semantic Fields and Lexical Structure.* Amsterdam

Levine, N. E. 1987 Differential childcare in three Tibetan communities: beyond son preferences. *Population and Development Review* 13: 281–304

Lévi-Strauss, C. 1949 *Les Structures élémentaires de la parenté.* Paris

Lévi-Strauss, C. 1963 *Structural Anthropology.* London (French edn 1958)

Lévi-Strauss, C. 1964–71 *Mythologiques,* 4 vols. Paris

Lévi-Strauss, C. 1965 Le triangle culinaire. *L'Arc* 26: 19–29 (English transl. P. Brooks 1966, *Partisan Review* 33: 586–95)

Lévi-Strauss, C. 1970 *The Raw and the Cooked.* London (French edn 1964)

Lévy-Bruhl, L. 1923 *Primitive Mentality.* London

Lewis, I. M. 1986 *Religion in Context: cults and charisma.* Cambridge

Lewis, O. 1962 *The Children of Sanchez: autobiography of a Mexican family.* London

Libéra, A. de 1991 *Penser au Moyen Age*. Paris

Lightman, B. V. 1987 *The Origins of Agnosticism: Victorian unbelief and the limits of knowledge*. Baltimore, MD

Lindemann, M. 1981 The regulation of wet-nursing in eighteenth-century Hamburg. *Journal of Family History* 6: 379–95

Lloyd, G. E. R. 1979 *Magic, Reason and Experience: studies in the origin and development of Greek science*. Cambridge

Lloyd, G. E. R. 1990 *Demystifying Mentalities*. Cambridge

Lu Wenfu 1988 *Vie et passions d'un gastronome chinois*. Arles

McCosh, J. 1884 *Agnosticism of Hume and Huxley; with a notice of the Scottish School*. New York

McDermott, J. n.d. Of gods and gangsters: the political economy of Suzhou in the sixteenth century (paper given at the Hong Kong University of Science and Technology conference on Chinese Management, October 1995)

Macdonell, A. A. 1922 *Hymns from the Rigveda*. London

Macfarlane, A. 1978 *The Origins of English Individualism: the family, property and social transition*. Oxford

McNicoll, G. and Cain, M. 1990 Institutional effects on rural economic and demographic change. In G. McNicoll and M. Cain (eds) *Rural Development and Population: institutions and policy*. New York

Malinowski, B. 1914 *The Family among Australian Aborigines*. London

Manuel, F. and Manuel, F. 1979 *Utopian Thought in the Western World*. Oxford

Margolin, J.-C. and Sauzet, R. (eds) 1982 *Practiques et discours alimentaires à la Renaissance*. Paris

Marx, K. 1958 Preface to *The Critique of Political Economy*. In Karl Marx and Frederick Engels, *Selected Works*, vol. 1. Moscow

Marx, K. [1867] 1970 *Capital* (transl. S. Moore and E. Aveling). New York

Mayer, A. C. 1966 *Caste and Kinship in Central India*. London

Mennell, S. 1985 *All Manners of Food: eating and taste in England and France from the Middle Ages to the present*. Oxford

Mintz, S. W. 1985 *Sweetness and Power: the place of sugar in modern history*. New York

Mitchell, J. and Goody, J. 1997 Feminism, fatherhood and family in late twentieth-century Britain. In A. Oakley and J. Mitchell (eds) *Who's Afraid of Feminism?* London

Mo, T. 1982 *Sour Sweet*. London

Montanari, M. 1994 *The Culture of Food*. Oxford

Mordacq, P. 1989 *Le Menu: histoire illustrée*. Paris

Morgan, L. H. 1877 *Ancient Society*. Chicago

Morris, B. 1987 Are there any individuals in India? A critique of Dumont's theory of the individual. *Eastern Anthropologist* 365–77

Morris, B. 1990 Indian materialism. *The Secularist* 123: 63–72

Morris, C. 1972 *The Discovery of the Individual, 1050–1200*. London

Needham, J. 1954 *Science and Civilization in China*, vol. I: *Introductory Orientations*. Cambridge

Needham, J. 1956 *Science and Civilization in China*, vol. II: *History of Scientific Thought*. Cambridge

Needham, J. 1959 *Science and Civilization in China*, vol. III: *Mathematics and the Sciences of the Heavens and the Earth*. Cambridge

Needham, J. 1985 *Science and Civilization in China*, vol. V: *Chemistry and Chemical Technology*. Cambridge

Newman, F. X. (ed.) 1967 *The Meaning of Courtly Love – papers of the first annual conference of the Center of Medieval and Early Renaissance Studies*. Binghampton

Ng, Chin-Keong 1983 *Trade and Society: the Amoy network on the China Coast 1683–1735*. Singapore

Nygran, A. 1953 *Agape and Eros*. London

Ogburn, W. F. and Nimkoff, M. F. 1955 *Technology and the Changing Society*. New York

Orme, R. 1805 [1792] *Historical Fragments of the Mogul Empire, of the Mosrattoes, and of the English concerns in Indostan, from the year M.DC.LIX*. London

Ousmane, S. 1974 *Tribal Scars*. London (French edn originally published as *Voltaique*, Paris 1962)

Ozouf, M. 1995 *Les Mots des femmes*. Paris

Parker, L. M. 1989 Medieval traders as international change agents: a comparison with twentieth-century international accounting firms. *The Accounting Historians Journal* 16: 107–18

Parrinder, G. 1961 *West African Religions*, 2nd edn. London

Parsons, T. and Bales, R. F. 1955 *Family, Socialization and Interaction Process*. Glencoe, IL

Pateman, C. 1988 *The Sexual Contract*. Stanford, CA

Patlagean, E. 1977 *Pauvreté economique et pauvreté sociale à Byzance 4e–7e siècles*. Paris

Paulucci di Calboli, R. 1996 [1909] *Lacrimi e Sorrisi dell'Emigrazione Italiana*. Milan

Person, E. S. 1991 Romantic love: at the intersection of the psyche and the cultural unconscious. *Journal of the American Psychoanalytic Association* 39 (supplement): 383–411

Peterson, T. S. 1994 *Acquired Taste: the French origins of modern cooking*. Cornell, NY

Pinchbeck, I. 1930 *Women Workers and the Industrial Revolution, 1750–1850*. London

Pirenne, H. 1925 *Medieval Cities*. London

Pitte, J.-R. 1991 *Gastronomie française: histoire et géographie d'une passion*. Paris

Popkin, R. H. 1964 *The History of Scepticism from Erasmus to Descartes*. New York

Postan, M. M. 1952 The trade of medieval Europe: the North. In M. M. Postan and E. E. Rich (eds) *Trade and Industry in the Middle Ages*, vol. II of the *The Cambridge Economic History of Europe*. Cambridge

Postan, M. M. 1987 The trade of medieval Europe: the North. In M. Postan and E. Miller (eds) *Trade and Industry in the Middle Ages*, 2nd edn, *The Cambridge Economic History of Europe*. Cambridge

Radcliffe-Brown, A. R. 1922 *The Andaman Islanders: a study in social anthropology*. Cambridge

Radhakrishnan, S. (ed.) 1952–3 *History of Philosophy, Eastern and Western*. London

Radhakrishnan, S. and Moore, C. A. (eds) 1957 *A Source Book in Indian Philosophy*. Princeton, NJ

Rattray, R. S. 1932 *Tribes of the Ashanti Hinterland*. Oxford

Redding, S. G. 1990 *The Spirit of Chinese Capitalism*. Berlin

Reik, T. 1949 *Of Love and Lust: on the psychoanalysis of romantic and sexual emotions*. New York

Revel, J. 1984 Forms of expertise: intellectuals and 'popular' culture in France (1650–1800). In S. L. Kaplan (ed.) *Understanding Popular Culture: Europe from the Middle Ages to the nineteenth century*. Berlin

Ribeiro, A. 1995 *The Art of Dress: fashion in England and France 1750–1820*. New Haven, CT

Richards, A. I. 1939 *Land, Labour and Diet in Northern Rhodesia*. London

Robertson, D. W., Jr 1966 *The Concept of Courtly Love as an Impediment to the Understanding of Medieval Texts in the Meaning of Courtly Love*. Albany, NY

Rodinson, M. 1949 Recherches sur les documents arabes relatifs à la cuisine. *Revue Etudes Islamiques* 95–106

Roover, R. de 1956 The development of accounting prior to Luca Pacioli according to the account books of medieval merchants. In A. C. Littleton and B. S. Yamey (eds) *Studies in the History of Accounting*. London

Ross, E. 1983 Survival networks: women's neighbourhood sharing in London before World War One. *History Workshop Journal* 15: 4–27

Rougement, D. de 1949 The crisis of the modern couple. In R. N. Anshen (ed.) *Family, Function and Destiny*. New York

Rougement, D. de 1956 *Love in the Western World*. New York

Rowe, W. T. 1984 *Hankow: commerce and society in a Chinese city, 1796–1889*. Stanford, CA

Rudner, D. 1992 *Caste and Capitalism in Colonial India*. Berkeley, CA

Rutherford, R. B. 1989 *The Meditations of Marcus Aurelius*. Oxford

Ruzin, P. and Nemeroff, C. 1990 The laws of sympathetic magic: a psychological analysis of similarity and contagion. In J. W. Stigler, R. A. Shweder and G. Herdt (eds) *Cultural Psychology: essays on comparative human development*. Cambridge

Sabean, D. W. 1990 *Property, Production, and Family in Neckarhausen 1700–1870*. Cambridge

Sahlins, M. 1976 *Culture and Practical Reason*. Chicago

Samuel, R. (ed.) 1981 *East End Underworld: chapters in the life of Arthur Harding*. London

Sangren, P. 1989 Comment on J. Goody, Cooking and the polarization of social theory. *Foodways* 3: 207

Sarris, M. 1995 Death, gender and social change in Greek society. *Journal of Mediterranean Studies* 5: 14–32

Saussure, F. de 1966 [1916] *Course in General Linguistics*. New York

Scafolgio, D. 1997 *Il Carnevale Napoletano: storia, maschere e rituali del XVI al XIX secolo*. Rome

Scafolgio, D. and Lombardi-Satriani, L. M. 1990 *Pulcinella: il mito e la storia*. Milan: Leonardo

Schmandt-Besserat, D. 1992 *Before Writing*. Austin, TX

Schneider, J. 1997. Was there a precapitalist world system? *Peasant Studies* 6: 20–9

Schofield, M. 1986 Cicero for and against divination. *Journal of Roman Studies* 76: 47–65

Scorgie, M. 1994a Accounting fragments stored in the Old Cairo Geniza. *Accounting, Business and Financial History* 1: 29–41

Scorgie, M. 1994b Medieval traders as international change agents: a comment. *The Accounting Historians Journal* 21: 137–43

Scott, J. 1985 *Weapons of the Weak*. New Haven, CT

Seccombe, W. 1992 *A Millennium of Family Change: feudalism to capitalism in northwestern Europe*. London

Seccombe, W. 1993 *Weathering the Storm: working class families from the Industrial Revolution to the fertility decline*. London

Sen, A. 1996 Family fortunes of Bronze Age mint, review of J. Goody, *The East in the West* in *Times Higher Educational Supplement* 31 May: 20–1

Shah, A. M. 1973 *The Household Dimension of the Family in India*. New Delhi

Shorter, E. 1975 *The Making of the Modern Family*. New York

Skinner, W. (ed.) 1977. *The City in Late Imperial China*. Stanford, CA

Smith, R. M. 1979 Some reflections on the evidence for the origin of the 'European marriage pattern' in England. In C. Harris (ed.) *The Sociology of the Family*. Keele

Smith, R. T. 1956 *The Negro Family in British Guiana: family structure and social status in the villages*. London

Southall, A. W. 1956 *Alur Society: a study in processes and types of domination*. Cambridge

Spearing, A. C. (ed.) 1993 *The Medieval Poet as Voyeur: looking and listening in medieval love-narratives*. Cambridge

Speiser, J.-M. 1985 La christianisation de la ville dans l'Antiquité tardive. *Ktema: civilisations de l'orient, de la Grèce et Rome antiques* 10: 49–55

Sperber, D. 1985 Anthropology and psychology: towards an epidemiology of representations. *Man* 20: 73–89

Srinivas, M. N. 1952 *Religion and Society among the Coorgs of South India*. Oxford

Stendhal 1830 [1938] *Scarlet and Black* (transl. C. K. Scott Moncrieff). London (Everyman edn)

Stenning, D. J. 1958 Household viability among the Pastoral Fulani. In J. Goody (ed.) *The Developmental Cycle in Domestic Groups*. Cambridge

Sterling, C. 1931 *L'Amour de l'art*. Paris

Stock, B. 1983 *The Implications of Literacy: written languages and models of interpretation in the eleventh and twelfth centuries*. Princeton, NJ

Stone, L. 1977 *The Family, Sex and Marriage in England, 1500–1800*. London

Stone, L. 1986 'Illusions of a changeless family', review of Alan Macfarlane, *Marriage and Love in England*. *Times Literary Supplement* 16 May 1986: 525

Stone, L. 1987 *The Past and Present Revisited*. London

Stone, L. 1988 Passionate attachments in the west in historical perspective. In W. Gaylin and E. S. Person (eds) *Passionate Attachments*. New York

Stone, L. 1989 Epilogue: Lawrence Stone – as seen by himself. In A. L. Beier, D. Cannadine and J. M. Rosenheim (eds) *The First Modern Society: essays in English history in honour of Lawrence Stone*. Cambridge

Stouff, L. 1970 *Alimentation et ravitaillement en Provence aux XIVe et XVe siècles*. Paris

Szreter, S. 1995 *Fertility, Class and Gender in Britain, 1860–1940*. Cambridge

Taylor, J. (ed.) 1911 *Kishamira: Prabod'h Chandro'daya, or The Moon of Intellect*. London

Tenbruck, F. H. 1975 Das Werk Max Webers. *Kölner Zeitschrift für Soziologie und Sozialpsychologie* 27

Thapar, R. 1966 *A History of India*. Harmondsworth

Thomas, K. 1983 *Man and the Natural World*. London

Thompson, E. P. 1977 *William Morris: romantic to revolutionary*. London

Thrower, J. 1971 *A Short History of Western Atheism*. London

Thrower, J. 1980 *The Alternative Tradition: religion and the rejection of religion in the Ancient World*. The Hague

Tocqueville, A. de [1945] *On Democracy in America*, edited P. Bradley. New York

Tosh, J. 1994 What should historians do with masculinity? *History Workshop Journal* 38: 179–202

Troelsch, E. 1931 *Social Teaching of the Christian Churches* (transl. Wyon). London

Trumbach, R. 1978 *The Rise of the Egalitarian Family: aristocratic kinship and domestic relations in eighteenth century England*. New York

Tucci, G. 1926 Linee di una storia de materialismo indiano. *Atti della Reale Accademia Nationale dei Lincei*, serie 6, vol. II. Rome

Tylor, E. B. 1871 *Primitive Culture*. London

Vincent, D. 1981 *Bread, Knowledge and Freedom: a study of nineteenth-century working class autobiography*. London

Viviani, V. 1969 *Storia del teatro napoletano*. Naples

Wack, M. F. 1990 *Lovesickness in the Middle Ages: the Viaticum and its commentaries*. Pennsylvania, PA

Wallerstein, I. 1997 Eurocentrism and its avatars: the dilemmas of social science. *New Left Review* 226: 93–107

Ward, J. 1899 *Naturalism and Agnosticism: the Gifford lectures: delivered before the University of Aberdeen in the years 1896–1898*, 2 vols. London

Watson, J. L. 1975 *Emigration and the Chinese Lineage: the Mans in Hong Kong and London*. Berkeley, CA

Watson, J. L. (ed.) 1977 *Between Two Cultures*. Oxford

Watt, I. 1996 *Myths of Modern Individualism: Faust, Don Quixote, Don Juan, Robinson Crusoe*. Cambridge

Weber, M. 1951 [1916] *The Religion of China* (transl. H. Gerth and D. Martindale). New York

Weber, M. 1957 The social psychology of the world religions. In H. H. Gerth and C. Wright Mills (eds) *From Max Weber: essays in sociology*. London

Weber, M. 1958 *The Protestant Ethic and the Spirit of Capitalism*. New York

Weber, M. 1968 *The City*. New York

Weinsinck, A. J. 1953 Entry on *Khamr*. In H. A. R. Gibb and J. H. Kramers, *Shorter Encyclopaedia of Islam*. Leiden

Westermarck, E. 1926 (repr. 1968) *A Short History of Marriage*. New York

Whitelock, D. (ed.) 1979 *English Historical Documents*. Vol. 1: *c. 500–1042*, 2nd edn. London

Whittaker, C. R. and Goody, J. forthcoming. Proto-industrialisation in the Rouergue from antiquity to the present

Wickham, C. 1981 *Early Medieval Italy: central power and local society, 400–1000*. London

Wittvogel, K. A. 1957 *Oriental Despotism: a comparative study of total power*. New Haven, CT

Wolf, A. P. 1995 *Sexual Attraction and Childhood Association: a Chinese brief for Edward Westermarck*. Stanford, CA

Wolf, A. P. and Hanley, S. B. 1985 Introduction. In S. B. Hanley and A. P. Wolf (eds) *Family and Population in East Asian History*. Stanford, CA

Wolf, E. R. 1982 *Europe and the Peoples without History*. Berkeley, CA

Wootton, D. 1985 Unbelief in early modern Europe. *History Workshop Journal* 20: 82–100

Young, M. and Wilmott, P. 1957 *Family and Kinship in East London*. London

Yu, Chang-jiang 1998 The 5th Symposium on Chinese Dietary Culture, The Foundation for Dietary Culture, Taiwan

Yver, J. 1966 *Egalité entre héritiers et exclusion des enfants dotés: essai de géographie coutumière*. Paris

Zarcone, T. 1993 *Mystiques, philosophes et Francs-maçons en Islam: Riza Tevfik, penseur ottomane (1868–1949), du soufisme à la confrérie*. Paris

INDEX

absolutism, 14, 47, 205, 263 ff.
acephalous polities, 274
adevism, 212
adoption, 53, 56, 70
adultery, 116, 117 (and gender),
    118, 136, 143, 256
'affective individualism', 50, 106
aggregate data, 67, 69, 83
agnosticism, 183, 204 ff., 208, 209,
    219, 220–1
Ahmadabad, 37, 40, 272 ff.
alternative traditions, 211, 214, 216
Althusser, L., 16
ambivalence, 126, 137, 141, 143,
    173–4, 179, 181, 183, 184, 189,
    192, 198, 203, 206, 208, 229,
    231–2, 236–7, 241, 245, 246,
    250, 251, 259, 260
    about love poetry, 111, 116
ancient society, 3–4, 8, 12–13, 14,
    15, 18, 38, 127, 139, 142, 167,
    175, 192, 210, 232–3, 235
Anderson, P., 3, 7, 10, 11, 12, 13, 14,
    15, 25
Anglo-Saxons, 132, 148, 152
animism, 230

Arab society, 15, 30, 34, 56, 105,
    107, 110, 120, 122, 129, 130,
    199, 200
Ariès, P., 45, 52, 57, 59, 80, 100,
    144
Aristotle, 33–4, 218, 221–2, 241–2,
    264
articulation, 15
asceticism, 212, 213, 214
atheism, 204 ff., 208, 209, 219
Aubin, Saint, 53
Averroës, 34

Bagre myth, 184, 219, 230, 247 ff.
bankers, 41 ff.
    Chettiar, 41
banquets, 129, 154, 164 ff., 187
beer, 175 ff., 178, 179
beings of the wild, 219, 230, 250,
    251, 253–4
belief systems, 218–19, 255 ff.
black-is-beautiful problem, 226–7
book-keeping, 34 ff., 64, 66
booty production, 9, 152, 155, 191,
    193
Brenner, R, 3, 7, 11, 25, 47

love, 2, 27, 95, ch. 5, 136
  congruent, 98 ff., 111
  conjugal, 59, 98, 102, 115, 144
  courtly, 111, 113
  discourse of, 106, 107, 110, 118,
    121, 122, 123, 142
  and literacy, 106 ff.
  passionate, 98 ff.
  poetry of, 101, 103, 107, 110, 111
    (Chinese), 120, 122
  romantic, 97 ff., 105 ff.
  unhappy, 111
lover, 113, 114 ff.
lust, 105, 107, 108, 112–13, 116
luxury cultures, 2, 4, 24, 71, 126,
    128, 134, 143, 147, 173–4,
    179–80, 181, 183, 188 ff., 190,
    192, 193, 196, 199, 202, 235,
    236–7, 241, 259

Macfarlane, A., 31, 38, 51, 59, 82,
    144
male breadwinners, 88
marginalised men, 91–2
marriage, 56, 59, 64, 72, 81, 83, 89
    (neighbourhood), 92
    (property), 98, 99 (elite), 100,
    104, 108, 121, 195 (close), 223,
    224, 242
  arranged, 61, 76, 102, 116
  choice, 106, 107, 121
  early, 61, 76, 89, 102, 115–16
  hypogamous, 113
  incestuous, 53
  in, 201
  late, 51, 61, 70, 74, 75, 76, 84, 85,
    98, 115–16
  out, 200

plural, 114
  of widows, 53
Marx, 1, 2, 3, 4, 6, 7, 10, 12, 16, 23,
    24, 25, 26, 27, 29, 32, 33, 40,
    45, 74, 90, 95, 223, 237, 241,
    262, 266, 268, 273
  Marxist, 80, 81, 86, 191, 202,
    222
mass media, 123, 192, 194 ff.
materialism, 206, 213, 214, 220
  'colour-blind', 10, 13, 23
  cultural, ch. 7
  material factors, 23
matrifocal, 88, 89, 91
matrilocal, 89
meaning, surface, 257
memory, 226
mentalities, 2, 45, 50, 51, 80, 81, 96,
    100, 104, 145, 232, 236, 237,
    266
mercantile capitalism, 5, 6, 7, 9, 11,
    14, 24, 30, 32, 37, 42, 78, 79,
    80, 267, 271
military technology, 1, 5, 19, 30, 33
    (Portuguese), 152
modernisation, 27, 29, 31, 38, 43,
    45, 47, 48, 49, 58, 79, 91, 95,
    96, 97, 98, 100, 101, 102–4,
    109, 114, 121, 122, 123, 166,
    169, 184, 228, 232, 236, 261,
    264, 270
monasteries, 54 ff., 175
motherhood, 88, 91, 92, 99, 100, 101
  invention of, 99, 100
  moral, 82, 100
  unmarried, 84–5
myth, 184, 213, 217, 223, 244,
    247 ff., 257–8

Renaissance, 14, 25, 30, 32, 37, 39,
    40, 49, 96, 129, 133, 139, 142,
    147, 148, 187, 193, 195, 201,
    206, 208, 210, 227, 232–3, 236,
    237, 246
representation, 121, 122–3, 141,
    183, 189, 214
    iconic, 180, 209, 220–1, 234
    political, ch. 14, 264–5
resistance, 56, 103, 134, 185 ff., 188,
    193, 194, 223, 270, 277
restaurants, 154, 167, 188
    British, 133, 166
    Chinese, 125, 161 ff., 163, 165,
        166, 169
    culture, 162 ff., 164
    French, 139
    immigrant, 163
    Indian, 161, 163
Restoration, 134 ff., 147, 227
    in France, 139
retirement, 61, 63, 64, 66, 69, 70, 72,
    73
Robinson Crusoe, 42, 43
role playing, 121
romance, 102, 104, 109
rules, 67, 69

Sabean, D., 63 ff., 72, 76
scepticism, 2, ch. 11, 203 ff., 207,
    216 ff., 219, 248
sceptics, 207
secularisation, 14, 25, 39, 48, 49, 56,
    122, 181, 195, 204, 210, 269
sensibility, 228–9
    attack on, 138
servants, 51, 60–1, 62, 65, 66, 67, 68,
    69, 70, 73, 74, 75, 76, 84, 98

sexuality, 97 ff., 99, 100 ff., 108, 114,
    141, 143, 213
sheep–*mouton*, 150 ff., 158
Shorter, E., 45, 51, 52, 144
silk, 13, 25, 37, 38, 167, 168, 192,
    233
slavery, 6, 14, 68, 225
snake, as procreator, 256
social stratification (including
    class), 2, 6, 23, 24, 25, 27, 66,
    67, 69, 71, 83, 87, 94, 99, 106,
    108, 113, 121, 125 ff., ch. 7,
    152 ff., 158, 167, 180, 183,
    185 ff., 196, 197 ff., 200 ff., 237
song, 103, 105, 106, 110, 114,
    118–19, 195, 197, 216
specialists, full time, 1
state, 68, 262 ff., 266 ff.
    African, 274 ff.
    agrarian societies, 71
    despotic, 24, 184, 262, 266, 272
    formation, 4, 20
    Indian, 267 ff.
    reach of, 10, 269, 276
    tributary, 4, 273
steam power, 8, 23, 88
Stone, L., 45–6, 48 ff., 52, 57, 59–80,
    82, 98, 106 ff., 121, 144
succession, to office, 87
sufism, 211
sumptuary legislation, 129
syllogism, 33

temporary advantage, 1, 5, 33, 34,
    184, 266
thin rituals, 235
thought, mode of, 205
    laws of, 240